UPHOLSTERY
TECHNIQUES
& PROJECTS

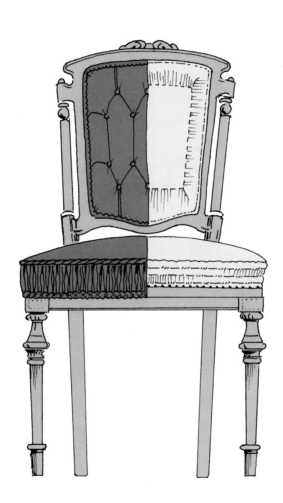

UPHOLSTERY
TECHNIQUES
& PROJECTS

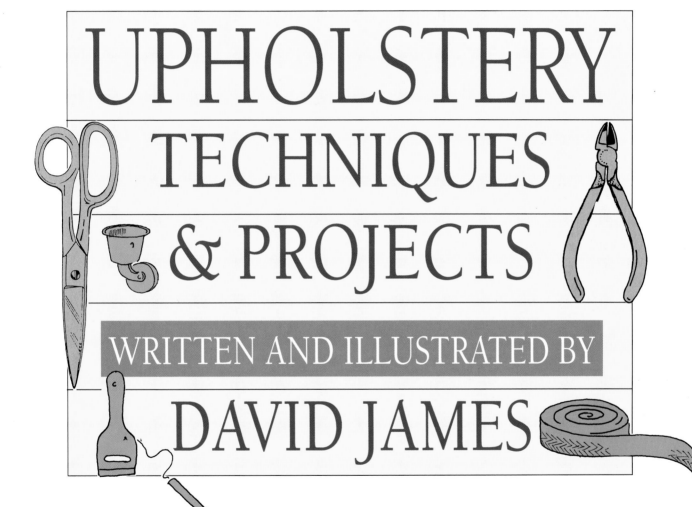

WRITTEN AND ILLUSTRATED BY

DAVID JAMES

GUILD OF MASTER CRAFTSMAN PUBLICATIONS

First published 1994 by
Guild of Master Craftsman Publications Ltd,
166 High Street, Lewes, East Sussex BN7 1XU

Reprinted 1995, 1997, 1999, 2001

© David James 1994

ISBN 0 946819 41 6

Illustrations © David James 1994
Photography by David James, except where credited otherwise.

Designed by Teresa Dearlove

Printed in Hong Kong
by H & Y Printing Limited.

Contents

Dedication

To E, R, D, C, J, J, P and R

Acknowledgements

I have been fortunate to have the help and advice of friends and colleagues while writing this book. My sincere thanks to all those who became involved in any way whatsoever. My thanks especially to Allan Hill and Ray Chapel at Vitafoam, Geoff Hughes, Maureen Batey and Dominic Jones at Bucks College, Len Rentmore for his immeasurable enthusiasm, Caroline Allaway for her help in allowing me access to the showroom of Parkertex, G P & J Baker Ltd, Richard Cook of Isaac Lord Tools Ltd, Ed Wilson and Angela Burgin for continually providing interesting pieces of work for drawing and restoration, Ivor Jones for the lunchtime floor level calculus which rubs off, and Dennis Cutten for the use of his catalogue.

A very sincere thank you to all of the upholsterers who agreed to be photographed at work in their own workshops. Their views, their enthusiasm and deep interest in the craft will inspire others to be like them. They are Dorothy Gates, Heather Gilbey, Vicky Lane, Angela Burgin, David Edgar, David Haines, Peter Humble and Bevan Guy. My thanks also to Mark Kelly from Manchester and Craig Green of Greengate Furniture for agreeing to be photographed.

I wish to acknowledge and thank the following companies for information and for access to their products: Farbo Contract Fabrics; Wardle Storeys plc; Makita Electric Works Ltd; Parkertex Ltd; G P & J Baker Ltd; Isaac Lord Ltd; A & C Valmic; Hamilton Colour; Bosch Tools; Senco (UK) Ltd; Singer (UK) Ltd; Andrew Muirhead & Sons; Connolly Bros (Curriers) Ltd; Trimproof Ltd; Laronde Fabrics; ICI Fibres Ltd.

My thanks also to the many students both past and present whom I have spent time with and whose work continues to inspire and fascinate me: at the Buckinghamshire College; the John Makepiece School, Parnham; the Rural Development Commission; and the Missenden Abbey Weekend School and Summer School.

Finally a very special thank you must go to Eirlys for her understanding and unfailing support, and also to my editors Alex Woolf and Elizabeth Inman.

Introduction

The craft of upholstery requires many different skills, some simple and many complex, and a feel for the work, together with some artistic flair, can produce outstanding pieces of work.

The techniques can be learned, skills developed and tips remembered, and the combination of these with the individual's aspirations and experience, no matter how brief, can achieve interesting and satisfying results.

Upholstery involves the use of a wide range of materials, and while skills are developed with tools, techniques have to be adapted to suit many different situations. Materials which have been cut, joined and shaped are eventually assembled and built into a piece of furniture's anatomy.

In many ways the upholstery of a large piece of work such as a settee or *chaise-longue* can be likened to the building of a house. A suitable foundation is needed, on to which more and more layers are fixed and built. As scrim-covered shapes are filled and stitched, or foams are engineered and wrapped, proportion and dimension become important. For new designs a working drawing, a sketch or a model is needed as a guideline. However, in restoration and reupholstery the aims are more clearly defined: frame shapes and different styles are recognizable or can be researched.

This book has been written for the practising furniture upholsterer. It covers everything from fillings and foams to cushion making, and from the tools of the trade to trade calculations. But it is not solely concerned with the practical. There are also sections which aim to inspire. Hopefully people will be encouraged by this book to work in a range of styles and materials, both traditional and modern, conventional and unconventional.

Part One

Chapter 1 Tools

Familiarity and skill in the handling of tools used for upholstery are the first requirements. Getting to know all the materials and fabrics comes a close second.

Hand tools

A basic tool kit for upholstery consists of:

Two pairs of **scissors**, one large and one small.

Two **hammers** - a tacking hammer with a single face and claw, and a two-face magnetic hammer; each should be about 8-10oz (*see* Fig 1.1).

A **ripping chisel**, a cross between a screwdriver and a wood chisel, is essential for stripping upholstery from wood frames; it is used together with a mallet to lift out tacks and staples.

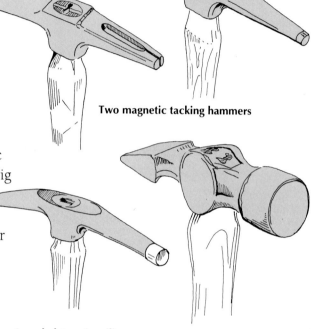

Fig 1.1

Two magnetic tacking hammers

An upholsterer's nailing hammer

A Warrington hammer

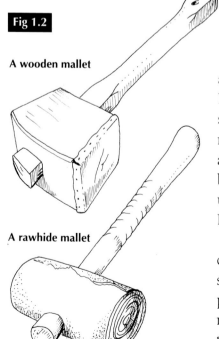

Fig 1.2

A wooden mallet

A rawhide mallet

A **mallet** which is easy to grip, not too large and easy to swing - 9oz is about average. Mallet heads may be wood (barrel-shaped or square), rubber, or rawhide. Wooden are much cheaper, usually made from beech, and are adequate. The life of a wooden mallet can be prolonged by gluing or tacking a piece of upholstery leather or rawhide to one face (*see* Fig 1.2).

A **webbing stretcher** or **strainer**: there is a choice of three equally good types. Fig 1.3 shows the bat and peg type which is the most popular, and probably the easiest to use. It is made from hardwood and has a large slot in the face to accommodate a loop of 2in (51mm) webbing. The ⅝in (18mm) dowel

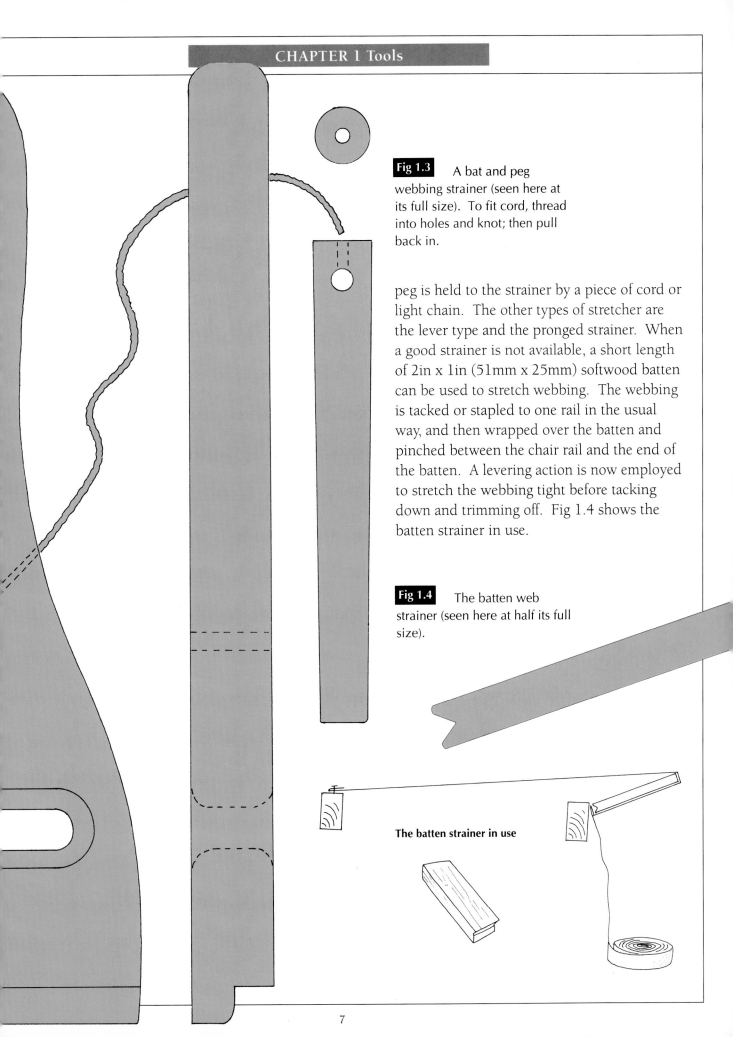

Fig 1.3 A bat and peg webbing strainer (seen here at its full size). To fit cord, thread into holes and knot; then pull back in.

peg is held to the strainer by a piece of cord or light chain. The other types of stretcher are the lever type and the pronged strainer. When a good strainer is not available, a short length of 2in x 1in (51mm x 25mm) softwood batten can be used to stretch webbing. The webbing is tacked or stapled to one rail in the usual way, and then wrapped over the batten and pinched between the chair rail and the end of the batten. A levering action is now employed to stretch the webbing tight before tacking down and trimming off. Fig 1.4 shows the batten strainer in use.

Fig 1.4 The batten web strainer (seen here at half its full size).

The batten strainer in use

Needles

These are very specialized, and a selection of different sizes and types is needed (*see* Fig 1.5).

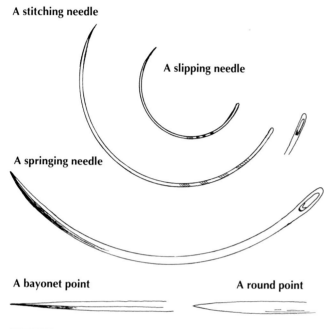

A stitching needle

A slipping needle

A springing needle

A bayonet point

A round point

Fig 1.5 Above: upholstery needles. Below: a needle gauge.

common. The gauge size varies according to length, which is measured around the curve. The higher the gauge number, the finer the needle becomes, e.g. a 3in (76mm) needle would be 18 or 19 gauge, and a 6in (152mm) would be 14 gauge.

A 2 ½in (64mm) by 20-gauge **cording needle** is useful for very fine stitchwork, particularly for trimming and joining fabrics and sewing decorative cords in place.

A **skewer**, used to hold materials and covers in place temporarily while they are being fitted or fixed: 3in (76mm) and 4in (102mm) are the common sizes; a box of several dozen will have many uses.

Plated pins, 1¼in (32mm), will be needed for finer work, particularly with covers. They have many uses when closing and stitching or machine sewing fabrics. Often under strain when fixing facings and outer covers to chairs, they need to be more robust than a typical dressmaking pin.

The **regulator** has a single round point and

A **two-point bayonette needle** is the largest, and at least two of these will be needed for bridling and stitching work, one about 8in (20.3cm) long, and the other 10in (25.4cm). A round point can be adequate, but a sharp bayonette point will cut its way through tough materials more easily.

Buttoning needles may be single- or two-point; one of each type is best.

A 5in or 6in (127mm or 152mm) **springing needle** is half round, with a single bayonette point. This heavy 10-gauge needle is used to tie in springs to webbing bases.

Fine-gauge curved **mattress needles** for hand-stitching work come in various sizes; 3in (76mm), 5in (127mm) and 6in (152mm) are

a flat end. Lengths range from 6in (152mm) to about 12in (30.5cm). The 8in (20.3cm) and 10in (25.4cm) are the most common, and will be in frequent use for adjusting and moving fibre fillings and stuffings. The regulator is essential in traditional stuffover work, and has many other uses.

Measuring and marking-out tools

A 60in (1m 52cm) linen tape measure

A 2m (6½ft) or 3m (10ft) **retractable steel tape**.

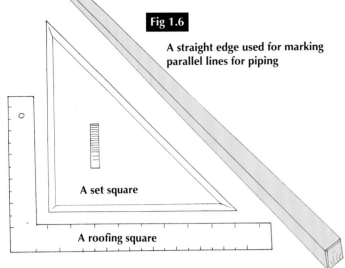

Fig 1.6

A straight edge used for marking parallel lines for piping

A set square

A roofing square

A **yard stick** or **metre stick**.

A 2m (6½ft) rule or **straightedge** (*see* Fig 1.6) may at first seem a luxury, but will be well used when marking out upholstery covers and fabrics. A simple alternative is a straight length of timber, 1.5m (5ft) or 2m (6½ft) long and 37mm (1½in) square. This should be made of a stable hardwood, e.g. mahogany, to remain serviceable, straight and accurate. The 37mm (1½in) thickness has two advantages: it is easy to handle and use, and it is the perfect width for marking out strips of fabric for making piping. Once the first two lines have been marked each side of the stick, it can simply be rolled over and the next chalk line drawn, to give a quickly marked, accurate set of lines.

A large **plywood set square** (*see* Fig 1.6) with 90° and 45° angles is an essential tool for marking out covers, as it gives instant right

Fig 1.7 Leather trimming scissors. The long handle and short blade produces a powerful cutting action, ideal for upholstery bench work.

Small wire snips

angles to an edge or a previously marked line, and can be used to find the true bias of any fabric.

A **steel square**, similar to a carpenter's roofing square (*see* Fig 1.6), is preferred to the set square by many upholsterers.

This basic equipment of about 20 tools can be added to as the need arises and as work and experience demand. Some of the more common household and woodworking tools will swell the kit:

A **carpenter's hammer**, Warrington or claw (*see* Fig 1.1), is ideal for heavier work, e.g. chair frame repairs and wire bending and forming.

Craft knives and **trimming knives** with spare blades.

A pair of **pincers** and a pair of small **wire snips** (*see* Fig 1.7) are very useful for easing out broken staples, old tacks and nails when cleaning up frames for reupholstery.

A medium-sized **wood rasp** will be needed for cleaning up old and rough wood frames after stripping, and removing sharp inner edges from newly machined timber rails. In traditional stuffover stitched edge upholstery, a clean, even chamfer is made on the outer edges of chair rails with the rasp. Seats, arms and backs where a stitched edge is to be built are all treated in this way. The chamfer provides a sloping tacking surface for fixing scrims before stitching.

Large and medium-sized **screwdrivers**, both slotted and Posidriv.

Different designs of **staple lifter** are available. Because staples seldom come out of frames cleanly, the pincers or snips will help to clean up after a stripping operation.

Leather trimming scissors (*see* Fig 1.7) are perfect for general upholstery bench work. Their short blade design produces a powerful cut at the blade's tip, which makes trimming tough materials easy.

Power tools

Although not essential for hand-crafted upholstery, power tools can assist enormously in drilling, cutting and fixing upholstery materials.

Fast, clean and effortless fixing is provided by the air-powered **staple gun**. However, a constant pressure of around 70lb/sq in is needed, which means a fairly high investment. An electric staple gun is not as expensive, and can be run off a normal 13-amp mains supply. It will fire 5mm (³⁄₁₆in), 10mm (³⁄₈in) and 13mm (¹⁄₂in) leg-size staples, and is a convenient substitute for hammer and tacks. In the small workshop, preparation and temporary fixing are worked with tacks, and the final fixings are completed by stapling.

A **foam saw**, though quite expensive, will be worth the investment if cutting and shaping foams is to be done.

An electric **meat slice** or **bread slice**, designed for kitchen use, makes a good foam cutter where only small amounts of foam work are planned. This tool works in the same way as a foam saw, with two long straight-toothed blades oscillating together to produce a powered cutting edge. Templates and guides made up from timber and plywood can be used where cutting has to be precise, or where the depth of foam is more than 2in (51mm). Deep straight cuts through foams can be made using a straight table edge and a length of timber used as a straight edge, placed as a cutting guide on top of the foam. Shaped work can be done freehand or with templates; upholstery foams are easily marked out with coloured felt pens.

The **cordless drill/driver** is able to drill holes quickly and drive screws into furniture with reasonable ease. Frame repairs and frame building are necessary parts of the traditional upholsterer's work - in fact, most reupholstery framework is constantly in need of strengthening or adjustment, e.g. corner blocks, castors and facings.

The electric **hot-melt glue gun** converts solid sticks of adhesive into hot liquid

A selection of power tools.

extruded through a fine nozzle. The glue produces a strong bond to most porous surfaces, particularly fabrics, making it ideal for fixing braids, fringes and other trimmings. The glue cools and sets in a few seconds, so the work should be well prepared beforehand.

There may be instances when fast fixing of trimmings with a very hot adhesive is not required, e.g. where more time is needed on very intricate or difficult work. In such cases, **cold contact glue** applied from a tube would suit the work best.

Safety and safe working are particularly important when using power tools of any kind. Great care should be taken at all times, and protective clothing worn as recommended. Make regular checks on the condition of wiring and cables, and switch off the mains supply whenever the tools are not in use.

Sewing machines

Machine sewing is divided into domestic and industrial; most upholstery sewing falls into the area of industrial, because the fabrics and materials used are medium to heavy weight.

The **domestic sewing machine** can generally only be used for small amounts of basic upholstery sewing, because of the limitations of its needle size and the height to which the presser foot can be raised. Piping feet for upholstery work have grooved soles of ³⁄₁₆in (4.5mm) and ¼in (6mm), but these are rarely available as domestic accessories and when several plies of heavy upholstery fabric are to be sewn together, the domestic machine is *very* limited.

Industrial sewing machines can deal with the whole range of fabric weights and thicknesses, from fine cotton to upholstery leathers. Needle sizes can be changed to give good quality seaming for various applications, e.g. size 18 and 19 needles for relatively light work, and size 20 or 21 for denser, heavier coverings. Thread sizes can also be varied, e.g. size 75 thread for light work, size 50 for most medium applications, such as loose covers, and size 36 for general and heavy upholstery.

Industrial machines for upholstery sewing are the lockstitch type, and produce a strong interlocking seam using a needle thread and a bobbin thread. This is the conventional stitch type and the strongest of all machine stitch formations. Other stitch types, e.g. zigzag, chain stitch and overedge, are more specialized and have their own particular applications, mainly in soft furnishings, clothing manufacture and sail making.

The single needle lockstitch industrial sewing machine with needle feed is typical of the type used in the industry. It has standard and additional features such as:

- Reverse feed
- Knee lift
- ⅜in (9.5mm) presser foot clearance
- Maximum stitch length of ³⁄₁₆in (4.2mm) (6spi)
- Bobbins can be refilled during work
- L-shaped extension tables with cupboards can be added

The simplified diagram in Fig 1.8 shows a Singer 211U model, which is a rugged workhorse with an all-round capability for heavy furnishing:

The **compound needle feed action** gives positive feeding of fabric plies and good seam quality.

Sewing speeds can be regulated up to 4000spm (stitches per minute).

A **courtesy curtain** has been fitted to the back of the unit for extra comfort to the machinist.

The **extension table** provides better work handling, especially for large covers.

See Chapter 2 for a full description of sewing machine techniques.

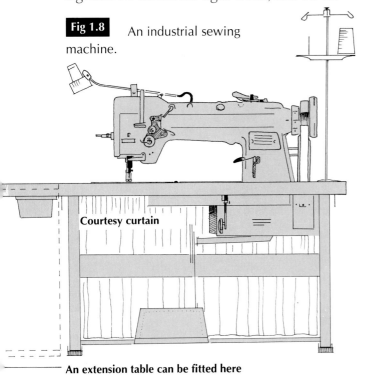

Fig 1.8 An industrial sewing machine.

Courtesy curtain

An extension table can be fitted here

Chapter 2
Sewing
Machine
Techniques

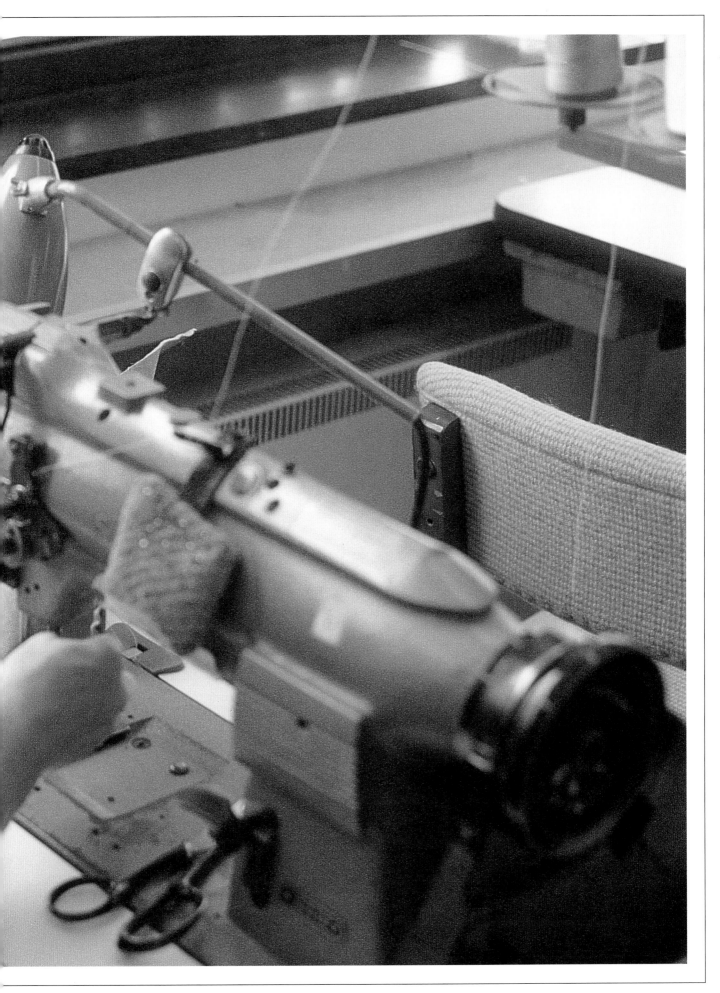

Modern upholstery increasingly relies on the sewing machine for its design, make-up and production methods, whereas period work and reproduction upholstery depend largely on the ability of the upholsterer to manipulate and fix separate pieces of fabric over stuffed and stitched shapes, and demands a good degree of skill with the needle and thread for finishing and trimming. Traditional and modern upholstery have become quite distinct, and the craftsman who is competent in both fields will always be in demand.

Presser feet for the industrial sewing machine.

Setting up

Setting up a sewing machine involves correct threading and understanding the thread path from reel to needle. On its route the thread must pass through tension discs, which are adjustable, and through the take-up lever, which takes up slack in the thread after each stitch is formed.

The second part of setting up is filling the bobbin and setting it in place. This will vary with different makes of machine, but the variation is usually easy to follow once the principles of lockstitch formation are understood. Adjustments to bobbin tension are rarely needed, and in most cases should be quite minimal. Bobbin thread tensions are kept quite low, which allows the upper thread tension to be balanced. The two threads are brought together at the needle, and the machine is ready for work.

Once the setting up is done, the stitch can be checked and balanced by sewing a sample length. Stitch length can then be adjusted if necessary to suit the cover and seam requirements.

Basic stop/start procedures

Begin by placing the fabrics under the needle at the start of the sewing line, then lowering the presser foot on to the cloth. Ensure that both threads are under the foot and pulled out beyond and away from the fabric to be sewn; this avoids any build-up of thread and makes for a clean start. The needle is initially brought down into the fabric by turning the drive wheel by hand towards the sewer, which puts the take-up lever in the up position and avoids snatch. The foot control then takes over, and sewing begins slowly. A quick glance after an inch or two will show whether the seam is good before continuing, checking the tension balance, stitch length and seam allowance.

Stopping procedures are equally important. Running off the fabric should be avoided, as most machines will clog if run without fabric. This is also likely to cause damage to the teeth on the feed dogs and burr the underside of the presser foot. At the end of a seam a back tack may be needed to seal the end of the seam. If so, the reverse lever is depressed and the seam oversewn. When there is no reverse fitted, then the normal stop procedure is used, by lifting the presser foot off the cloth and raising the needle by hand to its maximum height. The cloth is then free and can either be completely removed and the threads trimmed, or if the seam is to be sealed, then the cloth is simply slid back toward the operator by about ¾in (20mm) and the seam quickly oversewn by bringing the presser foot and the needle down by hand and sewing over to the end of the seam.

Both the bobbin thread and the needle will only run free when the take up lever and the presser foot are in their highest position, and the tension release should then work. With the fabric removed, the threads can be trimmed off, leaving the machine ready to begin sewing again. Many of the more sophisticated new generation machines have automatic needle positioners and underbed thread trimmers designed specifically for industrial high speed sewing.

Keeping the sewing machine running

Nothing is more frustrating than poor seam quality and recurring faults when there is work to be done and a reliable seam line is needed. Regular checks and simple maintenance are usually the answer to the majority of problems, combined, with knowing your own machine intimately. A quick check of every function from the very simple and obvious to the more complex, e.g. timing, is vital. Some 90% of sewing problems are remedied by easily adjusted functions. A good formula to follow is the three R's - readjust, reset, replace - and if this is followed by cleaning and lubrication, then most regularly occurring faults will be quickly corrected or avoided.

The following is a useful checklist:

Needle thread path:	correct, with no snagging or twisting.
Bobbin thread:	good even tension, evenly wound, smooth running.
Needle condition:	sharp, not bent, free of burrs, fully set into needle bar, correctly aligned running clear of presser foot and throat plate.
Bobbin condition:	no rough edges, correctly set in case, not distorted
Needle size:	compatible with thread size and work to be sewn.
Upper thread	tension spring and take-up spring still strong and runs smoothly during sewing; tension is well balanced.
Stitch	correct tension and stitch length for fabric.
Stitch length	7-8 stitches per inch (25mm), is a good average. Can be adjusted for: (a) very fine fabrics, 9-10 spi. (b) very heavy fabrics, leathers or vinyls, 6 spi.
Presser foot:	adjust pressure of presser foot according to work being sewn, i.e. light for light, heavy for heavy.

Needles should generally be as fine as possible, to avoid unnecessary damage to fabric yarns; use 7-9 stitches per inch (25mm) for most applications. Seam allowance should be ⁷⁄₁₆in (10mm) for most types of work. For very open weave fabrics and those which fray easily, use a half inch (13mm) seam allowance.

There are three types of needle point used in upholstery. The cloth point is universal and will deal with almost all covers and applications. For specialized areas of sewing, a ball point is used for stretch fabrics at about 9-10 spi. Several cutting points are available for use with leather, e.g. the twist point, which cuts its way through the leather and produces an interesting angled stitch. To avoid perforations which may weaken the leather, stitch lengths are generally large, 6-8 spi.

Chapter 3
Frame
Making
& Styles

Most upholstery is built on a frame or structure. This is the skeleton of a piece of upholstered furniture and may be a box, a frame or simply a board. In the UK, timber was always the most popular material used in frame making, and this remains the case today.

Beech is the first choice timber for the construction of upholstery frames, with joints such as mortice and tenon, dowel, and housings used to ensure sound construction. It is mainly the case that horizontal rails are jointed into uprights and shaping pieces are applied where needed. Rail dimensions range from 2½in x 2in (65mm x 50mm) for Chesterfield seat rails, down to 1⅛in x 1in (27mm x 25mm) for stuffing rails in small chairs. Seat rails for upholstered chairs should generally be a minimum thickness of 1⅛in (27mm): this allows for adequate webbing fixings and strong main rail construction.

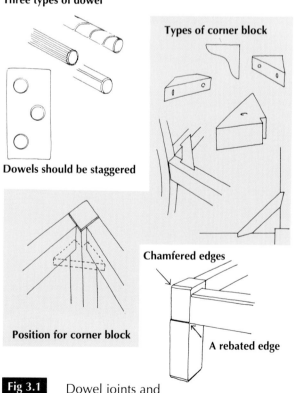

Three types of dowel

Dowels should be staggered

Types of corner block

Position for corner block

Chamfered edges

A rebated edge

Fig 3.1 Dowel joints and corner blocks.

Dowel joints and corner blocks

Fig 3.1 shows a selection of dowel joints and corner blocks. Dowel sizes are usually ⅜in (10mm), and the dowels are reeded or grooved with a straight or spiral groove. Where possible, dowel holes are countersunk to allow extra glue space.

Corner blocks of various types are fitted into chair frames to brace the structure and add strength to main joints. The blocks are cut with the grain running along the greatest length or from corner to corner. Because frame movement is inevitable, the blocks are glued or glued and screwed in place. The larger corner blocks used in seat frames often have a dual function, and are drilled to house castors or glides. Rebates and chamfers are produced by removing timber from rail edges and faces. Both techniques are essential in traditional frame making - they provide tacking surfaces and locating grooves and allow for cover thicknesses, all of which helps the upholsterer achieve a good line and finish.

Scroll arm and back shapes

These are a prominent feature of traditional work, providing profile and shape as a basis for upholstery. The larger scrolls are usually an indication of quite shallow upholstery, while finer scroll shapes are typical of antique and period styles requiring a deeper build-up.

Scroll uprights may be jointed in or dowelled on to the surrounding framework. Cross-rail positions are important for providing fixing for upholstery materials and correctly placed tuckaways between arm and seat or back and seat.

In Fig 3.2, the seat rails are shown crosshatched to illustrate different thicknesses and applications: **A** and **C** are modern reproductions, and **B** and **D** are typical period designs, with firm and spring edge seat styles.

Fig 3.3 Some examples of variations of scroll and C scroll framework can be seen below. Access to seat rail fixing is vital so that upholstery material can be positioned easily. All joints may be dowel, or seat rails could be tenoned into the main uprights.

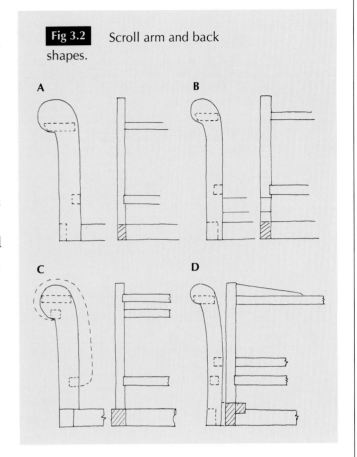

Fig 3.2 Scroll arm and back shapes.

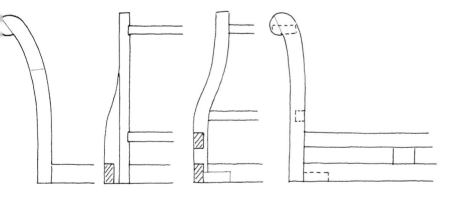

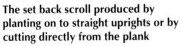

The set back scroll produced by planting on to straight uprights or by cutting directly from the plank

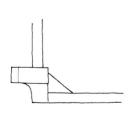

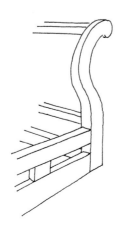

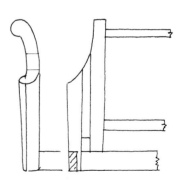

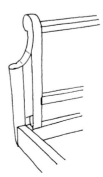

A typical example of C scroll framing construction

Fig 3.4 Examples of rail positioning.

Aligning seat and main rails with the outer face of legs; stuffing rails particularly should be kept to inner edges

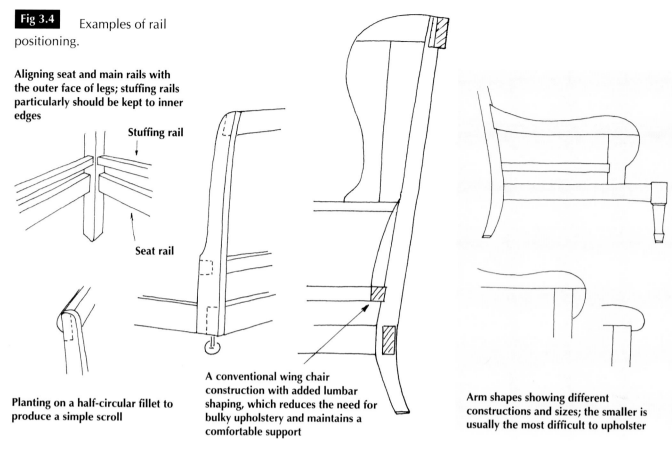

Stuffing rail

Seat rail

Planting on a half-circular fillet to produce a simple scroll

A conventional wing chair construction with added lumbar shaping, which reduces the need for bulky upholstery and maintains a comfortable support

Arm shapes showing different constructions and sizes; the smaller is usually the most difficult to upholster

Fig 3.5 Stretchers.

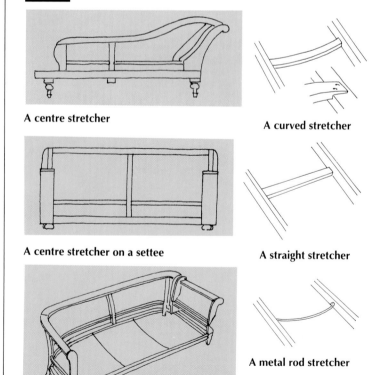

A centre stretcher

A curved stretcher

A centre stretcher on a settee

A straight stretcher

A metal rod stretcher

Two stretchers on a settee

Stretchers

Stretcher rails or rods are needed in the long seats and backs of settees and couches (*see* Fig 3.5). They are usually placed at approximately 24in (609mm) centres, to support the span of the main rails. A stretcher may be straight or curved and can be made from beech or steel rod; webbed or sprung upholstery exerts a great deal of pulling force which would bend unsupported main rails. A two-seater settee generally needs one stretcher rail in the seat and back, and three-seater versions will require two. Where seats are fairly shallow, a curved rail helps to avoid bottoming when the seat is in use.

Joints may be dowel, lap and screw, or housed and screwed. Corner blocks are often used at each end of the stretcher to brace seat rails when compression is likely to be severe.

Fig 3.6 Drop arm action.

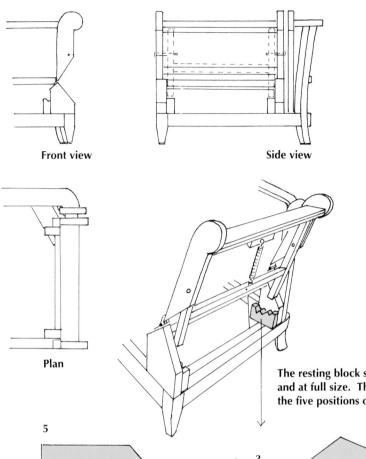

Front view

Side view

Plan

Drop arm action

Many different mechanisms for the adjustable drop arm on sofas were designed and developed during the Victorian era, most of which are based on a ratchet system which allows the arm to drop at intervals to four or five different levels. This approach to the sofa bed or day bed allows a small upholstered settee to be quickly converted to a *chaise-longue* or daytime place for resting.

Most of the actions had wooden mechanisms, though some quite complex all-metal versions still exist. Fig 3.6 shows one of the simplest forms of action, based on the traditional pivoting arm fixed to blocks. The mechanism is all wood, except for bolts,

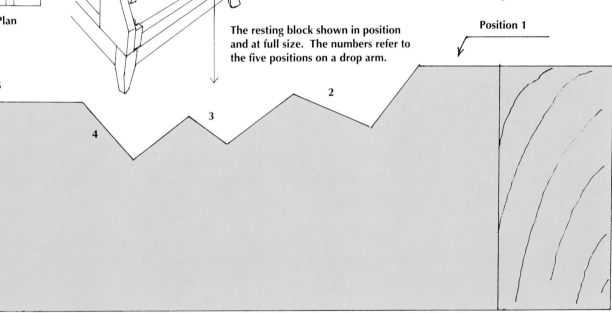

The resting block shown in position and at full size. The numbers refer to the five positions on a drop arm.

Position 1

5

2

3

4

A

hinges and a large tension spring. A wood or metal knob to operate the pivoting frame was fixed through the upholstery at the base of the tension spring.

The full-size drawing **A** of the resting block shows the five resting positions: position 1 is upright, and position 5 shows the arm fully down, level with the seat.

Eighteenth-century wing chair construction

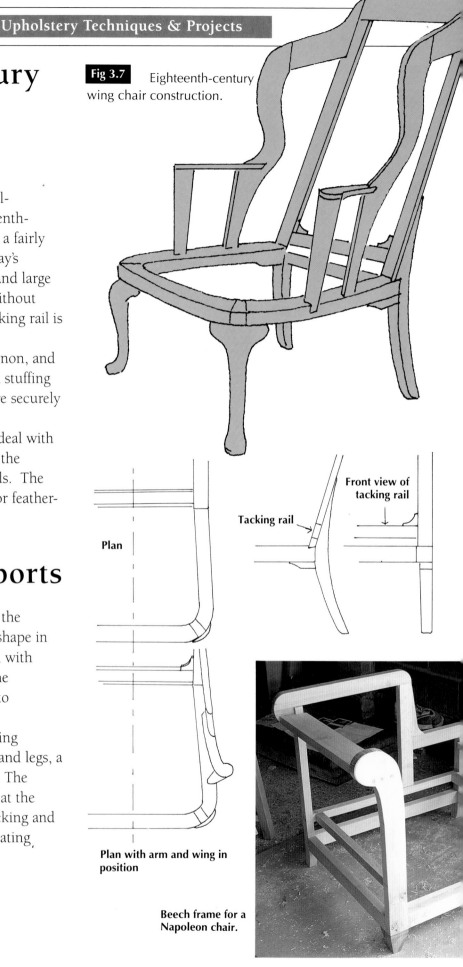

Fig 3.7 Eighteenth-century wing chair construction.

Fig 3.7 shows an interesting and well-proportioned chair, typical of eighteenth-century upholstery. It is designed as a fairly upright chair and is quite tall by today's standards, with short arm supports and large wings. The construction is strong without being cumbersome and only one tacking rail is fitted, at the base of the inside back.

Joints were mainly mortice and tenon, and corner blocks were fitted to the back stuffing rail. The long back upright rails were securely housed into each side seat rail.

The upholsterer was expected to deal with the stuffing and tacking by fixing all the materials to the strong seat frame rails. The seat is firm and flat, and has a hair- or feather-filled squab.

Shapes and supports

The frames in Fig 3.8 show many of the variations used to produce line and shape in framing. Distinct styles are achieved with inserts, fillets and peg frames, and the upholsterer uses fabrics and fillings to accentuate and hug the frame lines.

Detail **A** in Fig 3.8 shows a blocking technique used around arm stumps and legs, a method used particularly in France. The blocks are nailed and glued in place at the right height to provide a shelf for tacking and finishing in the traditional French seating style.

Plan

Tacking rail

Front view of tacking rail

Plan with arm and wing in position

Beech frame for a Napoleon chair.

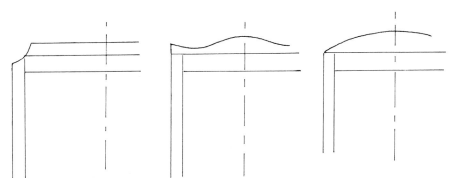

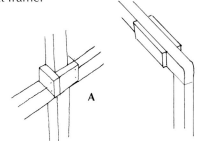

Fig 3.8 Examples of shapes and supports. Inset: a peg-fixed seat frame.

Board materials and box constructions

Modern constructions for upholstered furniture rely to some extent on the use of board materials, particularly plywood and medium density fibre board (MDF). In addition, hardboards and millboard are often used as stiffeners and linings in frames.

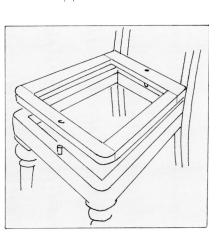

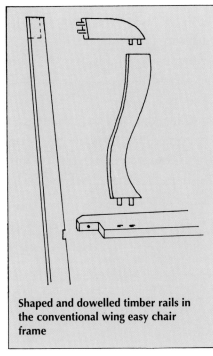

Shaped and dowelled timber rails in the conventional wing easy chair frame

Fig 3.9 Wing frame alternatives.

A wing cut from ⅝in (15mm) plywood or MDF, screwed and dowelled in place after being upholstered

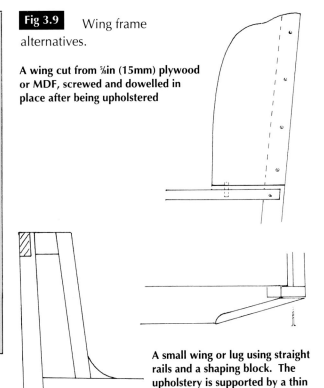

A small wing or lug using straight rails and a shaping block. The upholstery is supported by a thin plywood or millboard panel, pinned and glued to the inner face, which is an optional alternative to a webbing and hessian support.

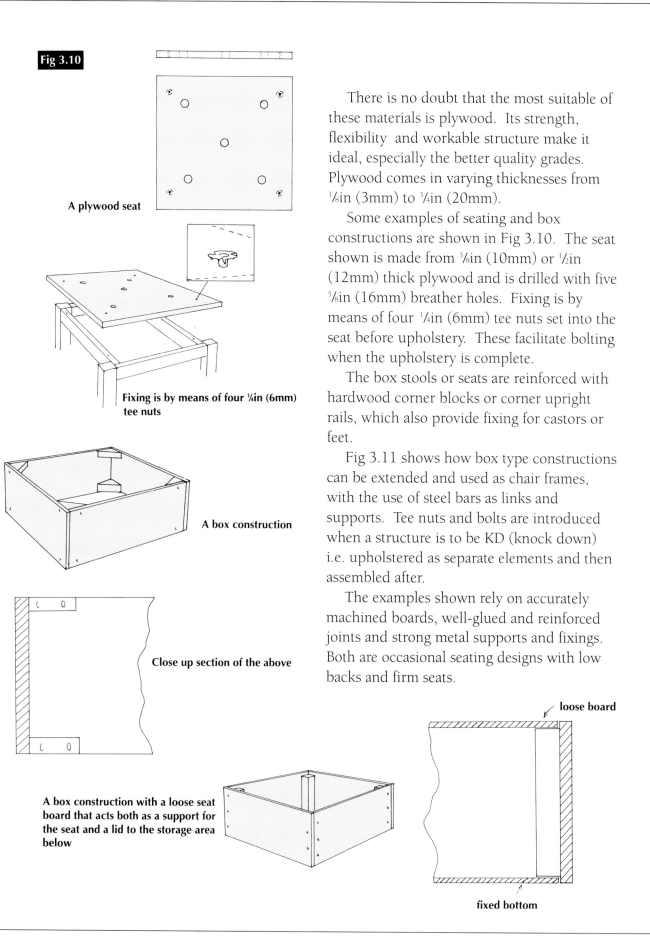

Fig 3.10

A plywood seat

Fixing is by means of four ¼in (6mm) tee nuts

A box construction

Close up section of the above

A box construction with a loose seat board that acts both as a support for the seat and a lid to the storage area below

loose board

fixed bottom

There is no doubt that the most suitable of these materials is plywood. Its strength, flexibility and workable structure make it ideal, especially the better quality grades. Plywood comes in varying thicknesses from ⅛in (3mm) to ¾in (20mm).

Some examples of seating and box constructions are shown in Fig 3.10. The seat shown is made from ⅜in (10mm) or ½in (12mm) thick plywood and is drilled with five ⅝in (16mm) breather holes. Fixing is by means of four ¼in (6mm) tee nuts set into the seat before upholstery. These facilitate bolting when the upholstery is complete.

The box stools or seats are reinforced with hardwood corner blocks or corner upright rails, which also provide fixing for castors or feet.

Fig 3.11 shows how box type constructions can be extended and used as chair frames, with the use of steel bars as links and supports. Tee nuts and bolts are introduced when a structure is to be KD (knock down) i.e. upholstered as separate elements and then assembled after.

The examples shown rely on accurately machined boards, well-glued and reinforced joints and strong metal supports and fixings. Both are occasional seating designs with low backs and firm seats.

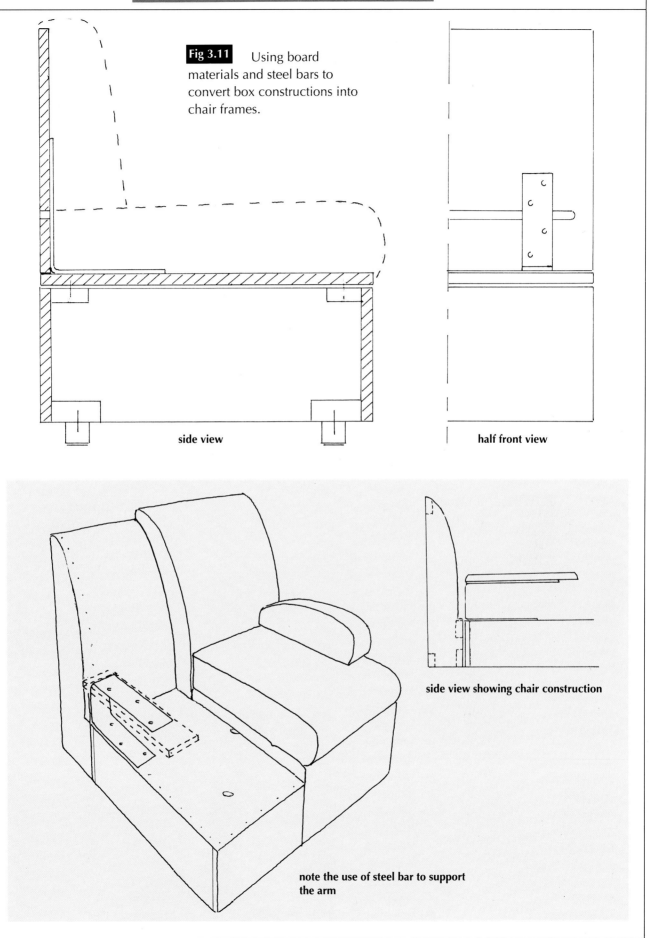

Fig 3.11 Using board materials and steel bars to convert box constructions into chair frames.

side view

half front view

side view showing chair construction

note the use of steel bar to support the arm

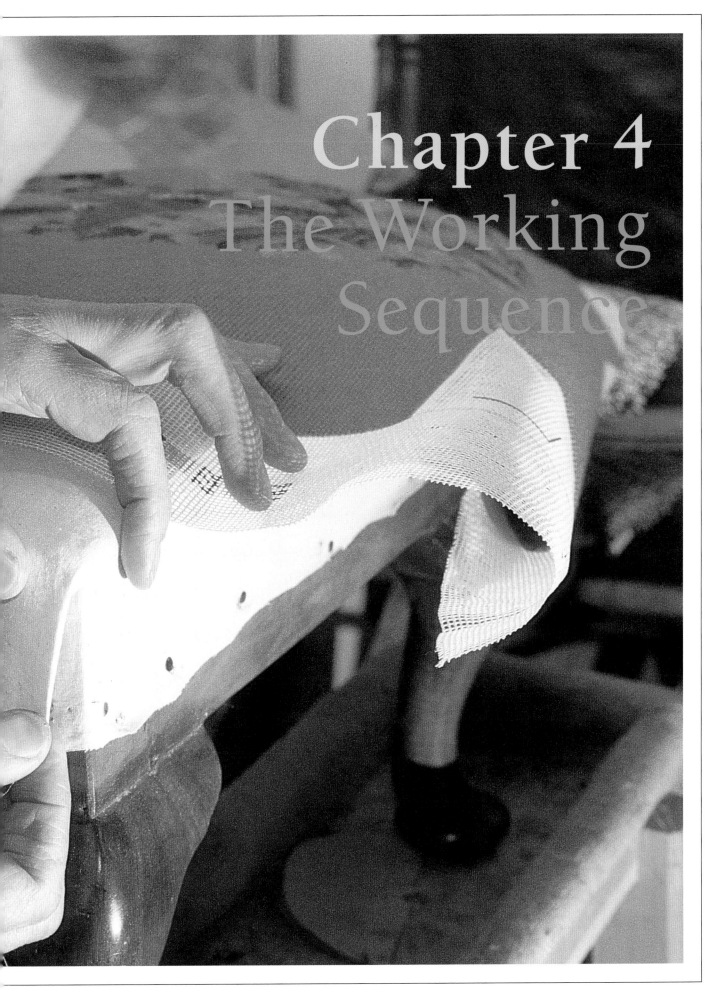

Chapter 4
The Working Sequence

A chair has two main areas, the insides and the outsides, each of which has its upholstered and covered parts. The insides are soft, comfortable areas and the outsides are the lightly padded and covered parts which cover the framework. There is a conventional sequence to the stages of upholstery, beginning with the inside parts.

Fig 4.1 The parts on some conventional upholstered pieces.

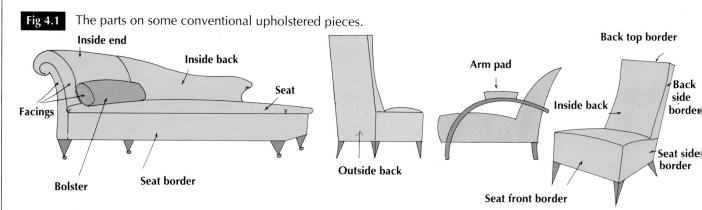

Insides

The upholstering of settees and chairs which have upholstered arms is nearly always begun by webbing up and lining the inside arms; in models without arms the inside back is completed first. When wings are built into a frame, these can be webbed and lined with hessian after the inside arms are completed. When the inside wings and inside arms are ready for covering the inside back can be webbed, lined, upholstered and covered in the same way. The inside work is completed by building and covering the seat. Trimmings, pipings and facings etc. are added where appropriate before tacking off and starting work on the outside coverings.

Tacking off

This is often a tedious task but it must be done with care as it can affect the appearance and evenness of the insides and tuckaways. All the

layers of linings and cover are tacked or stapled off, then trimmed off leaving about 2in (51mm) to fold back and tack again (*see* Fig 4.2).

Fig 4.2 Tacking off.

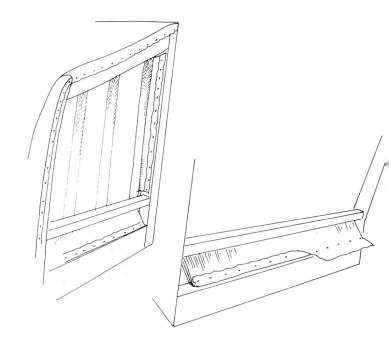

Outsides

The outside coverings are dealt with in the following order: outside wings, outside arms and outside back. The outer fabric coverings on upholstered furniture should be supported and lightly padded. This can be done with any strong lining cloth, but a medium-weight (10oz) hessian is usually a good choice. Skin wadding will provide a suitable padding, but in some cases, e.g. iron frame chairs, where a generous depth is more in keeping with the style, a cotton felt filling is used.

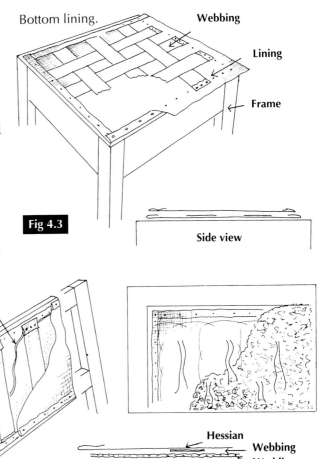

Fig 4.3

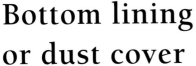

Bottom lining or dust cover

The traditional choice for chair undercovers is hessian or a black cotton lining cloth. Woven or spun bonded polypropylene cloths are widely used in modern production.

Stripping

Taking a piece of upholstery apart, to discover its condition or to strip it for reupholstery, is done in the exact opposite order to the work sequence. Removing the dust cover gives access to the underside, and taking the outside back off allows the back upholstery to be checked. The process can be continued by removing the outside arms and wings; this then allows the important supporting materials to be assessed for wear and tear. If the inside upholstery is to be stripped, the tacking-off work is lifted to free the inside coverings.

Varying the order of work

Some cases do not follow the normal work sequence. The upholstered seats of small dining chairs and stools, which are unsprung, can be lined with a black lining before they are webbed. This leaves the underside of the seat clear and uncovered. In such cases the inner surfaces of the seat rails are sanded smooth and given a coat of stain and sealer.

Fig 4.3 shows how the black lining cloth is tacked on and turned, and then webbed in the normal way. The upholstery then continues as for a normal seat, with hessian, stuffings and scrim, etc. Care has to be taken during the later stages that the bottom lining is not pierced by stuffing ties or bridle ties.

First stage: webbing inside arms and back.

A similar treatment is given to the back upholstery on many show-wood chairs. The outside back covering is first applied and fixed to the inside of the frame, then a layer or two of cotton wadding is placed over the cover, followed by webbings and the usual layers.

The upholstery can be traditional or modern, but in the cases of traditional work the bridle ties will need to be set into the hessian before any stuffing is put in. These ties can be in the form of a few single twines which can eventually be needled through on to the face of the scrim. This avoids having to take a needle through the outside back covering.

Examples of the working sequence

Only a generalized view of the working sequence can be gained by looking at the more common examples of upholstery. The order of working has to be adapted to suit the many different types and styles. However, the following routines form a sound basis, enabling an accessible and convenient method of working.

The following pieces are all conventional styles which crop up time after time in the workshop, either as new work or as reupholstery:

The stool

1. Web under the rails for traditional sprung work or on top of the rails for unsprung upholstery.
2. Spring up and lash.
3. Line with hessian.
4. Apply and fix filling. Build first and second stuffings in traditional work. Build, stitch or fix edges.
5. Apply soft topping, such as waddings or felts.
6. Cover in calico.
7. Cover with covering fabric.
8. Fix trimmings.
9. Fit bottom lining or dust cover.

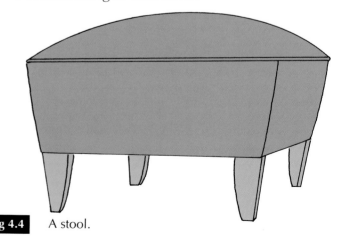

Fig 4.4　A stool.

Fig 4.5   An ottoman.

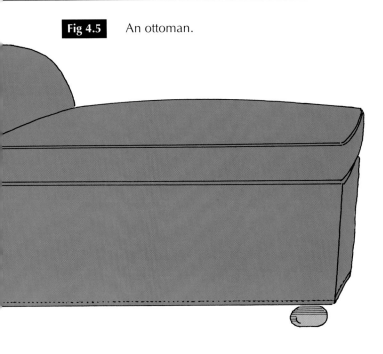

The nursing chair

1. Web and hessian the inside back.
2. Apply edgings or stuff and stitch.
3. Add second stuffings and cover in calico.
4. Cover the inside back with fabric.
5. Fit suspension to seat - traditional or modern.
6. Build first and second stuffings to seat or cut and glue foam fillings in place.
7. Complete the seat to calico.
8. Cut and sew seat cover.
9. Cover the seat and temporarily tack in place.
10. Tack off inside back and seat.
11. Line the outside back with hessian.
12. Position and back tack the outside back cover in place.
13. Cut and fit wadding to the outside back, then tack and pin before slipping to close.
14. Turn the chair over to tack off permanently and fit the black bottom lining.

The ottoman

1. Unscrew and remove the hinged lid.
2. Web and hessian the scroll end.
3. Occasionally an end may be sprung.
4. Build edging and apply fillings.
5. Cover in calico and trim off.
6. Pad and line the box base. Some ottomans have removable bottom boards to make lining easier and more accessible.
7. Cover the end with the covering fabric.
8. Cover the outsides of the base. Pin and slip stitch where necessary.
9. Apply facings and fix trimmings.
10. Tack off where necessary and line the outside end.
11. Pad and cover the outside end.
12. Upholster the lid, which may be sprung or firm.
13. Cover the lid in calico and position on to the box to check for fit.
14. Cover in fabric and line to match the base lining, then refit the lid.
15. Slip stitch and add more trimmings as they are needed.
16. Fix black bottom lining cloth to underside of base.

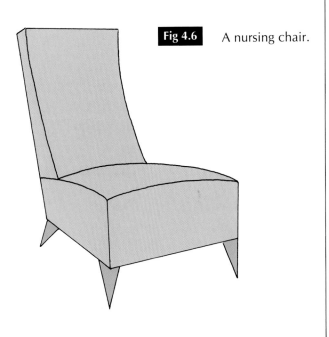

Fig 4.6   A nursing chair.

Fig 4.7   A wing arm chair.

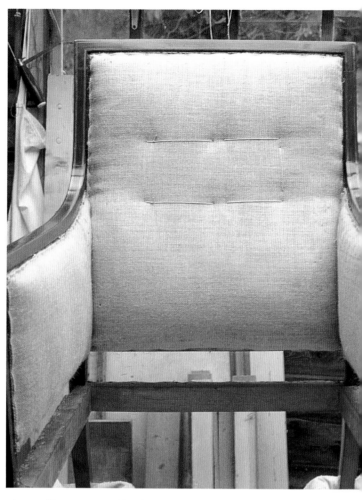

First stuffings: arms and back, covered in scrim.

The wing arm chair

The insides

1. Web and hessian the inside arms.
2. Apply edgings and then first and second stuffings.
3. Complete both inside arms in calico.
4. Repeat process on the inside wings to the calico stage.
5. Cover both arms and both wings.
6. Upholster the inside back which may be sprung or unsprung, by using modern or traditional materials as appropriate.
7. Cover the inside back in calico and the top cover.
8. To complete the insides, make up the seat - which will support the reversible cushion - with a platform, usually sprung.
9. Pull down the seat in calico and then cover.

The cushion

10. Measure for the bordered cushion, cut out the cover and machine sew.
11. If the seams are to be piped, make up the piping first and then sew it around each cushion panel.
12. Join the borders together and sew them around the first cushion panel and then to the opposite panel.
13. When zip closing is to be used, prepare the back border separately before the cushion is made up, by inserting a zip along its centre.
14. Fill and close the cushion and place it into the seat to check for shape, size, and good fit.
15. Complete the covering of the insides by tacking off and trimming.

The outsides

16. Add any decorative trimmings to the chair before the outside wings are lined, padded and covered.
17. Set on outside arms, trim to size and back tack under the arms. Line and pad each outside arm before tacking off.
18. To complete the outsides, line, pad and cover the outside back. Turn and pin edges ready for slip stitching or else secure with tacking strip.
19. Finally, turn the chair over and trim and tack the bottom lining or dust cover in place.

The *chaise-longue*

The single end

1. Begin by building the foundation of the single end, often called the scroll end, which may be sprung or unsprung. Complete this up to calico.
2. Web, line and stuff the inside back.
3. Both the end and the back may be buttoned or plain. In the case of a buttoned *chaise-longue* do not use calico, but cover both the end and the back and button them directly into the second stuffing.

The seat

4. The seat may be firm edge or spring edge. Web, spring, lash and then stitch up in scrim.
5. Build second stuffing and then pull this down in calico.
6. Cut and carefully fit the seat cover before tacking down over cotton felt or skin wadding.
7. Use decoration, facings and trimmings as required before the tacking off commences to permanently secure the insides at their tuckaways.

The outsides

8. Finishing off begins by lining and padding the outside back before covering. This is followed by the outside end where the process is repeated.
9. Slip stitch edges and corners which have been pinned before the work is turned over and tacked off on the underside.
10. Fit a hessian or black lining cloth to the underside of the seat.

Fig 4.8 A *chaise-longue*.

Chapter 5 Marking Out & Fitting Covers & Fabrics

Marking out the cover for a piece of upholstery brings the cutting plan from a small sketch on paper to real size on the fabric. Measurements become more critical at this stage, and at the same time have to be kept within the parameters of the cover: the cover width and length, and any texture, pile, pattern or design.

Each fabric or covering presents a different situation, which has to be dealt with at the time of marking out and cutting. With the fabric laid out on a cutting table face side up, the arrangement and particular treatment of the covering can be visualized.

Grain or thread direction must be considered, as it is very important to 'cut to thread' in both the warp and the weft directions. In some fabrics the grain will be strong and very obvious, whereas in others, e.g. velours and printed fabrics, it is hidden below the pile or colouring.

A mental check list is useful:
- Is the face side of the cover obvious? The fabric should have been rolled up with the face inside.
- Which is the top (or bottom) of the surface design or pattern? Now is the time to get it right.
- Check the grain or thread of the cover, and trim the leading edge straight with the thread before starting to mark out and cut.
- Does the fabric have a pile, and is the pile direction obvious? If not, lay a small coin on the surface and tap the table; the coin will travel in the direction of the pile.
- What is the size of the pattern repeat, and how does it relate to the main areas and sizes to be cut?
- Check the position of stripes or cords in the cover, and choose a centre which can be used throughout the job.

- What does the half width measure and how does it tie up with the sizes to be cut? Can the half width be used to advantage so that cover parts will match across and be mirrored?
- Will there be extension pieces to be added to the width or half width, and where will they conveniently come from?
- Is the centre of the fabric obvious, and can it be chosen now?
- Are stripes dominant? If so, how can they be best placed for effect?
- Should any bold stripes be used or avoided for small parts such as facings and buttons?
- Where will pipings be cut from?
- Can unseen cushion borders be cut from oddments for economy?
- Are fly pieces being used to make savings on the cover?

Bias

Upholstery covers are best marked out on the face side so that the features of the cloth are always visible.

Woven and printed patterns become very important when they are bold and large, as they will be central to the main areas of the work, e.g. inside backs and seats. Smaller, all-over patterns and fine stripes are generally not as dominant and therefore more flexible in the cutting layout; however, it is usually advisable to select a centre line early on and to stick to it throughout the layout.

Plain covers are of course much more flexible and easier to deal with, but the same

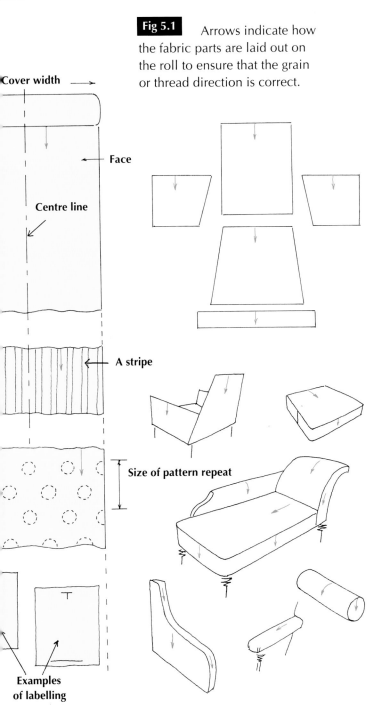

Fig 5.1 Arrows indicate how the fabric parts are laid out on the roll to ensure that the grain or thread direction is correct.

Cover width

Face

Centre line

A stripe

Size of pattern repeat

Examples of labelling

Labelling

Once a length of fabric has been cut into smaller parts, each part should be labelled so that all parts remain in order and ready for use without delay or confusion. Pairs can be kept together and those parts to be matched or sewn can be pinned. Labelling in industry is done with chalk on the reverse side of the cover: the top is marked with a large T, and the positions of flies and extensions are marked with a thick straight line just inside the edge. Where two pieces are to be sewn into shapes, edges are marked with V-notches as balance marks. An alternative method of labelling is to use pins, which are always placed in the same position on each piece, e.g. the top left or bottom left corners. Small slips of paper, marked with the part's name and always pinned in the same place, are another good way to deal with labelling.

Marking and cutting sequence

If space is limited, covers can be marked piecemeal and parts cut when they are needed. The best sequence in this case will depend on the type of work being done: for chair work, the inside arm pieces and inside backs will generally be needed first, followed by, for example, the inside wings and then the seat cover. Cushion panels and borders should be marked out and cut together, and then rolled up until needed.

Accuracy

Cover parts to be upholstered and tacked into place will need an allowance of 2-3in (52-75mm) for pulling and tacking down. This is a fairly generous amount, and can be carefully

code of practice should be followed as a matter of habit, especially when face side and grain direction are being checked.

White dust-free chalk is an ideal marking medium, and allows for adjustments if errors are made, when used with light pressure on the cover. Tailor's crayon is also used extensively, but this gives a more permanent line and is difficult to remove.

reduced where the positioning is precise and the part is relatively small.

Where cover parts are to be fitted or are shaped ready for machine sewing, the allowances need to be much smaller and more accurate: ⅜in or ½in (10 or 13mm) maximum is the normal margin, and must be accurately kept to during marking and cutting (see Fig 5.2). The machinist automatically follows an imaginary line of this margin just inside and parallel to the edge of the fabric. Most sewing work of this kind in upholstery is done with an allowance of ⅜in (10mm), and everyone involved in the producing of a made up cover works to the recognized margin. This practice can be adopted for both small and large-scale work, and results in well-made and accurately fitting covers. Occasionally allowances are varied for certain difficult coverings, e.g. ½in (13mm) for very loosely woven fabrics, and ¼in (6mm) for some leather work.

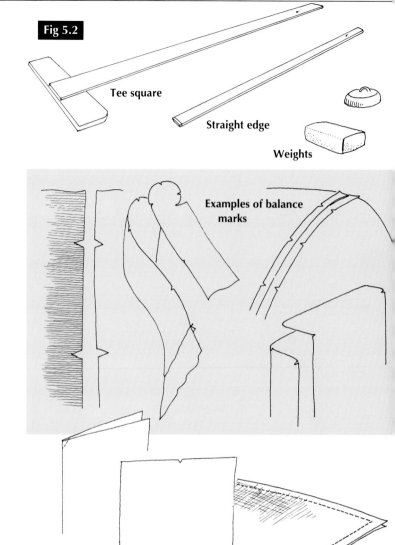

Fig 5.2

Tee square

Straight edge

Weights

Examples of balance marks

Centring

The ⅜in (10mm) margin

Fig 5.3 A comparison between the conventional layout of fabric on to chairs and settees and the 'railroad' technique. In large-scale production of upholstered furniture the technique of running fabric along the length of large pieces of furniture, called railroading, can be more economical in the fabric used, and will also save time in matching and joining.

This method is being used more and more as textiles are being designed and produced to suit this kind of work. Furnishing fabrics with woven or printed stripes or patterns could not usually be treated in this way; this system calls for special fabrics to be made so that patterns will be upright when a fabric is used sideways on. However, this is still a very specialized area of upholstery manufacture, and the bulk of fabrics used for furnishing remain of the conventional type, with an average width of 125cm (49in) and with repeats of the pattern running up and down the roll length.

A number of different plain surface coverings can be adapted to the railroad system quite easily, e.g. vinyl-coated cloths, plain wool tweeds and suede nylon cloths.

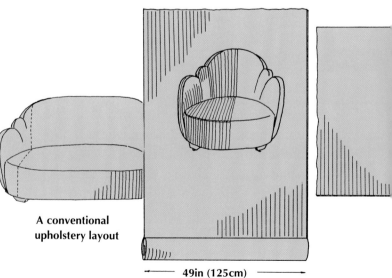

A conventional upholstery layout

49in (125cm)

Cuts, collars and corners

The safest and most reliable method used to cut and trim covers is to cut after the first temporary tack fixing. This is a standard sequence which requires the cover first to be set on and checked for straightness of thread and then pulled down and temporary tacked.

Once the cut or cuts are made there is often very little allowance for the cover to be moved or readjusted. The setting on and temporary fixing is therefore a fairly critical time: the grain or thread of the cloth needs to be straight and designs and patterns aligned and matched where necessary. When the temporary tacks are in place, the cover can be pushed over and tucked lightly to left and right up to the points where the cuts will be made.

Fig 5.4 Most cuts around rails, uprights and stumps etc. are made with the cover edge folded back and with the fold lined up closely to the point of cut. Here are several examples.

An allowance must often be made for the depth of the tuckaway, so the cut may initially seem short of the rail to be cut round; a good example of this can be seen at **A**, showing the corner cut at the back of the chair seat. This allows plenty of tuckaway before the back leg is reached. With the initial cut made, the position can be checked for accuracy by pushing the cover down and into place. Once checked it can easily be pulled back and cut further or adjusted before finally being positioned.

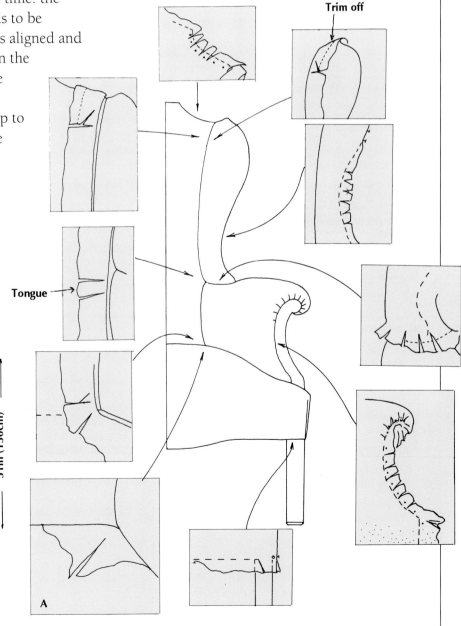

Tongue

Trim off

A 'railroaded' fabric

51in (130cm)

A

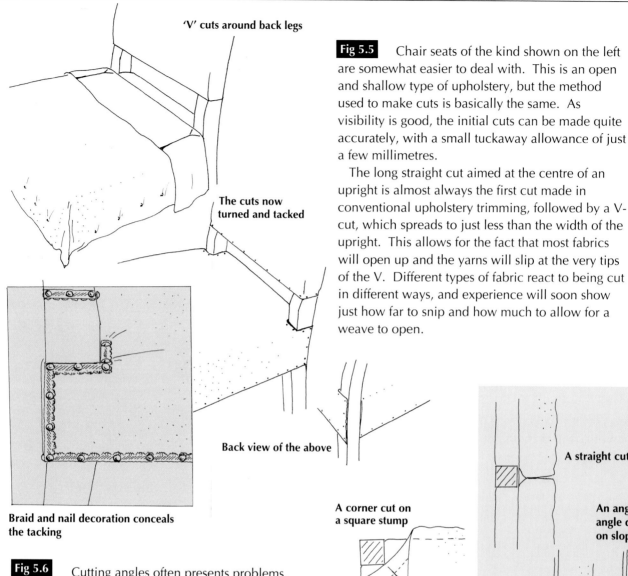

'V' cuts around back legs

The cuts now turned and tacked

Back view of the above

Braid and nail decoration conceals the tacking

Fig 5.5 Chair seats of the kind shown on the left are somewhat easier to deal with. This is an open and shallow type of upholstery, but the method used to make cuts is basically the same. As visibility is good, the initial cuts can be made quite accurately, with a small tuckaway allowance of just a few millimetres.

The long straight cut aimed at the centre of an upright is almost always the first cut made in conventional upholstery trimming, followed by a V-cut, which spreads to just less than the width of the upright. This allows for the fact that most fabrics will open up and the yarns will slip at the very tips of the V. Different types of fabric react to being cut in different ways, and experience will soon show just how far to snip and how much to allow for a weave to open.

Fig 5.6 Cutting angles often presents problems. Angle cuts have to be judged correctly to give the right amount of cover in the right place after cutting; sloping arm rests and chair legs set at an angle need particularly careful assessment before cuts are made. It often helps to try to visualize the finished position of a seat or back cover, and sometimes a dry run using a newspaper or an odd piece of calico will show exactly the best cutting angle. The grain of a fabric can help, giving a visual line which either has to be followed or, in the case of an angled cut, crossed.

Some interesting examples are shown on the right; the cuts at **A** are angled well to provide good turnings each side of the upright, and the very wide stump or leg means that a tongue is produced, rather than a Y-shaped cut. The tongue can then be pushed well down into the upholstery, and, if possible, fixed by tacking or by a holding stitch.

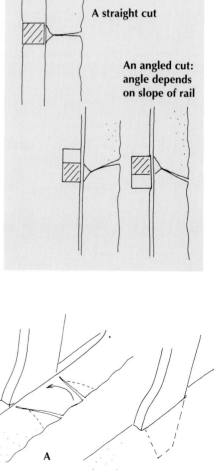

A straight cut

An angled cut: angle depends on slope of rail

A corner cut on a square stump

Cutting fabric around a turned stump

A

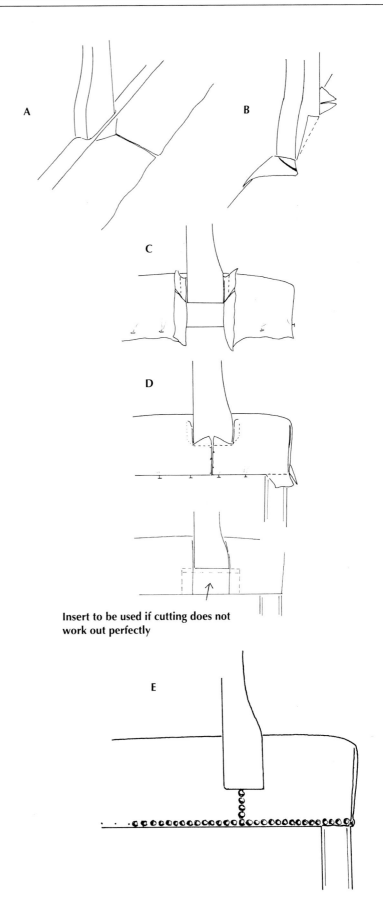

Fig 5.7 The Gainsborough-style chair with arm supports set along each side of the seat provides a cutting challenge: a series of five careful cuts (A to E) around the upright will bring the two cut edges of the first cut back together. If cut well, these two edges will butt together and can be gimp-pinned before finishing with upholstery nails or a braid.

Should the cutting not work out perfectly, an insert of extra fabric can be back-tacked below the arm stump, and the seat cover can be trimmed and turned to lay straight down either side over the insert. However, with some thought and careful manipulating and trimming, a good cut is easier than it would first appear.

Insert to be used if cutting does not work out perfectly

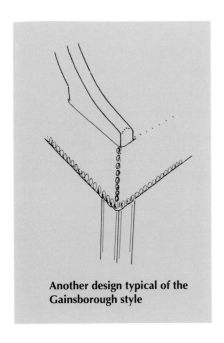

Another design typical of the Gainsborough style

The inside back panel is trimmed and fitted to the arm shape.

If the panel is carefully centred, only one side need be shaped to the arm curve; the panel can then be folded down the centre line and the opposite shape cut from the first.

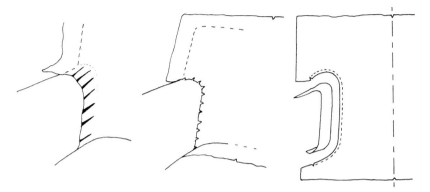

The collar strip is measured for and cut AxB.

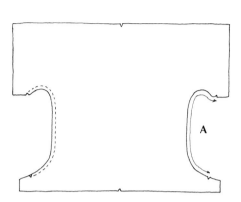

Balance marks are cut at each end and a sewing allowance of about ⅜in (10mm) is made.

Fig 5.8 How to cut and sew a full collar into an inside back. Collars are made up and used in upholstery covers in much the same way as they are for clothing; they provide a sealed and turned edge which hugs and fits neatly around a shape. The collar is purely functional, and is added to a seat or back cover to produce good line and shape; where collar strips are not used, covers have to be cut around arm tops and fronts (for example) and are more vulnerable to wear and tear. A well fitted and machined collar often indicates that care has been taken to produce a cover that looks professional and sits well on its foundation. Collars may be full collars or half collars, and can have plain or piped seams. Only full collars will have piped seams; those made up with plain seams are less obvious.

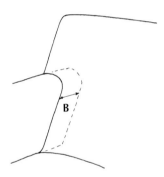

The collar strip is machine sewn in place around the shape.

If piping or any other seam decoration is to be used, this is sewn in around the collar opening before the collar strip is sewn in.

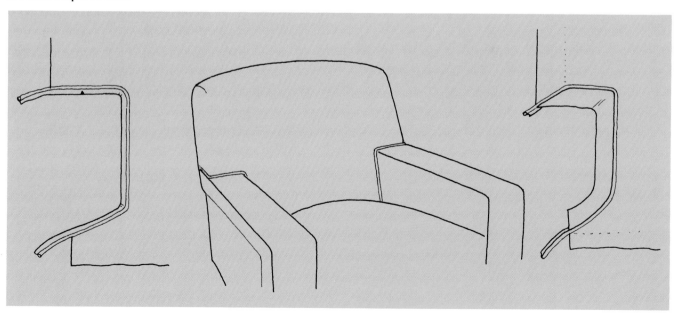

The length of the cuts is determined by the cover's position on the chair, and an allowance of ⅜in (10mm) is made for sewing.

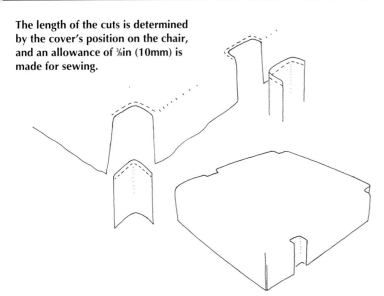

A collar being fitted ready for sewing.
Note the balance marks used for centring the collar.

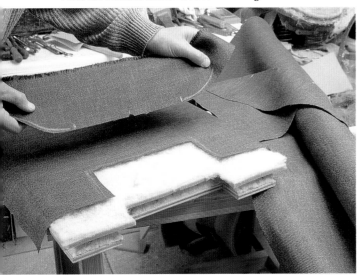

The collar now fitted and tacked in place.

Fig 5.9   The stages of fitting a half collar. This is a simplified version of the full collar, and is a small square of cover, trimmed and sewn into a cut. The cuts are first positioned and made into the panel by laying the cover on to the chair and carefully marking the cuts with chalk. Half collars of this type can be used in seat corners, platforms for seats, inside backs and in any place where long cuts may be vulnerable to wear and tear.

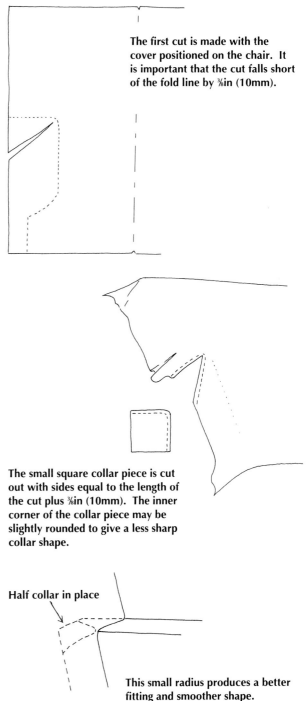

The first cut is made with the cover positioned on the chair. It is important that the cut falls short of the fold line by ⅜in (10mm).

The small square collar piece is cut out with sides equal to the length of the cut plus ⅜in (10mm). The inner corner of the collar piece may be slightly rounded to give a less sharp collar shape.

Half collar in place

This small radius produces a better fitting and smoother shape.

Collar face down

Face

Cut away centre and snip corners

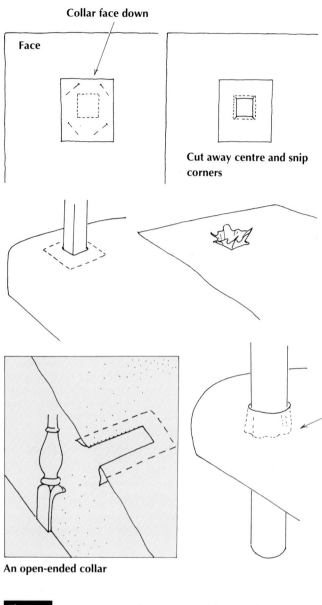

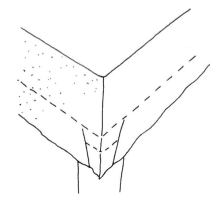

An open-ended collar

Fig 5.10 Shaping collars are easily fitted and can be made up to virtually any outline shape. They can be positioned anywhere on a panel or cover, and may be closed or open-ended.

Once the exact position has been decided on, the making up is simple and painless: use a few pins to position the collar piece directly over and central on to the up-facing panel. Place the collar face down and mark carefully the shape to be sewn. Machine sew around the marked shape and tie off the thread. The collar is completed by cutting away the centre of both layers of cover, leaving a small allowance. Any corner should be carefully snipped up to the sewing, to allow the collar to be turned easily and flat. Finally, unpin the collar and push it through the panel, to produce a neatly sealed edge with the collar on the underside.

This technique is used around timber and steel uprights, legs and stumps in both traditional and modern upholstered furniture.

Collar is pushed down where it meets the tube

Cutting and turning fabric on a back leg

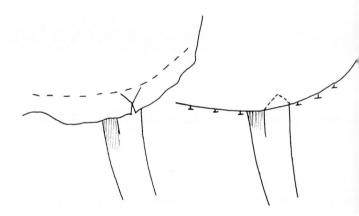

Fig 5.11 Some typical cuts around legs and corners. Trimming should be precise and clean, using sharp scissors, and any excess bulk should be removed wherever possible before tacking down.

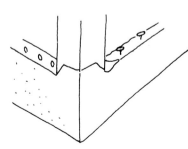

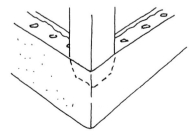

Cutting and turning fabric on a square corner

Fig 5.12 Covering and pleating a square corner (right); the arrows indicate the direction of pull. A corner of this type is worked after the cover has been set on and temporary tacked. When the corner has been positioned and tacked, as much excess cover as possible is cut away, to leave the minimum amount of turning. Final covering should be neat and tight, leaving one sharp upright pleat.

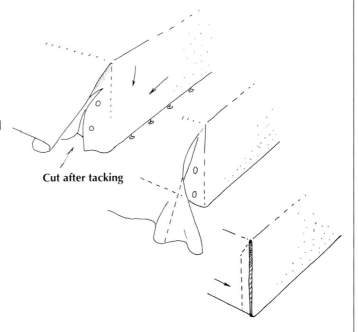

Cut after tacking

Fig 5.13 Rounded corners are best treated with two or four inverted folds: the larger the radius, the more pleats that can be used to form a pleasing detail. The first pull is centred on the corner with equal fullness on each side, and a tack is fixed in the centre. Two more tacks are fixed on each side of the centre, and the excess cover below the tack line is cut away. To allow the pleats to form in a sharp V formation, a vertical cut of about 1in (25mm) is made on each side of the outer tacks.

The tack and cut method is used to produce a corner with four or more pleats: as each pleat is formed and tacked in place, the excess cover is cut away, avoiding a build-up of bulky fabric. The next pleat can then be folded and set, followed by more trimming. Short vertical cuts can also be used to help ease the tension from the fabric as work ˋ progresses.

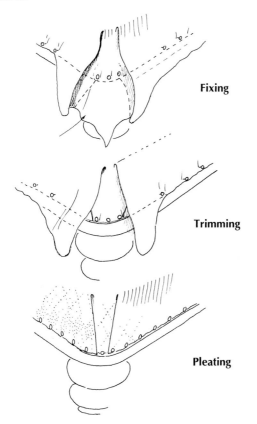

Fixing

Trimming

Pleating

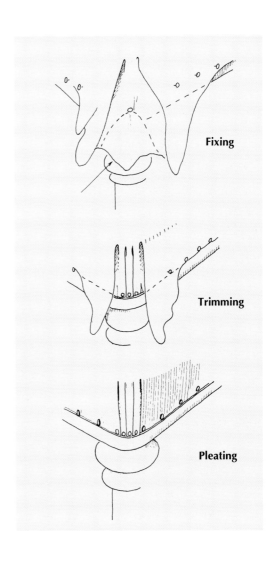

Fixing

Trimming

Pleating

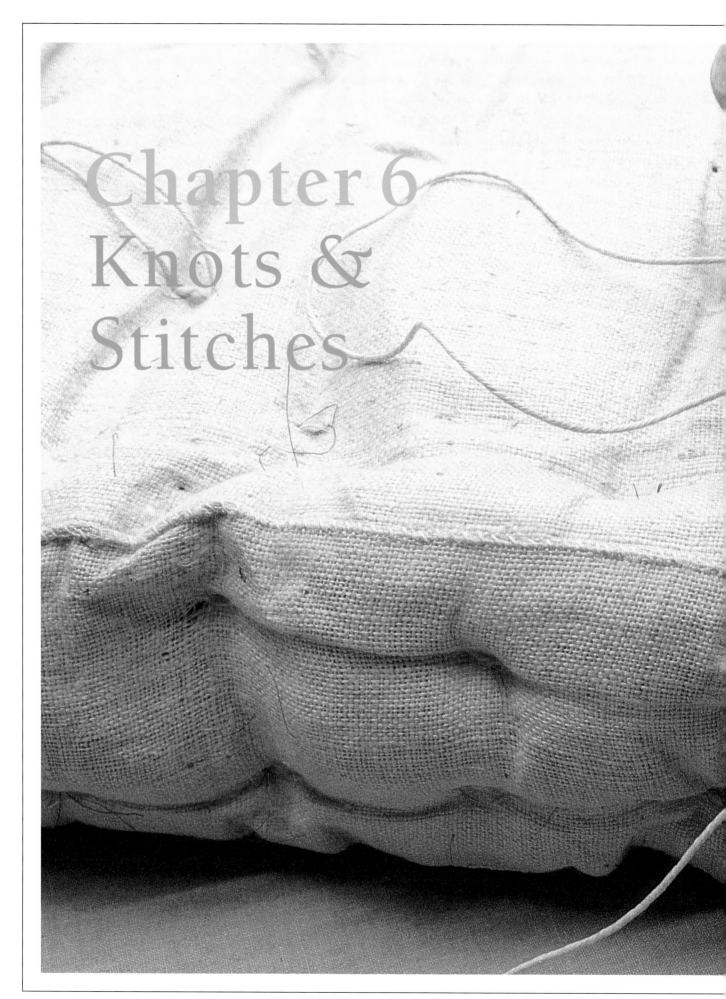

Chapter 6
Knots &
Stitches

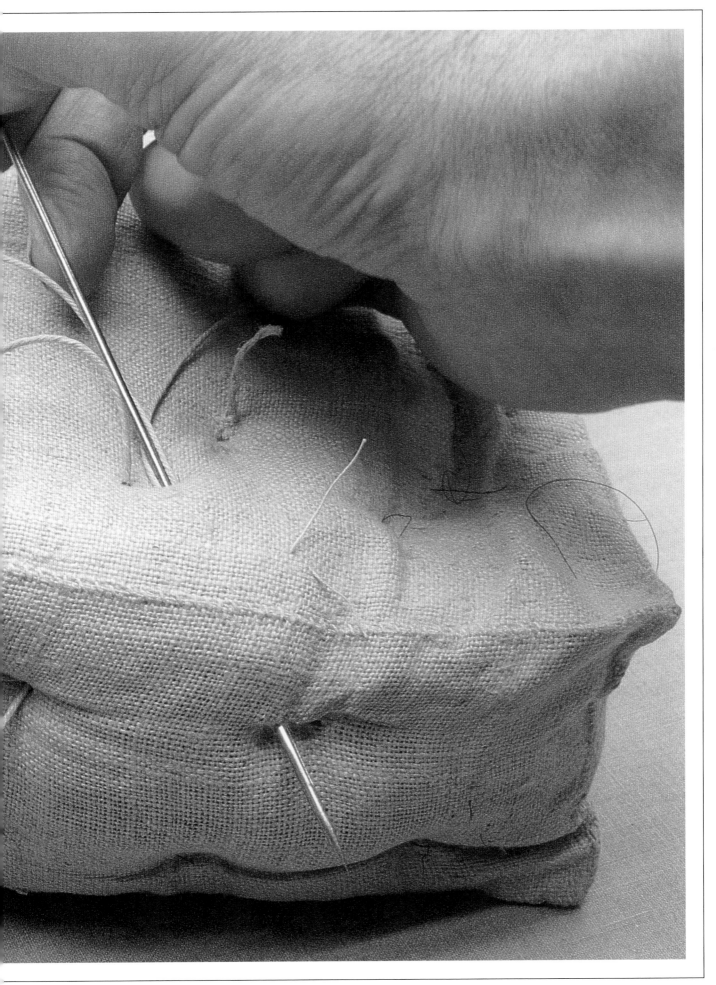

Quite a range of knots and stitches is used in upholstery, some very basic and some intricate and special to the craft. Once mastered and perfected they can be applied as the need arises. Some of the more basic knots and stitches are needed repeatedly and become second nature, while others such as the Chesterfield stitch and the feather edge are less common and are only used when the work demands them.

There are a number of adapted stitches and knots which are very traditional and have obviously been developed and used by craftsmen and then passed on in one form or another. It is a fascinating and important facet of the craft, but an area which is no longer needed in today's upholstery production. Various glues, tacking strips and the general use of foam fillings have created a branch of upholstery where knots and stitches are no longer necessary.

It is mainly in reupholstery and period upholstery restoration that knot tying and hand stitching skills are still part of the craft. These skills and techniques are also very much in evidence where handcrafted design is produced.

In the fashion trade particularly, many quite amazing hand stitching techniques are used to tailor, design and style new clothes. To a lesser extent many similar skills are used in the upholstering of furniture.

Most knots and stitches in upholstery are used to join and to hold materials together in a familiar way. Many, however, are used to create shape and to build and hold a shaped piece of work in place. Making shapes with loose fillings is a form of sculpture, with the knots and stitches holding and supporting the basic medium to give shape and design to the upholstery.

Jute, hemp and linen are the natural fibres used in the manufacture of threads, twines and strong cords. Nylons and polyesters also make excellent and very tough twines, often used for buttoning etc.

Fig 6.1(a) Everyone working in upholstery uses the slip knot; so much so that it would be difficult to cope without it. The slip knot may be single or double and is adjustable until locked off with a half-hitch. Its main uses are when starting off bridling, tying in stuffing ties, stitching edges and when buttoning or tufting. The double knot is needed whenever strain is likely, e.g. in buttoning, and particularly when beginning stitched edge work. A single slip knot is otherwise quite adequate and works in the same way: the more the knot is pulled the tighter it becomes.

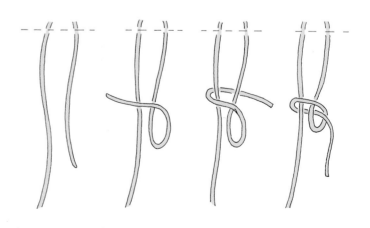

Fig 6.1(b)   A double-tied variation of the slip knot.

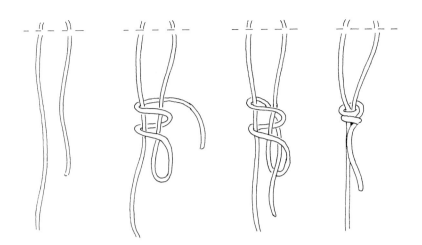

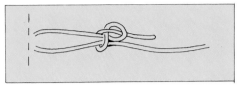

Fig 6.2(a)   An example of how the slip knot is used to secure buttons in a chair back, with a toggle of cloth or webbing for the knot to grip and slip on. The depth of buttons for surface buttoning and for deep buttoning needs to be adjustable until the work is even and tight and ready to be finished off. Each knot is finally locked off and secured with the hitch or double hitch.

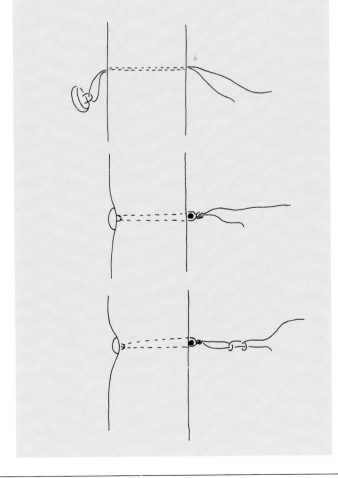

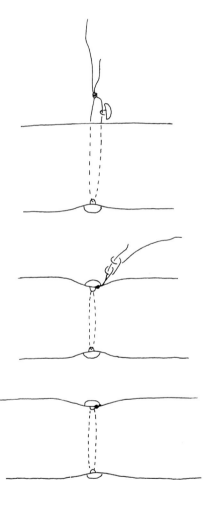

Fig 6.2(b)   Surface buttoning in a reversible cushion is dealt with in a similar way, but with a button on either side. The depth is temporarily set and then adjusted down to suit the product and filling.

When all the buttons are in place, each can be pulled to a finished position and well tied off with a double hitch. All the twines can finally be snipped and then tucked under the head of the button.

Fig 6.3 Tufting (right) is a technique used in cushion, futon and mattress making. There are a number of variations which basically do the same job of stabilizing the fillings and setting the depth of the cushion or mattress. The traditional cotton-filled futon is a good example of a tufted mattress which is filled entirely with layers of natural fibre filling.

The simple tuft or tie is needled through the case or covering with strong linen thread or twine. A small amount of the cover is caught on the surface, preferably at an angle to the grain of the cover yarns, and the twine is then tied off with the slip knot. Once all the ties are in place they can be pulled evenly to depth, and the work is then turned over for final adjustment and knotting off with the hitch. Setting the ties diagonally on the surface helps to avoid any splitting of the case covering.

Special tufts made from wool or leather and decorative tufts of cotton or silk yarns are normally used when the surface of the work is to remain visible.

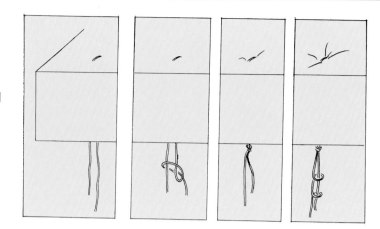

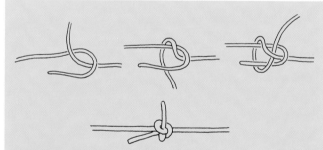

Fig 6.4 Making the hitch and the double hitch. Both knots are used extensively to knot and to tie off upholstery stitch work of all kinds.

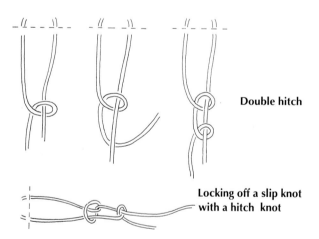

Double hitch

Locking off a slip knot with a hitch knot

Fig 6.5 The reef knot is familiar and easy to make. To form the reef correctly using two ends of twine or thread, the right hand thread is laid over the left and turned under, then the left is laid over the right and turned under. The knot has to be tightened to make a secure join.

Fig 6.6 The sheet bend is a quickly made and useful knot; to join two ends together, the left is turned into a loop and the right twine is threaded into and around the loop.

The reef and the sheet bend knots are both used to extend a twine or cord in lashing and stitching.

Before a stitching or lashing sequence is started, the length of twine or cord cut off for the job has to be judged. Short lengths can be annoying, and lengths that are too long can cause handling problems. The span of a person's open arms is a good single length, but most stitching operations need about two of these lengths (something over 2m); anything much beyond this becomes cumbersome and difficult to control.

Fig 6.7   The various sorts of hitches make interesting and useful knots for fixings and lashings in upholstery. They depend in most cases on the friction created at the point where the cord or twine crosses over. Although a hitch can be made free, it is most effective when tied around something.

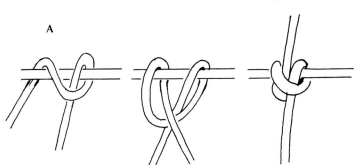

A

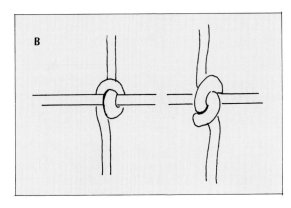

B

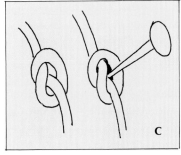

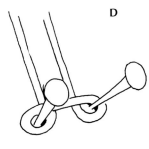

C

D

A The clove hitch produces a strong and reliable grip on wires and springs. Its reliability makes it perfect for lashing down rows of springs in the seats and backs of chairs.

B The simple hitch or spring hitch works in a similar way, but is less reliable. It is very much easier and quicker to form, and relies on a laid cord remaining taut. The simple hitch is ideally used alternately with the clove hitch or thumb knot.

C A thumb knot, otherwise known as the overhand, is a relatively simple knot which has a strong grip once tightened. It is ideal for lashing purposes in spring and tying work of all kinds.

D A simple hitch is basically a loop, and can be effectively used in twin for fixing down and tying off.

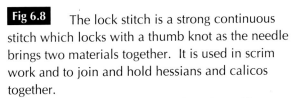

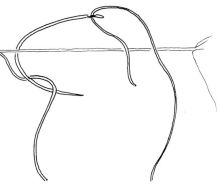

Fig 6.8   The lock stitch is a strong continuous stitch which locks with a thumb knot as the needle brings two materials together. It is used in scrim work and to join and hold hessians and calicos together.

The knot is formed by winding the trailing twine clockwise around the needle after it has passed through the cloth being stitched. There are variations of this stitch, but they all do the same job. The spacing of the knots, for example, will depend on the tightness needed and the type of scrim being used. When a good strong join is needed, the scrim should be well caught and knots should be about ½in (13mm) apart.

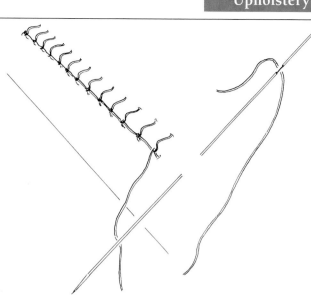

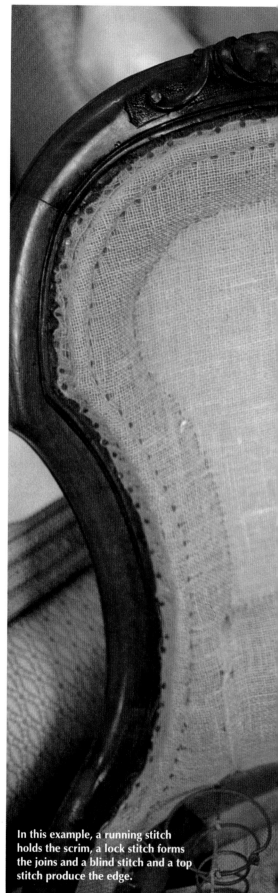

Fig 6.9 The blanket stitch is easily formed with a straight two-point needle or a curved mattress needle. It is basically an edging stitch and is quite often seen in early Victorian stitch edge work, where a fine feather edge is made around facings and shaped scrolls.

The stitch is spaced approximately ⅜in (10mm) without knots and is simply pulled into place as the scrim and stuffing are squeezed to a tight sharp edge (*see* Fig 5.13).

In sailing terms the blanket stitch is known as a marline hitch, and is used to maintain sails, bundles and packages in neat rolls by 'marling' them down with a light rope.

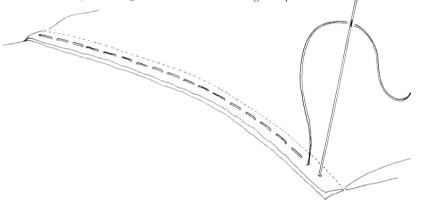

Fig 6.10 The running stitch is used by every upholsterer in all sorts of different ways: a fabric can be gathered on an evenly sewn running stitch; a platform in a chair seat is held in place by a running stitch before being filled, and a pull-in can easily be produced on an inside back or an inside arm by running through with a needle and twine in a neat even running stitch. The twine is eventually covered by a decorative upholstery cord which is slip-stitched along the pull-in.

A running stitch has a knot to start off and to finish with, and so has to be tightened down after the stitch line is in place.

In dressmaking and tailoring a running stitch is used to baste fabrics and hold them down so that they are aligned before being machine sewn.

In this example, a running stitch holds the scrim, a lock stitch forms the joins and a blind stitch and a top stitch produce the edge.

Fig 6.11 The back stitch is one of the strongest hand stitches and is worked from right to left. It can be used as a substitute for machine stitching as the continuous line of stitches resembles a machine sewn seam. However, for fixing fringes and braids the back stitch used in tailoring is extended and spaced so that a very small stitch appears on the surface about every ⅜in (10mm).

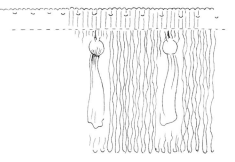

Fig 6.12 With care and precision, a slip stitch will be almost invisible when complete. It is universally used to join and finish covers on chairs and cushions and to close up fitted calico linings. In traditional upholstery work its use is unlimited and versatile.

The circular slipping needle and a waxed linen thread make a strong durable seam, particularly on shaped and difficult work. The stitch is formed by catching two cloths together in a ladder pattern. Seams can be hand stitched plain or through piping, or can be corded.

When a piped join is to be slipped the stitch remains basically the same, but the needle passes across under the piping cord between each stitch. Inset: to perfect the slip stitch, the circular needle is inserted just a millimetre or so back from its opposite stitch.

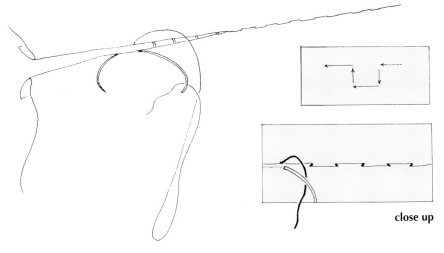

close up

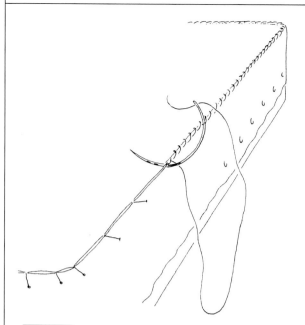

Spring lashing.

Fig 6.13   The overedge (overhand) stitch simply oversews together the two folded edges of a border and its main panel. It can be worked very close to form a fine but firm edge, or spaced out to make a softer join. Many bordered edges in 18th-century work were sewn in this way. The stitches were small and close to the edge.

Fig 6.14   The bridle is a stuffing tie in the form of a long running stitch which pierces the depth of a first stuffing and holds it firmly in place while other work proceeds.

Bridling begins with a slip knot on the surface of a scrim covering and runs through at 3- or 4-inch (75mm or 102mm) centres. When the pattern of stitches is complete, the stitches are tightened down and the twine end is half-hitched with a half bow. This allows for quick release and adjustment at a later stage. In some types of work, e.g. deep buttoning, the bridle stitch can be released to allow the stuffing to rise and create a loft if needed.

A whipping stitch is similar to the overedge, but has larger slanting stitches. The whipping creates a rolled edge which gives a stiff line when the stitches are drawn up very tight, or when the very tip of the edge is curled over with finger and thumb as the stitch progresses.

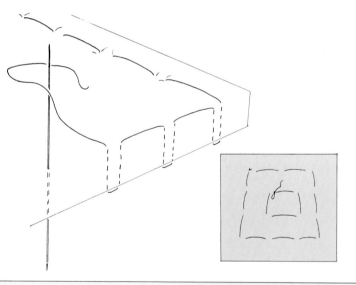

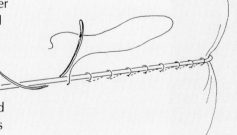

Fig 6.15   The holding stitch is a long overhand stitch adapted to produce a loose holding stitch over a cord or a heavy twine. The stitch allows the cord to be tightened and drawn to create a pull-in or waist around stuffed cushions and pouffes. The stitches are spaced at about 1in (25mm) centres while the cord is held in place.

A long, well-spaced slip stitch can also be used for the same purpose. Use a fine unwaxed mattress twine and a 4in (102mm) circular needle.

Fig 6.16   Lashing and whipping techniques are commonly used in upholstery to tie cane or wire edges to springs and to whip the ends of upholstery cords. Both techniques need to be tightly made.

Fig 6.16(a)   This shows a method used to lash cane in a spring edge. About 39in (1m) of mattress twine is folded in half and looped around to start the line of lashing, which when finished will be about 1¼in (32mm) long. The twine is kept double throughout as each subsequent loop is pulled through and laid tight against its neighbour. The lashing soon builds as each loop is pulled very tight, and it is finished off by parting the twines and tying a reef knot.

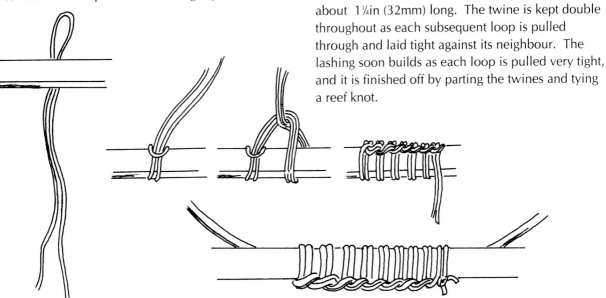

Fig 6.16(b)   Whipping the end of a cord or rope for upholstery purposes is done with a length of waxed linen thread. A short loop is held on to the cord as the thread is tightly wound from the end and worked back down the cord. To complete the whipping, the end is taken through the loop and held with finger and thumb while the short end is tightened to take the loop and its end well under the whipping. Both ends are snipped off close.

Fig 6.16(c)   Whipping can be used for cording into a button back to form flutes. The buttoning twines are pierced through the centre of the whipping and the button loop or shank eased into place before the button is pulled down and tied off.

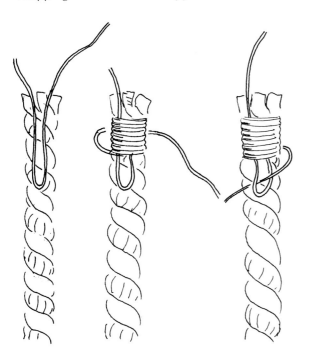

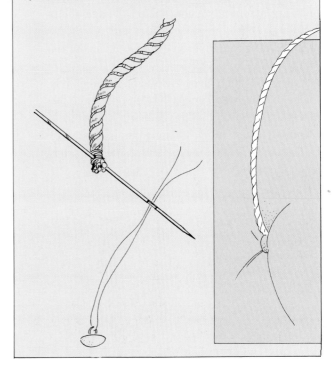

Fig 6.17   The blind stitch (right) is used to build and firm up the foundation of stitched edge upholstery. It is the first row of stitches put into a first stuffing in traditional work, to pull the stuffing into an edge in preparation for subsequent rows. Its use is common in stuffover seats of all kinds and in panel upholstery with show-wood surrounds. Arm fronts, facings and scrolls are all built using a blind stitch foundation.

A two-point needle, either bayonette or round, is used with a strong fine mattress twine. The blind stitch begins with a double slip knot and progresses along the edge from left to right. (Left-handed people may prefer to work in the opposite direction.) The blind stitch knot is wound around the needle and the needle removed and parked, while the stuffing is eased to the edge by tightening with a vertical pull followed by a horizontal pull. Fresh twine is begun with a new slip knot into which the end of the previous twine is overwound twice.

As the stitch progresses immediately above the scrim tacks, the edge changes shape and becomes firm. A second and third row can be used to give height to an edge and produce a very hard foundation for the roll or top stitches which may follow.

Fig 6.18   The upholsterer's top stitch (below) forms a roll edge by compressing and pinching the scrim and stuffing. Depth and tightness will vary with this technique: a very sharp stiff edge will be typical of 18th- and early 19th-century styles, while a softer more rounded roll edge would suit furniture of the late Victorian period.

The top stitch gives the outline and feel to a piece of upholstery, and will often determine the finish and the way that the covering is treated. Planning ahead and visualizing the finished work will usually dictate the type and shape of a stitched edge foundation.

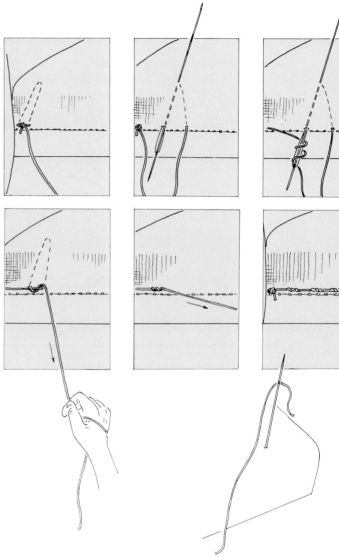

One, two, or even three rows of top stitch are quite common. These may be worked straight or diagonal; the stitch is basically the same for both.

Two rows of blind stitch and two rows of top stitch will give a good average edge about 2½in (63mm) high.

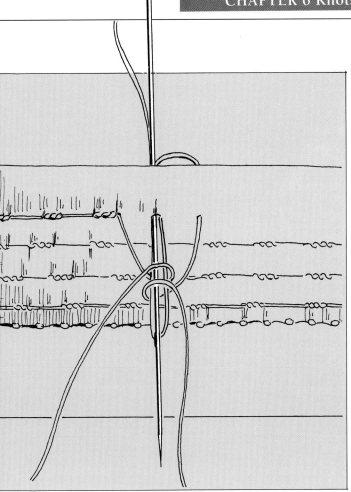

Fig 6.19 A row of top stitches being worked using an alternative English method of knotting.

As the needle leaves the scrim the left hand twine is brought under and over, followed by the right passing under and over. To tighten the stitch, the lead twine has to be pulled directly forward and is then locked off with a hard jerking pull to the right.

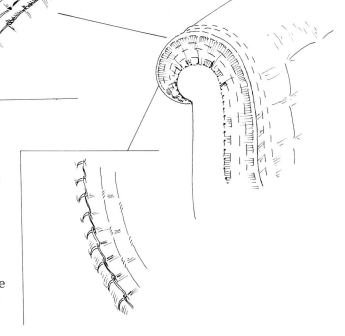

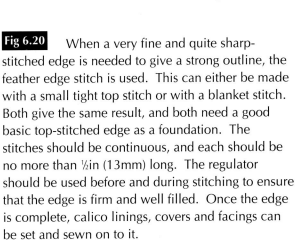

Fig 6.20 When a very fine and quite sharp-stitched edge is needed to give a strong outline, the feather edge stitch is used. This can either be made with a small tight top stitch or with a blanket stitch. Both give the same result, and both need a good basic top-stitched edge as a foundation. The stitches should be continuous, and each should be no more than ½in (13mm) long. The regulator should be used before and during stitching to ensure that the edge is firm and well filled. Once the edge is complete, calico linings, covers and facings can be set and sewn on to it.

Fig 6.21(a) The tack stitch is a very old type of blind stitch which is worked along the edge of chair backs and seats to draw quantities of first stuffing out to the edge, to create firmness and good line.

A fine mattress twine is used with a double-ended round-point needle. Scrim covering is temporary tacked along the centre of rails, with the tacks equally spaced approximately 1½in (38mm) apart. The stitch begins by winding the twine around the first tack and knocking it home. The threaded needle runs into the stuffing alongside the first tack and returns to take the twine around alternate tacks in a blind stitch formation. Before each tack is driven home the twine is pulled to ease the stuffing into the edge.

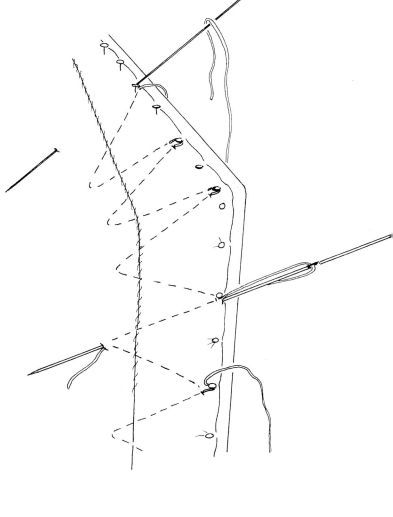

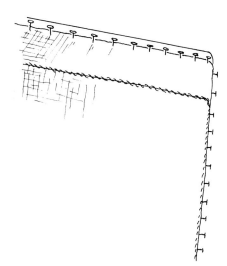

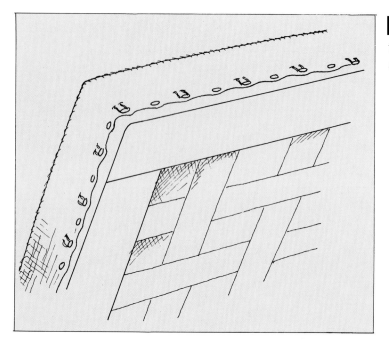

Fig 6.21(b) When the stitch is complete all the tacks will be permanent, with the twines just visible around each tack head.

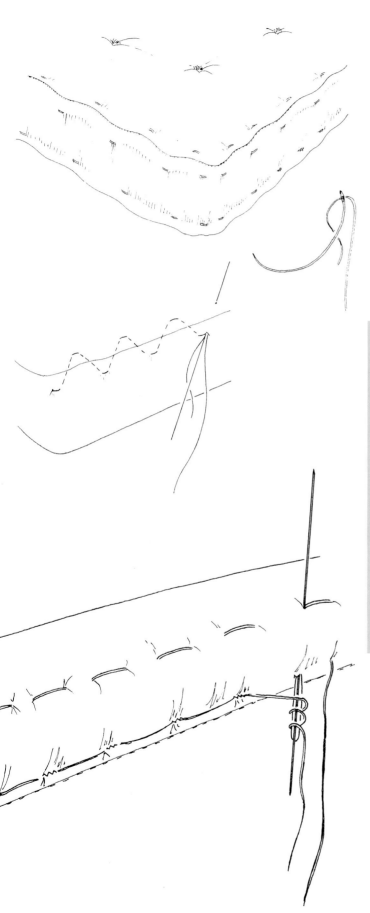

Fig 6.22 Two very similar edge stitches are used in mattress making to hold fillings into the borders and produce a durable shape.

Both stitches can be used in squab and mattress making to hold and support edges. In modern spring interior mattress production a version of both these stitches is used to give the mattresses a hand-crafted finish.

Fig 6.22(a) This shows a basic zigzag formation using the two-point needle, which is pushed and pulled through the edge in the form of a top stitch. This runs right through the corner of the edge and appears on the top of the mattress case as well as the border. This technique is commonly known as an English mattress stitch.

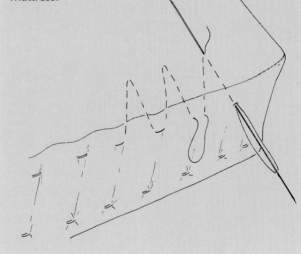

Fig 6.22(b) This is a variation traditionally used on the continent, particularly in France. This variation of the stitch shows only on the side or border of the mattress.

Fig 6.23 Large roll edges and bible-front seats are two examples of the use of the Chesterfield stitch (left). It takes its name from the fully sprung stuffover settees of the Chesterfield style.

The stitch is a very large top stitch (*see* Fig 6.18) which is set vertically into an overhanging roll edge. The stuffing is held and supported by the stitch, which is applied softly along arms, backs and seats. Light compression of the scrim and stuffing are all that is needed for the edge to remain flexible yet supported.

Chapter 7
Borders & Facings

Always interesting and decorative features of upholstered furniture, borders and facings allow the upholsterer a degree of freedom to design and create a finish to a piece, either as a replica of an original or to introduce a decorative effect.

The basic function of borders and facings is to cap and close off an arm front or an edge. Borders tend to be large and generally straight, while facings are mostly shaped and machine- or hand-stitched in place. Borders are often added to give extra detail and add line, and to break up large areas of fabric. They can be plain, pleated, gathered, buttoned or fluted. In the same way, a facing can be kept plain and functional or used for decoration.

Facings

The traditional facing added to the end or the edge of an upholstered arm is cut, fabricated and hand-stitched into place. Because of their position, facings are usually quite vulnerable to wear and tear and therefore need to be well fixed and finished.

The modern facing is very often a made up shape produced from a suitable thin board; this can be cut or laminated and then upholstered and trimmed before being fitted to a chair. Some facings of this type are made detachable by using push fasteners or snap fittings; these are occasionally used when loose covers are fitted or when replacement is going to be likely. Velcro and Cric-crac fasteners are also commonly used for fixing.

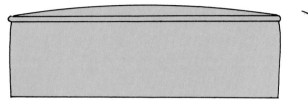

Fig 7.1 [a] A plain border with piped edge The piping can be contrast or self-piped, and is usually machine-sewn and capped on.

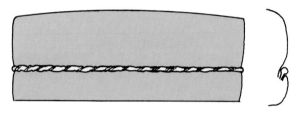

[b] A stuffover edge with a shallow border, back-tacked with a flanged cord.

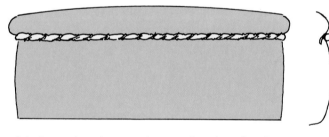

[c] An underedge seat front with a deep border slip-stitched below the lip. The sewing line is disguised with an upholstery cord hand-sewn under the edge.

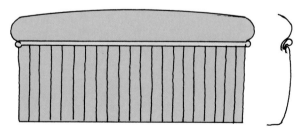

[d] A pleated border machine sewn to an underedge seat panel with a piped seam. The piping flange is either carefully hand-stitched into the seat or back-tacked to a firm edge before the border is filled and pulled down.

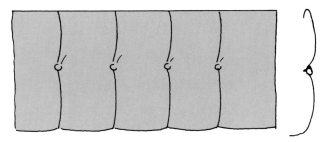

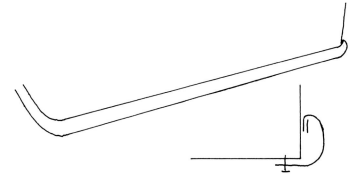

[e] A purely decorative pleated and buttoned border typical of Victorian upholstery. This is used on seat fronts and also arm and back edges. It is more effective if small (size 20) buttons are used.

[i] A simple and effective method of enhancing and finishing the outline of a chair frame base. The small padded border is back-tacked about ¾in (20mm) high, with either a light or heavy filling.

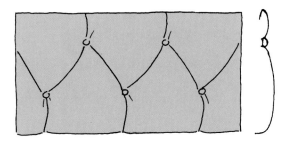

[f] A half-diamond buttoned and pleated border. A reasonable depth of filling is needed to produce a good result.

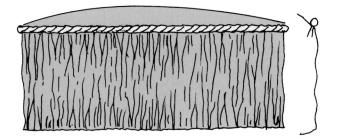

[g] The ruched border is tightly gathered and then hand-stitched to the top of a firm edge, e.g. a stitched edge. Upholstery cord sits snugly over the seam. This is typical of late Victorian and Edwardian upholstery.

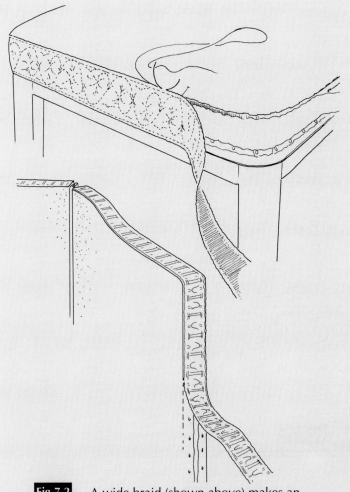

Fig 7.2 A wide braid (shown above) makes an attractive and easily applied border around small seats or back edges, replacing the conventional fabric border. Screens are an ideal subject for wide braid edging. Chair borders are slipped along the top edges and glued against the show-wood frame at the base.

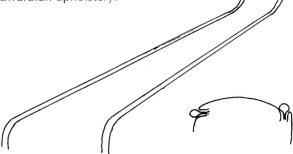

[h] A plain, narrow piped border hand- or machine-sewn to chair arms and wings, etc. This gives a clean and even finish to the edges of headboards and Edwardian drawing room chairs.

Fig 7.3 Upholstered headboards bordered for decorative effect.

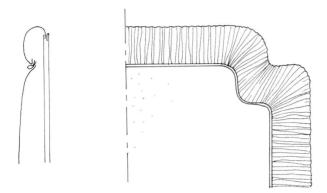

A pleated and corded facing.

Fig 7.3(a) Random pleating back-tacked against a line of welt or piping (above). Plain covers, especially the finer cottons and silks, are well suited to this treatment. Accuracy is important when setting and fixing the piping in place before the border is made.

The curves and corners shown can be difficult, and to ensure good even effect the three inner curves are built up with close or extra pleating so that there is ample fullness in the fabric for the outer three corners. 100% fullness will be needed to achieve the required effect.

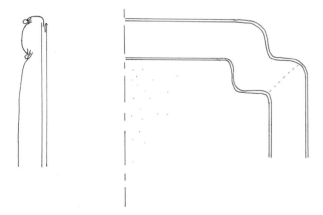

Fig 7.3(b) This plain unpleated border is constructed in the same way, but uses two rows of piping to give a clean, uninterrupted line to the edge of the board. Again, the corner areas can prove difficult to back-tack smoothly. If a join is used for economy of cover, it is best placed as a mitre seam at the first or second curve of the corner.

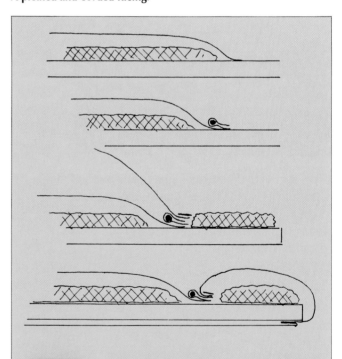

Fig 7.3(c) Joins will inevitably occur with the method shown in Fig 7.3(a), and these are easily introduced by turning the raw edge of the border strip of cover and laying the fresh strip well under as pleating continues. The join will be unseen among the random pleats.

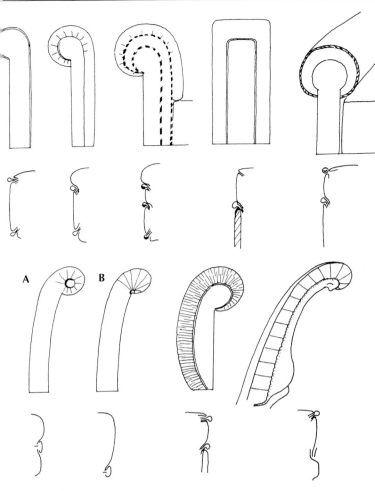

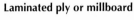

Fig 7.5(b) C scroll facing laminated and nailed ready for covering.

Laminated ply or millboard

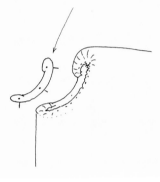

Fig 7.4 A selection of facings and their construction are shown above; **A** and **B** are not strictly applied facings but rather a manipulation of the inside arm fabric to produce pleating designs. Each is finished with a button or a medallion, and is in the French style; the other facings shown are mainly traditional English styles.

Fig 7.5 Details of the preparation work involved in three different types of facing.

Fig 7.5(c) Flat scroll facing cut and shaped from ¼in (6mm) plywood (below). The preparation for this type includes well-rounded edges and nail fixings which are pre-positioned and drilled with pilot holes. A large-headed wire nail is hammered into the facing and covered over with two layers of tacking strip stapled across the nail head. (An alternative fixing uses 2½in (64mm) bolts). The upholstery consists of a layer of cotton wadding and the top cover.

Fig 7.5(a) Simple shoulder facing slip stitched and tacked.

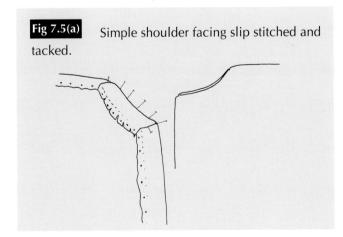

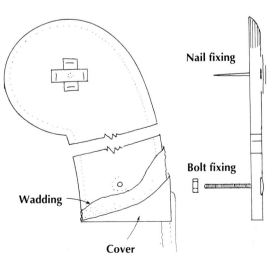

Nail fixing

Bolt fixing

Wadding

Cover

Chapter 8
Fillings, Foam &
Creating Shape

When loose natural filling fibres are being tied in and teased into a chair, the shape and build of the stuffing are obviously important. Each piece of work is different from another, and density, height and proportion have a bearing on the work as it progresses.

The topstuffed seat, which will have stitched edges, will need a good firm build of first stuffing, especially at the outer edges. All the examples shown are of firm edge upholstery: some depend simply on a firm dense padding pulled down with calico or scrim to create the shape. Others, e.g. the sprung seat or the well seat, are a combination of well-filled edges, which will be supported with rows of stitching, and good resilient layers of second or top stuffing.

There is an art in handling and working with natural fillings such as curled hair, coir fibre and wool felts. It begins with an ability to measure amounts of stuffing by feel, and progresses through set methods by which the fibres are worked under ties to create an even thickness and a density to suit each different piece of work.

Once height and firmness are established, an evenness of feel is then essential so that a 'bag of walnuts' is avoided. The filling takes on a friendly well-worked compactness, even to the touch and friendly to the eye. If a well-filled surface feels good then it will almost certainly look good; this is the basis of stuffing technique.

This must be combined with good proportion, which balances upholstery and upholstered areas with the surrounding framework and with the corresponding dimensions of the whole. The artist, the sculptor and the maker all have the same problem, and will often take a long look at their work from a distance so that their work can be seen in scale with the whole as it

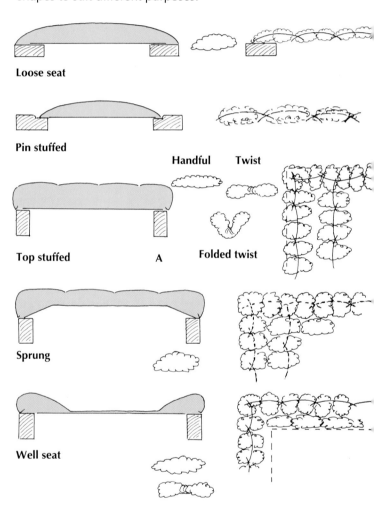

Fig 8.1 Examples of a variety of heights and edge shapes to suit different purposes.

Loose seat

Pin stuffed

Handful **Twist**

Top stuffed **A** **Folded twist**

Sprung

Well seat

progresses. This applies equally to plastic foams, polyester fibres or rubberized fillings.

Once loose fillings are in place they need to be teased and opened up so that each handful of fibres is blended with those around it. This will produce an overall evenness of feel and will make a good foundation for the first

Fig 8.2 Rubberized hair. Hair fibres are coated and rubberized to produce a sheet of even density filling, which is relatively easy and quick to use; the results are instant when staples or glue are used to fix it .

Rubberized hair is not recommended for seating, but is an ideal first stuffing for chair arms and backs. It can then be topped with felts and polyester waddings.

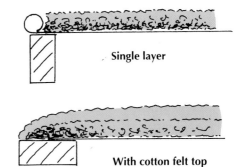

Single layer

With cotton felt top

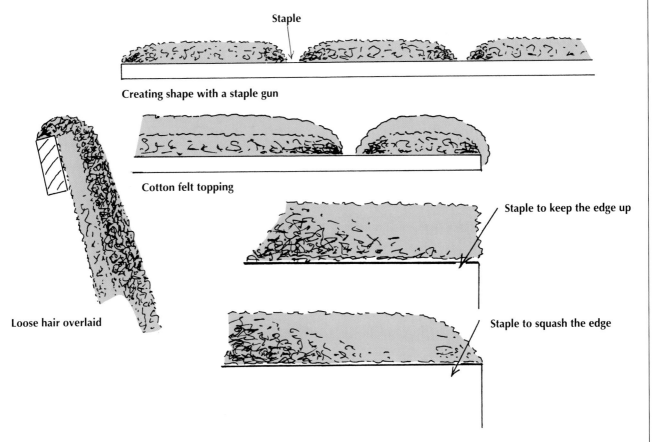

Staple

Creating shape with a staple gun

Cotton felt topping

Loose hair overlaid

Staple to keep the edge up

Staple to squash the edge

covering and any subsequent stitching.

Second stuffings are treated in the same way, but are less dense and have more resilience. The layers become softer and lighter as the work progresses, finishing with soft toppings of cotton wadding, cotton or wool felts, or feathers and down.

Stuffing ties are sewn into hessians with loops equal to approximately the width across the palm of the hand. One handful of teased out stuffing into each tie will produce a soft even filling suitable for a pinstuffed seat or back. Two handfuls into each tie will give a much more dense, firm filling more suited to a

loose seat. When a strong, well-filled edge is required, e.g. in preparation for stitching, each handful of filling can be given a twist before being inserted. At least three twists will then be pushed under each tie to produce a strong, dense edge. To increase the density further, each twist is folded in half to create a nose of fibre which is then tied in along a rail edge (as shown in Fig 8.1 **A**).

Three to four handfuls or twists should be put in each tie all over the area to be filled so that density is relatively even all over. The complete filling is then opened up by teasing in the usual way.

Fig 8.3 Felt, made from wool or cotton, is another prefabricated filling. It has very diverse uses and makes an excellent second and top filling.

Felts may be 2½oz or 5oz to the square yard (75g or 150g per square metre). A roll contains about 22 yds (20m), with an average width of 27in (686mm).

Both wool and cotton felts are easily teased or machine carded into loose fibre for use as hand fillings. The layers from the roll can be split for convenient variation.

Two or more layers will give good bulk in places where extra thickness is wanted. Felt edges are easily rolled in and firmed for shape, or they can be picked to a feather edge for good line.

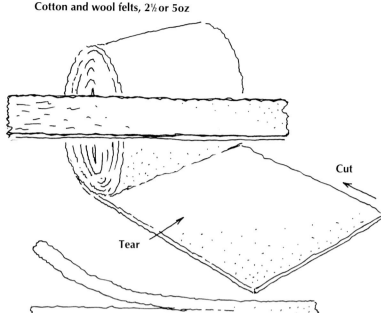

Cotton and wool felts, 2½ or 5oz

Cut

Tear

Split

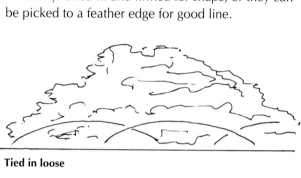

Tied in loose

Feathered

Layered

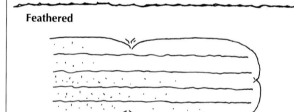

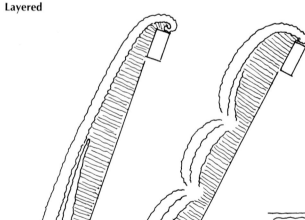

Folding and layering

Firming an edge

A well-shaped, upholstered scroll.

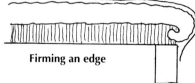

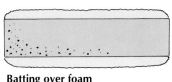

Batting over foam

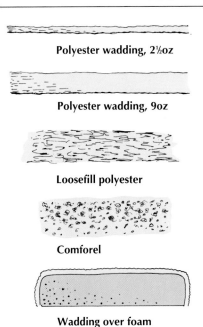

Polyester wadding, 2½oz

Polyester wadding, 9oz

Loosefill polyester

Comforel

Wadding over foam

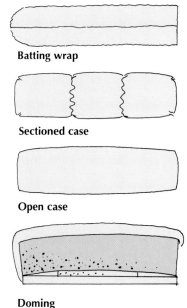

Batting wrap

Sectioned case

Open case

Doming

Fig 8.4   Polyester fibre filling. This very resilient filling is available in wadding weights from 2½oz to 14oz. Its tough nature gives it good flexibility, and it can be tacked, stapled, glued or loose laid over most base fillings. Its main application is as
  an overlay or wrap over foams and as a loose cushion filling.

 'Comforel' is the trade name for a recently developed loose filling designed particularly for use in loose cushions and pads. It has good shake-up qualities which keeps it fresh in use and has the feel and resilience of a curled feather filling.

Fig 8.5   Foams. Urethane combustion modified (CM) upholstery foams are flexible open-cell plastic materials which make excellent ready-to-use upholstery fillings. They are available in a large range of densities and hardnesses, and are easily engineered and fabricated. Here we see some basic techniques for layering and cutting to shape.

 Base foams are generally in the medium to firm range with toppings and overlays producing a smooth even surface. Cutting and shaping combined with minimal use of contact spray adhesives must be done with care and precision to get the best results.

 Before covering, modern foams are always wrapped with polyester waddings or stockinette cloths, or both.

 At **A** we see a simple wooden jig made up from two end blocks and two thin straight battens. The battens should be less than ⅜in (10mm) thick and located on to the blocks as shown, to set the depth and angle of cut. Jigs of this kind can be varied to suit the work and to make cutting precise and easily repeatable.

Medium

Firm

Shaping and laminating

Chamfering and curving

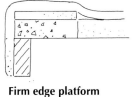

Shaping over rails

Firm edge platform

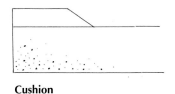

Cushion

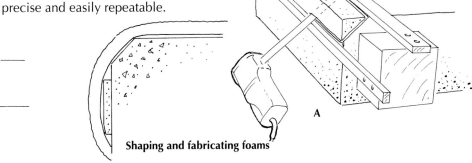

Shaping and fabricating foams

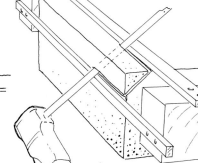

A

Chapter 9
Cushion Making
& Design

Cushions used in upholstery can be either loose or fitted. They are generally based on a few basic shapes and constructions defined by the piece of furniture they are intended for.

Loose cushions

Loose and decorative cushions for use with upholstered furniture come in all sorts of shapes and sizes. They will either form part of a piece of work or be added later for support or decoration.

Additional furnishings of this kind have filled interiors or pads made up from cotton calico, cambric or fine bonded polypropylene cloth. These are then stuffed with a chosen filling, e.g. loose feather or polyester fibre, and permanently closed by machine sewing.

Outer covers incorporating surface design features and decorative trimmings can then be made up to the same dimensions as the pad. Zip fasteners, press studs, and Velcro fastenings can be used along the opening side of the cover to make it easily removable for changing or cleaning.

Upholstery cushions of all types are either bordered or unbordered; Fig 9.1 shows several different constructions or styles.

Plain sewing is used as seaming for the making up of interior pads; if necessary it can be reinforced by sewing twice. The seams used for covers can be kept plain and simple or made quite complex by the introduction of pipings, cords and fabricated edges.

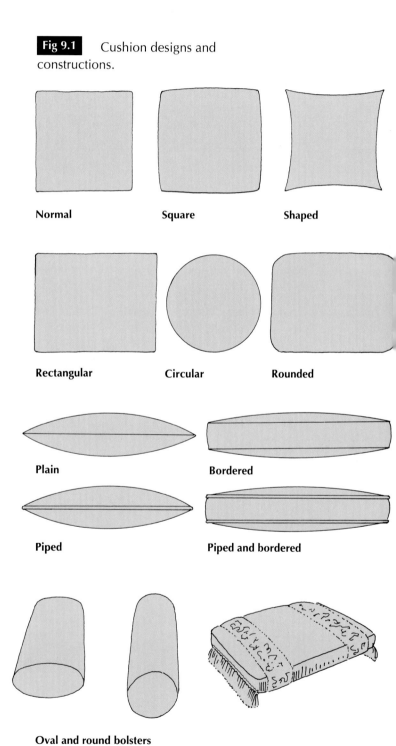

Fig 9.1   Cushion designs and constructions.

Normal   Square   Shaped

Rectangular   Circular   Rounded

Plain   Bordered

Piped   Piped and bordered

Oval and round bolsters

Fig 9.2   Shown here are the techniques for cutting out fabrics and piping construction. Piping strips are cut 1½in (37mm) wide and can be taken from the roll at 45°, which is known as bias cut. This makes a piping which is easy to work, has good flexibility and is particularly good for cushion work and shaping. It does, however, use up large amounts of fabric, where straight cut strips are more economical and can often be cut from the waste fabric alongside main panels. A useful rule to follow is to cut the strips across any strong grain, thus avoiding the need to cut and sew perfectly along the grain or thread of the cloth; pipings are visually more pleasing when cut to short grain effect.

After cutting, the first job is to join all the cut strips together and make up the piping in one continuous length, which can then be used up and cut off as needed. Joins may be angled at 45° or straight sewn. The straight joining of large amounts of piping can be speeded up by laying and feeding the strips face to face in a continuous run through the machine (*see* inset below).

The fasteners and flaps used to close cushion covers on bordered and unbordered cushions are generally put in first, so the method and type of closing must be decided early in the making up process; hand-sewing using a slip stitch will not affect this sequence. The openings need only be long enough to feed the pad into its cover, as most pads can be folded in half or squashed to one-third of their full size.

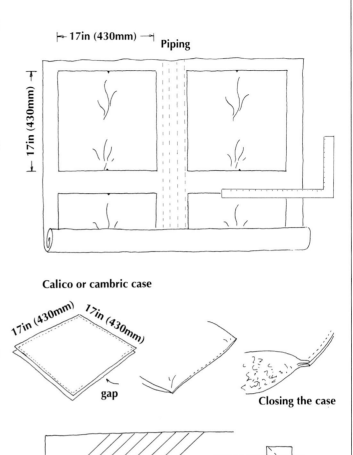

17in (430mm)   **Piping**

17in (430mm)

Calico or cambric case

17in (430mm)   17in (430mm)

gap

Closing the case

Bias cut piping

cut

sew

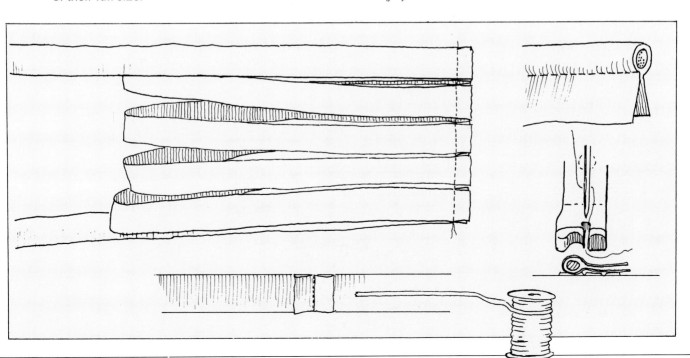

Fig 9.3 Some alternative methods of closing. The simplest of these is the pillow flap, which uses a little more fabric but avoids the need for more elaborate fastenings. Hand-closing with a slip stitch, using a curved needle and strong thread, is another very versatile and simple method: a fine slip stitch will blend easily and unobtrusively into a piped or trimmed edge.

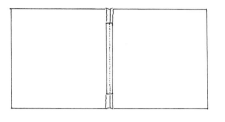

Zips go in first

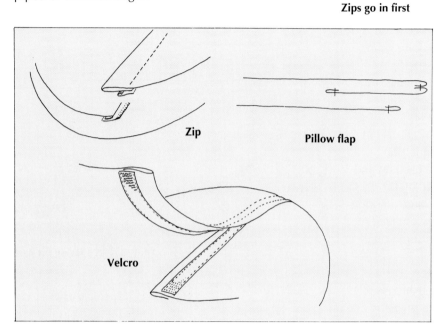

Zip

Pillow flap

Velcro

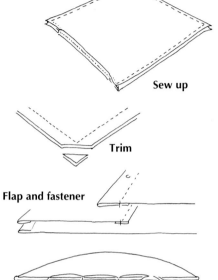

Sew up

Trim

Flap and fastener

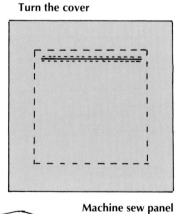

Piped and slipped

Fig 9.5 How to make a floppy cushion

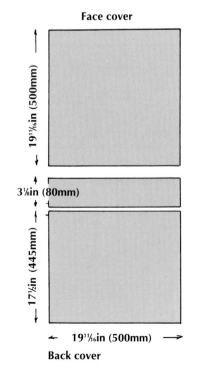

Face cover

19¹¹⁄₁₆in (500mm)

3¹⁄₈in (80mm)

17½in (445mm)

← 19¹¹⁄₁₆in (500mm) →

Back cover

Zip goes in first

Sew ⅜in (10mm) in all round

Turn the cover

Machine sew panel

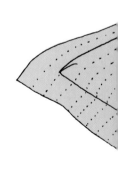

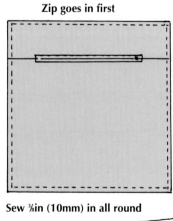

Fold and fill with feather pad

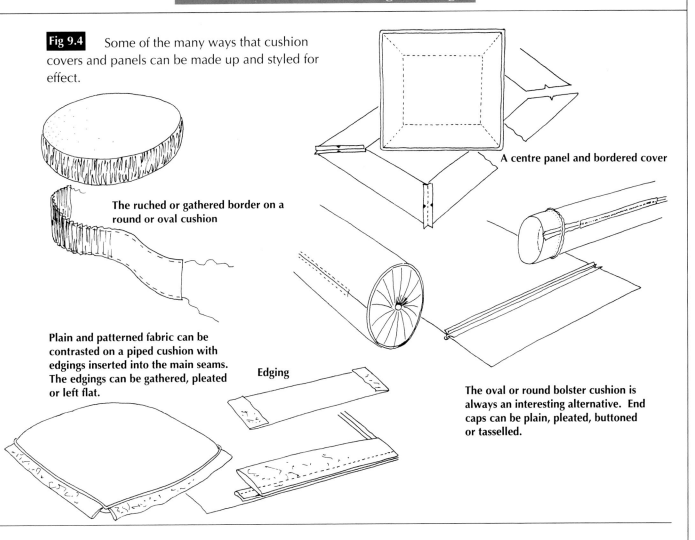

Fig 9.4 Some of the many ways that cushion covers and panels can be made up and styled for effect.

The ruched or gathered border on a round or oval cushion

A centre panel and bordered cover

Plain and patterned fabric can be contrasted on a piped cushion with edgings inserted into the main seams. The edgings can be gathered, pleated or left flat.

Edging

The oval or round bolster cushion is always an interesting alternative. End caps can be plain, pleated, buttoned or tasselled.

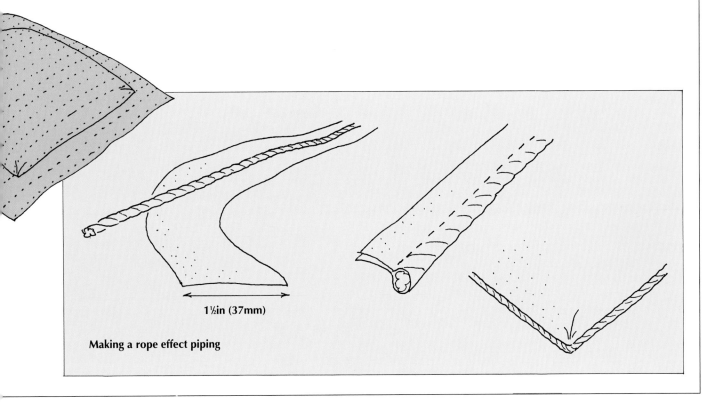

1½in (37mm)

Making a rope effect piping

Bordered and fitted cushions for upholstery

Constructing and making up large boxed and bordered cushions for upholstered sofas and chairs is a fairly precise business: heights and thicknesses need to be in proportion to their surroundings and will usually have to fit fairly exactly into a space in a seat or a chair back.

When the plan shape of a cushion consists of straight lines and the outline is precise and symmetrical, marking out for the cover and the interior can be done by measurement. If curves are predominant or the shape of the space is irregular, the process can be made easier by making a pattern from paper or a stiff card. The pattern can be adjusted and trimmed to the exact cushion shape, taking care to set the shape at the right level. This will provide a check that the pattern fits where the cushion first touches the surrounding upholstery.

Once a pattern is made or a set of measurements taken, a number of important allowances have to be made (*see* Table 9.1). The cover thickness should be considered first, followed by the normal sewing allowance - usually ⅜in (10mm) - which is added to the size all round. Piping or edge trimmings all take up space, and ¼in (6mm) can be deducted all round to allow for this. Cushions set into chairs need to be able to flex and to move without restriction; a large cushion squashed into a small space will soon result in bagging fabrics followed by creasing and unnecessary wear.

A combination of fitted and scatter cushions furnishing a *bergère*.

Table 9.1

Allowances chart for cushion covers and interiors

Cover

Pattern size or measurements	**example** 19^{11}/$_{16}$in x 19^{11}/$_{16}$in (500mm x 500mm)		
Cover thickness (heavy)	deduct	^{1}/$_8$in (3mm)	overall
Sewing allowance	add on	^{3}/$_8$in (10mm)	all round
Pipings, ruche etc	deduct	^{1}/$_4$in (6mm)	overall
Multiples of two or more, with space between	deduct	^{1}/$_8$in (3mm)	overall

Interior

Pattern size or measurements	**example** 19^{11}/$_{16}$in x 19^{11}/$_{16}$in (500 x 500mm)		
Foam and stockinette, 5%	add on	1in (25mm)	overall
Foam and polyester wadding wrap, 3%	add on	^{9}/$_{16}$in (15mm)	overall
Feather, 10%	add on	2in (50mm)	overall
Feather and down, 10%	add on	2in (50mm)	overall

Some examples using the chart

Cover

1 A single cushion measuring 19^{11}/$_{16}$in x 19^{11}/$_{16}$in (500mm x 500mm) deep, to be covered in a heavy fabric with piped seams, will be cut 20in (508mm) deep by 20in (508mm) wide.

2 A pair of cushions for a small sofa, each measuring 19^{11}/$_{16}$in x 19^{11}/$_{16}$in (500mm x 500mm) deep, to be covered in a light fabric with plain seams, will each be cut 20½in (520mm) deep by 20^3/$_8$in (517mm) wide.

Interior

For **1** above, feather filled, will be made 21^5/$_8$in (550mm) deep by 21^5/$_8$in (550mm) wide.

For **2** above, foam and polyester wrap, each will be made 20^7/$_8$in (530mm) deep by 20^3/$_8$in (518mm) wide.

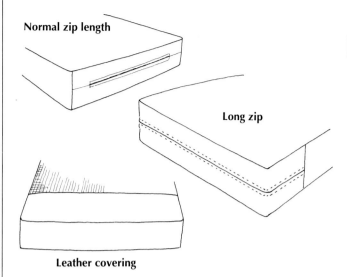

Normal zip length

Long zip

Leather covering

Fig 9.6 (a) The size and firmness of a boxed cushion interior will determine the length of the opening. A single opening the length of the back border will be adequate in most cases. For interiors which may prove difficult to fold, the opening should be extended round the corners; this method is commonly used in industrial upholstery, where cushion filling is done by machine. When this type of cushion is to be covered in leather or other non-porous covers, e.g. vinyl cloths, soft breathable panels of tweed are fitted and sewn to the underside.

Fig 9.6(b) The development and preparation of softly rounded corners are shown here, as well as two methods of dealing with the fabric fullness.

Elasticating the corner to achieve an evenly gathered fullness is produced by cutting the fabric to a radius of about 4in (100mm). A notch is cut at each end of the curve, and the distance from notch to notch is measured. A piece of strong flat elastic is cut to half the measured length and then stretched and pinned to the edge. The elastic is then flattened and stretched by being machine-sewn in place.

Each half of the cushion is worked in the same way before being lined up and sewn together to create a closely gathered corner.

A quite different way of dealing with a rounded corner is to pleat in a formal V formation. The corner is rounded and prepared in the same way and then notched to position the two pleats. The corner is set and sewn by pleating and pinning the notches together before finishing with the stitch line, which should be kept close to the cut edge.

All corners should be marked, cut and notched at the same time so that pleats will line up when the cushion panels are machined together.

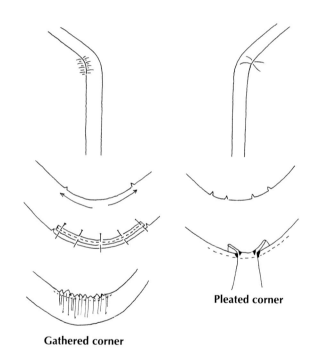

Pleated corner

Gathered corner

Fig 9.6(c) Basic construction of unbordered and bordered cushions using piped seams. In all cases the piping is sewn around the panel first.

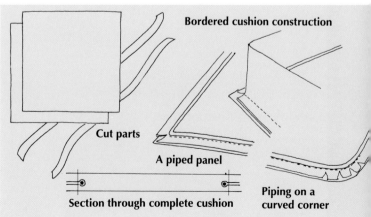

Bordered cushion construction

Cut parts

A piped panel

Section through complete cushion

Piping on a curved corner

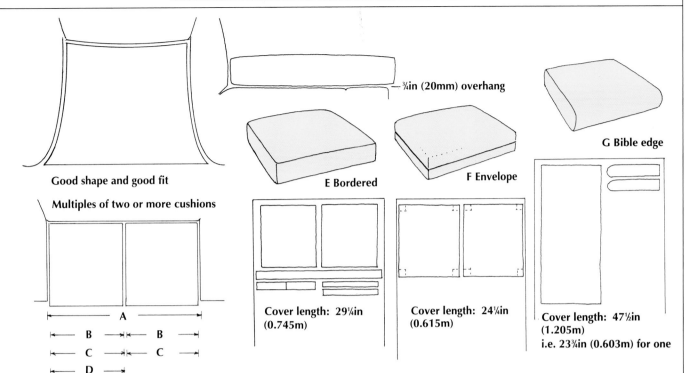

Good shape and good fit

Multiples of two or more cushions

¾in (20mm) overhang

G Bible edge

E Bordered

F Envelope

Cover length: 29¼in
(0.745m)

Cover length: 24¼in
(0.615m)

Cover length: 47½in
(1.205m)
i.e. 23¾in (0.603m) for one

A **Full width of the space, less ⅜in (10mm) for the centre gap**
B **Cover size, to cut** C **Interior size, to make** D **Finished size**

Fig 9.7 Cushions for upholstered furniture are generally made up to a set size to fit into a particular seat, back or arm space, unlike loose occasional cushions, which need not be rigid in their proportions or size. Seat cushions are one example of an integral part of the upholstery which should be made to fit well into the space provided.

Widths can be quite critical (e.g. when a chair has upholstered arms), and the depth or front to back measurement should be reasonably exact and include a good overhang at the seat front to allow the cushion to work properly under the pressure of use, to settle well into the seat and to provide support at the front of the seat where it is needed.

The choice of design and make-up will usually be influenced by the general style of the whole piece, and may in some cases be influenced by economy of fabric, time and labour.

E, **F** and **G** illustrate three conventional cushion styles: the bordered box-shaped cushion, the envelope cushion and the nosed or bible-edge type. The cutting plan with cover length requirements compares the difference in these styles when measured and cut to fit a space 20in square (500mm x 500mm): **E** requires 29¼in (0.745m) of cover, **F** uses 24¼in (0.615m) of cover, and **G** the longest length of 47½in (1.205m). However, if two or more type **G** cushions were to be made, the second cushion would fit conveniently into the waste side, including 8¼in (210mm) for two more side borders. This figure can then be halved for one cushion for comparison. All the measurements above can only be approximate.

Fig 9.8 Below: Upholstery cushion interiors.

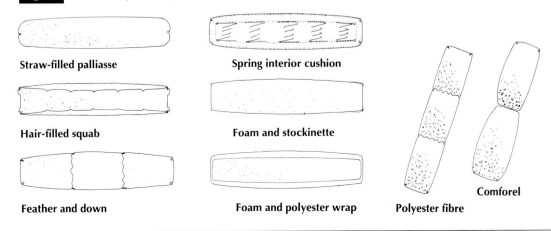

Straw-filled palliasse

Spring interior cushion

Hair-filled squab

Foam and stockinette

Feather and down

Foam and polyester wrap

Polyester fibre

Comforel

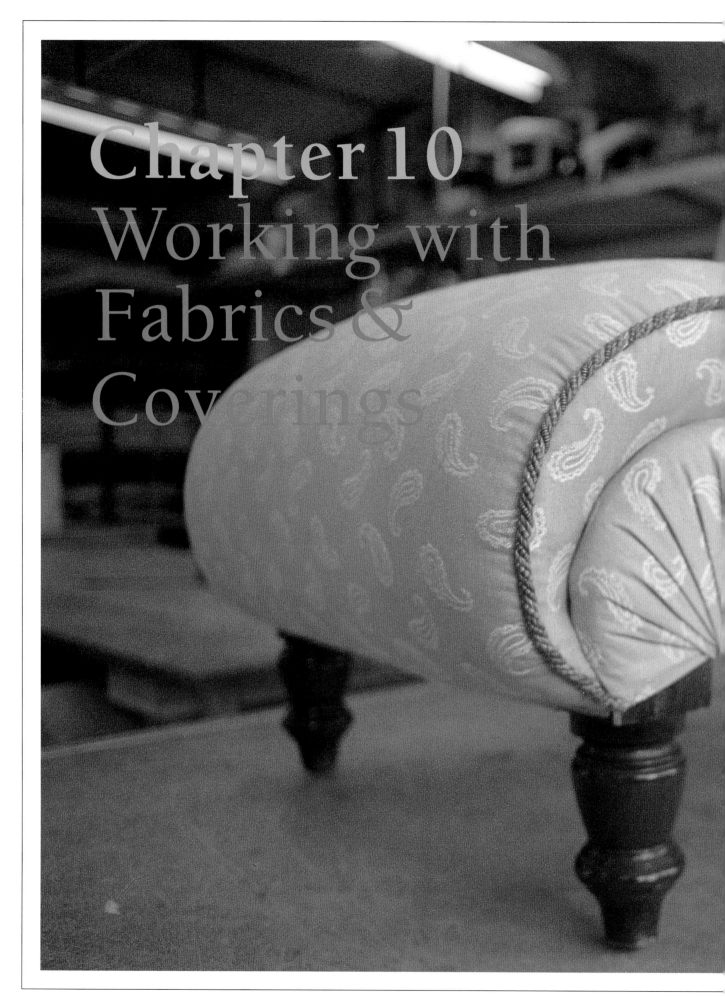

Chapter 10
Working with Fabrics & Coverings

A vital aspect of the upholstery process is the accurate and careful manipulation of fabrics. Understanding the many different types and how they react to pressure and stretch is all part of the covering process. Working closely with, and continually handling upholstery fabrics is the best way to gain this valuable knowledge.

The physical characteristics can vary enormously from one fabric to another. Some are immediately supple and friendly to the touch, while others can be much less flexible and more harsh to feel and work with. For example, cotton calico is a plain woven fabric made from strong cotton yarn which is universally used as a first covering in upholstered furniture. It is strong, yet has some flexibility and works well when pressure is applied: it creases and folds easily, and forms well to shapes and curves.

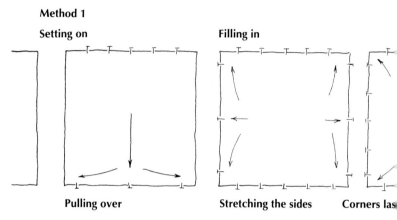

Fig 10.1 Here we see some of the techniques used to set coverings into place on a frame and the progression of stretching and fixing to get the best results. The three different methods illustrated can be used to suit different situations. There is, however, one similarity between them and that is the importance of the long pull to produce good line and smooth edges. The short pull is used to ease a cover over an edge and fix after the long pull has been made.

This can clearly be seen in Method 2 where the first fixing is at **A**, pulled to **B** then filled in at **C**. The covering continues with a stretch to **D**, then out to **E** and filled in at **F**. Any final adjustments or fullness can be taken out at the corners to finish off at **G**.

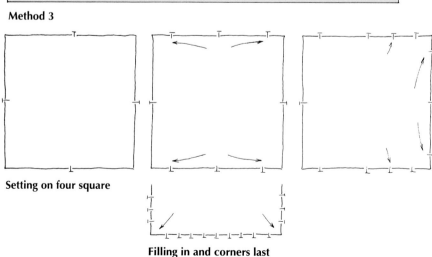

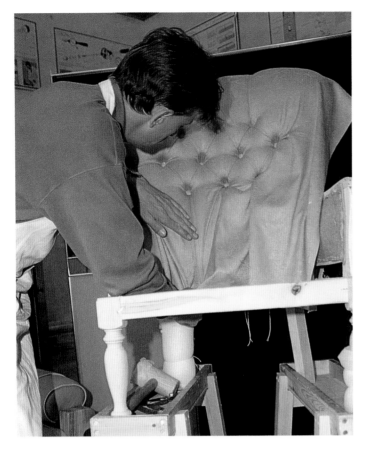

Covers and covering are both general terms used to describe the fabrics that we use to line and finish upholstery with. Top covers can range from heavy leather and vinyls to fine silks and cotton chintzes; in between there is a whole range of varying types and weights.

Velvets are a good example of heavyweight upholstery covers with a woven base supporting a soft thick pile. A good velvet with a linen or Dralon pile is by nature a quite difficult fabric to stitch and manipulate; the thickness of the pile and its nap tend to make it behave quite differently to a plain flat cloth such as calico.

Even the stiffest and most unforgiving of covers can be worked, but will need patience and firmness in the way that it is adjusted and pulled into a piece of work.

Pleating and pulling a buttoned back cover. Photo courtesy of Jan Jarosz.

Keeping the line of thread straight

Fig 10.2   A similar pattern emerges when setting and pulling covers up and over an arm or back shape. It is physically much easier to set a cover in place with tacks or staples at a low level and then to pull up and over a particular shape. The cover edge can then be temporary tacked at its centre, usually with two tacks to avoid the risk of tear, followed again by the long pull out to the ends.

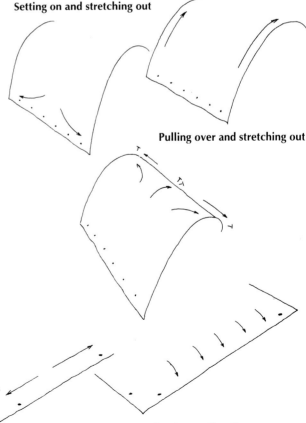

Setting on and stretching out

Pulling over and stretching out

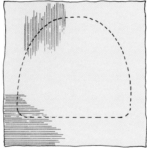

The long pull first

The short pull to fix

Fig 10.3   Any job which has long curves or is circular in shape will involve large amounts of fullness of cover. This has to be worked so that the grain of the cover remains straight and true to the shape and the fullness arranged evenly along the edge. Here we have a circular seat with the first fixings made four square at **A**, **B**, **C** and then **D**. These fixings are then followed by four intermediate tacking points halfway between. The fullness will then have been broken up but evenly placed into eight separate areas; each of these spaces can then be pulled down and tacked to arrive at a gathered edge which is even all round.

Pleating is a commonly used technique in upholstery covering to absorb the fullness in fabrics and to give accent to a corner or scroll. The cover should in most cases fall naturally into place with a little help by smoothing and some stretching. The underlying shape of the upholstery will determine exactly how the pleating should be arranged and how many folds are necessary to take out all the fullness. An odd number of pleats or folds will sometimes look more pleasing than an even number.

Scroll work on arms and ends of chairs and sofas is often made attractive by the amount and the arrangement of pleated covering. As can be seen, there is always a choice of styles; the variations are only limited by the shape of the scroll. when pleating is not intended to be a decorative feature, the long tight pull up and down the scroll is used and all the surplus is taken over at the top end and tacked. The cover is then snipped and the excess removed before one single pleat is folded and placed along the line of the scroll edge. This is pulled tight to set the pleat before tacking off.

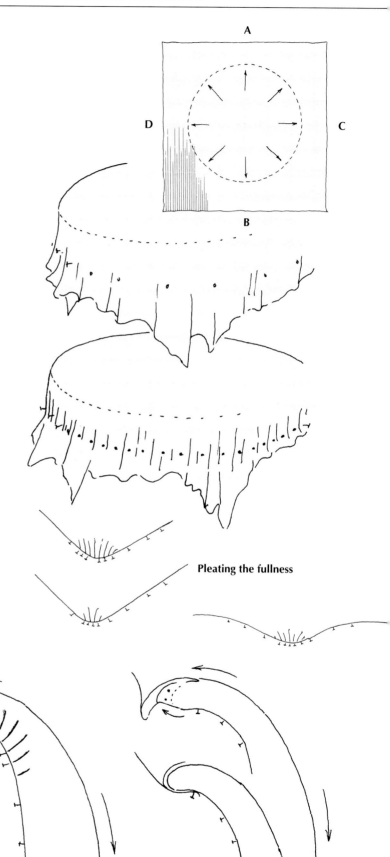

Pleating the fullness

Pulling, setting and pleating

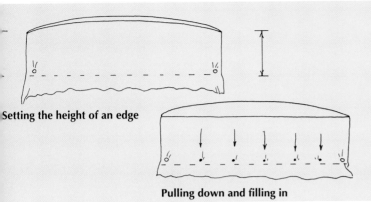

Setting the height of an edge

Pulling down and filling in

Fig 10.4 Capped and fitted covers rely on good line and the accurate setting of seams. The technique shown here begins at the ends or corners which are pulled down to the height required and temporarily fixed. This gives the eye an imaginary line to follow as the side is eased down to line up. Final tacking off can be checked with a rule or a short gauge stick marked with a pencil.

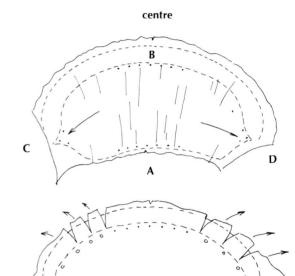

Fig 10.5 Desk chairs and tub chairs with concave backs can often prove difficult to cover when any fullness has to be cleared. The degree of difficulty will largely depend on the severity of the curve and the type of cover that is to be used.

Temporary tacking and setting in place begins at the centre, with a few tacks at the bottom and the top. The long pull is then used to stretch the cover end to end; this should be as tight as the cover and the fixings will allow. The outer edges are then cut carefully down to the tacking line; this will relieve the tension on the cover and allow the four corners to be pulled and eased out for tacking. More cuts are made into the edges where necessary, to help ease out any fullness that may persist. Final tightening, which will often be necessary, is done in a downward direction using the flat palms of the hands and replacing the original tacks at the base.

Taking out the tension by cutting and pulling

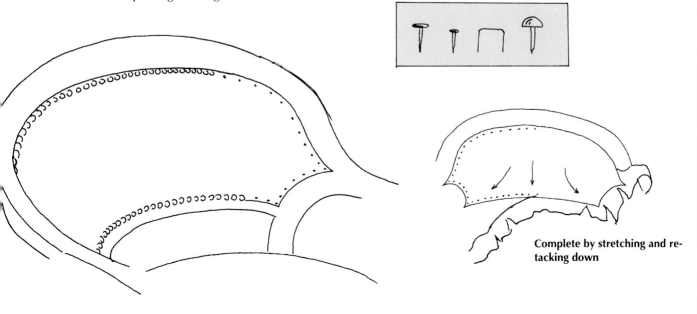

Complete by stretching and re-tacking down

Chapter 11
Trimmings
& Decoration

Silk, wool, cotton and fine synthetic filaments are twisted and gimped, woven or braided to make the familiar trimmings that we use on upholstered furniture. There is a host of different types and styles available to suit every kind of application.

Ready-made trimmings such as braid, cord and ruche are used to enhance, decorate and finish an edge or a border and often a tacking line so that the work is given some impact or the design is accentuated. This may not always be appropriate, in which case dark and subdued colours can be used to trim and finish in a purely functional way. Trimmings can either be made to feature prominently or be kept to the minimum on both traditional and modern work.

Selecting and using the different colours and styles that are available is part of the upholsterer's craft and makes the work satisfying and interesting. With some thought and careful experimenting quite ordinary pieces of work can be made to look more appealing. Contrast pipings and bias bound edges are two techniques which are commonly used and add very little extra cost to the job.

We should be more careful and restrained with our choices when exact replicas or pieces of antique period furniture are being upholstered and restored. Overdecoration or the wrong choice of trim can easily spoil good work.

Trimmings can be bought in different colourways so that on any one piece of work, cord, gimp, and fringe, for example, will match each other as a set. Companies specializing in this field offer an excellent service either direct from a pattern book or a matching up service from a fabric sample. Delivery is normally within days from their huge stocks of standard trimmings. There is

also a number of companies who will make up and dye a minimum order to the upholsterer's special requirements. It is well worth the extra cost when something unusual is needed.

There are a few small companies who spin and weave upholstery trimmings to individual requirements at their premises. They offer a valuable and very personal service and their work is generally of a high quality.

Spacing stick

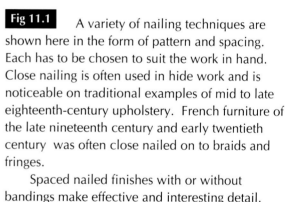

Fig 11.1 A variety of nailing techniques are shown here in the form of pattern and spacing. Each has to be chosen to suit the work in hand. Close nailing is often used in hide work and is noticeable on traditional examples of mid to late eighteenth-century upholstery. French furniture of the late nineteenth century and early twentieth century was often close nailed on to braids and fringes.

Spaced nailed finishes with or without bandings make effective and interesting detail. Many Victorian and Edwardian examples can still be seen finished or restored in this way. Bandings for use with nailing can be made up from cut and folded strips of leather offcuts. Firms specializing in leather work will, if asked, make up continuous lengths of banding from offcuts and strips. These are made to standard widths to suit nail sizes and are usually tooled with two embossed lines.

Preparation work for nailing is done with gimpins which are small coloured tacks with fine heads. These are covered over later with the large brass-headed upholstery nails. When spaced nailing is preferred the gimpins are set at evenly spaced centres. The traditional measurement is 1¼in (32mm) and the use of a marking stick with notches ensures even spacing. Distances are usually marked with white chalk which is easily removed later when the nails are in place. Even spacing of the nails in level and straight lines is essential because any form of brass or decorative nailing is a very prominent feature.

Brass, antique and decorative nails and studs should be applied with the least number of strikes with the hammer. This avoids excess damage and scuffing to the nail head. A sharp steel punch is often used to produce a pilot hole for each stud, so lessening the need for excessive hammering. However, this will often depend on the nature of the timber used for the framing and will not always be necessary. The technique of nailing requires a little practice and care in judging space and evenness of line to ensure a good result. A hammer with a clean, unmarked face is essential and ideally it will be used exclusively for this kind of work. The hammer should preferably weigh at least 9oz (255g) in order to make nailing easier and more positive. Toughened nylon-tipped hammers are available for this work with replaceable tips. Trimming knives with fine, sharp blades will also help enormously to produce accurately trimmed and prepared edges.

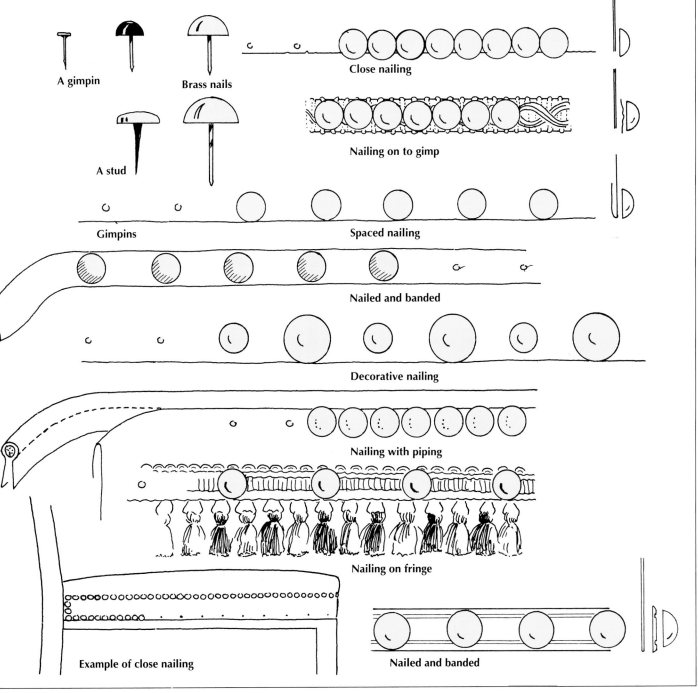

A gimpin

Brass nails

A stud

Gimpins

Close nailing

Nailing on to gimp

Spaced nailing

Nailed and banded

Decorative nailing

Nailing with piping

Nailing on fringe

Example of close nailing

Nailed and banded

Fig 11.2 Pipings can vary enormously in their size and make up, from fine ⅛in (3mm) welts for leather work to the large soft foam-filled pipings for some modern work. The traditional method of make up is still used as the best way of producing a prominent edge and a strong seam line. Sizes will usually depend on the cord available and the size of the machine piping feet that can be bought or specially made up. The following are those most commonly used: ⅛in (3mm); 3⁄16in (4.5mm); ¼in (6.3mm); 5⁄16in (8mm) and ⅜in (9.5mm). Machine presser feet in the form of half feet can be used for the larger soft-filled variations using foam or polyester fibre as fillings.

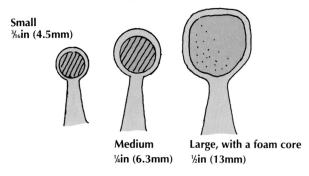

Small
3⁄16in (4.5mm)

Medium
¼in (6.3mm)

Large, with a foam core
½in (13mm)

Conventionally made piping, or welt as it is known in industrial upholstery, gives a fine but flexible corded strip for sewing or upholstering into a chair cover. In cushion-making the bias cut piping with a washable cotton twist cord insert remains the favourite. It is versatile, tough and has a stretch and flexibility which gives the final seam a good-looking and well-behaved edge. The bias cut fabric strip helps particularly on curved work and also where there are no rigid fixings. The bias cut direction in a cover is at 45° to the edge, thus making the cuts more expensive than straight cut strips. Straight cut strips of cover for piping can

usually make use of waste areas and edges and so are relatively economical in cover use.

Whichever method is used, the 1½in (37mm) strips are joined into one continuous length for quick and easy making up. The joins may be set at 45° or can be straight.

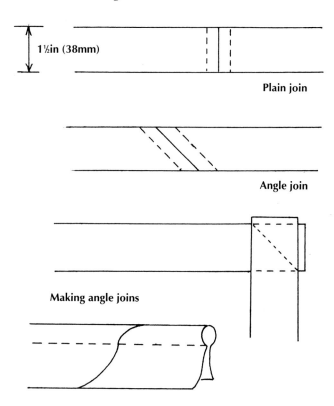

1½in (38mm)

Plain join

Angle join

Making angle joins

The illustrations show the variations and some techniques of application. Pipings can, for instance, be used as a finish against show-wood with the main cover slip stitched to it. This is a very traditional method which was commonly used in the early part of this century: the piping is tacked into place and the fixing is reinforced with a strip of card or buchram which holds the piping firmly in place after it has been stitched to.

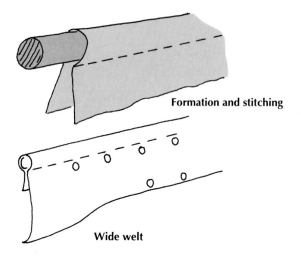

Formation and stitching

Wide welt

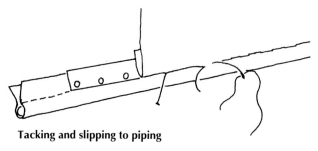

Tacking and slipping to piping

Also illustrated here are back tacking, double piping and self and contrast piping. These are all techniques used to close and finish upholstered edges.

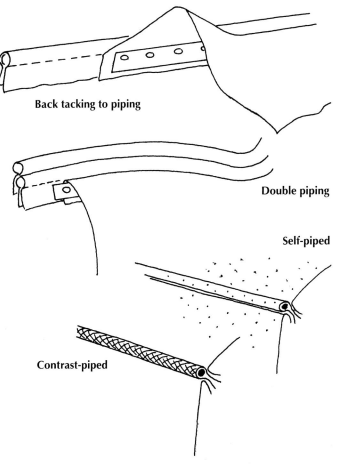

Back tacking to piping

Double piping

Self-piped

Contrast-piped

Large soft welts or pipings can be made up using narrow cut strips of foam or polyester fibre fillings. These are typical applications in modern upholstery and may be as large as ¾in (20mm) across. Such techniques are used around cushions and facings to give a soft and pronounced outline to the shape and design of a chair.

A good example of trimming a chair front using a medallion and tassel.

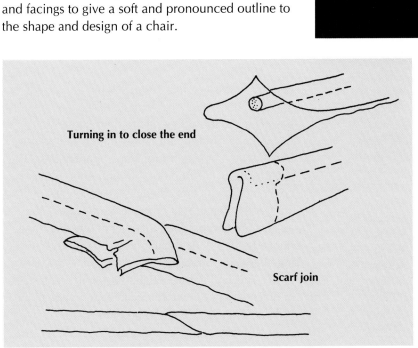

Turning in to close the end

Scarf join

Gimp

Braid

Border

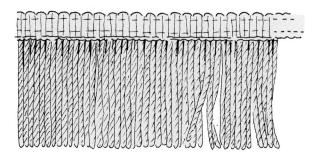

A rope fringe

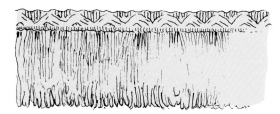

A loop fringe

A tassel fringe

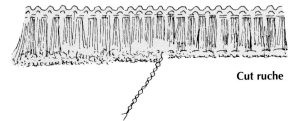

Cut ruche

Removing the holding stitch

Fig 11.3   Trimmings. Functional and decorative proprietary trimmings are used to enhance, close and to disguise tacked and stitched edges. They can also be added simply as a form of traditional decoration.

Here we see a few of the many different types available and some ways in which they can be used. Trimmings are fixed in place by stitching or gluing. Cold contact glues or hot melt glues are ideal for permanent fixing of cords, gimps and fringes.

When very old and valuable pieces of period upholstery are being restored it is worthwhile considering the use of needle and thread. Slip stitching and back stitching techniques were quite common in the past and do not take very much longer than glue methods. Early this century gimp pinning and animal wood glues were also in general use.

Braids, borders and gimps can be machine sewn into place for certain applications by carefully sewing the outer edges on to flat coverings which will then be made up into covers and cases for cushions and bolsters etc. Upholstery cords are generally available with or without a flange or tape sewn on them. Flanges make for easier and quicker machine sewing into seams and for stapling and tacking into chair edges. If a flanged variety is not available when needed then it is reasonably easy to apply your own tape or fabric strip.

Using a piping foot of the correct size, usually ¼in (6.3mm) or ⁵⁄₁₆in (8mm), the cord is laid out on to the tape just left of centre. By carefully sewing at a slow speed the needle will catch the very edges of the cord and sew it down on to the centre of the tape. A large stitch of eight stitches per inch should be used for best results. After sewing, the tape is folded in half and a check made to see that the cord has been caught sufficiently to hold it fast.

Another useful cording technique can be used to make up a large cord for some applications. This is particularly useful on pull-in upholstery or for covering difficult tacked edges. Two lengths of cord are twisted together to produce a rope effect, the lengths are tied or taped together at one end, then hooked round a fixed nail and twisted evenly together using opposite twist direction to the cord itself. This will ensure a tight twist which will stay in place and not unwind. Sticky tape or fine twine is then used to finish and bind the ends.

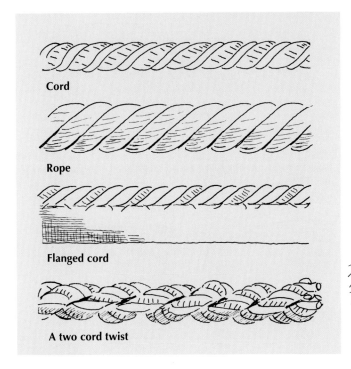

Cord

Rope

Flanged cord

A two cord twist

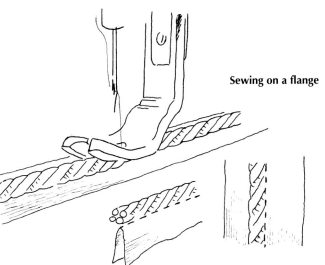

Sewing on a flange

Using gimp and braid

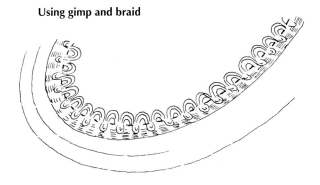

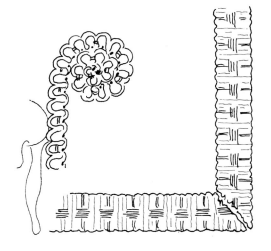

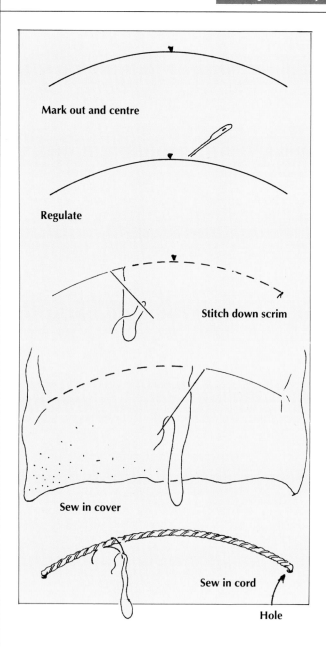

Mark out and centre

Regulate

Stitch down scrim

Sew in cover

Sew in cord

Hole

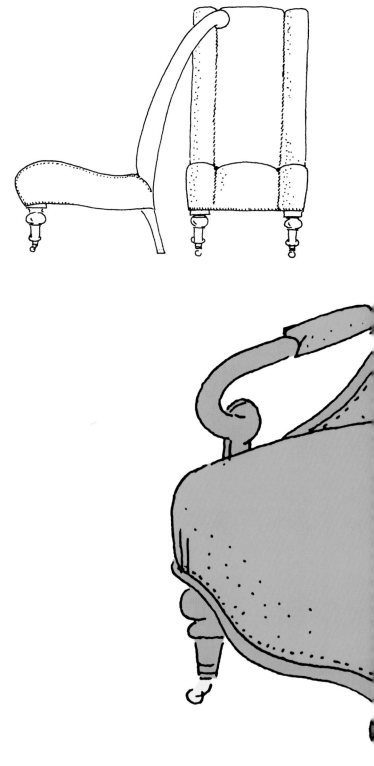

Fig 11.4   Pull-in or taped upholstery is a technique which is a common feature on Victorian upholstery and often appears on concave-shaped chair backs as an alternative to buttoning or tufting. This type of upholstery has to be planned in the early stages so that first stuffings and scrim coverings are prepared for the pull-in. The shape of the pull-in (often an arc) is centred and marked out on to the first covering, which may be scrim or foam depending on the age of the upholstery.

First stuffings are regulated to clear a space under the line and a running stitch is put in with a two point needle and strong twine. The stitch is adjusted to depth as it proceeds along the line and is tied off securely at each end. This forms a deep

channel in the upholstery into which subsequent coverings of calico and the top cover are secured. If surface cording is not to be used then a tape or calico strip can be machine sewn into the back of the cover for eventual stitching down and to leave the pull-in plain. When cording is to be used the ends are carefully pushed away into a small hole

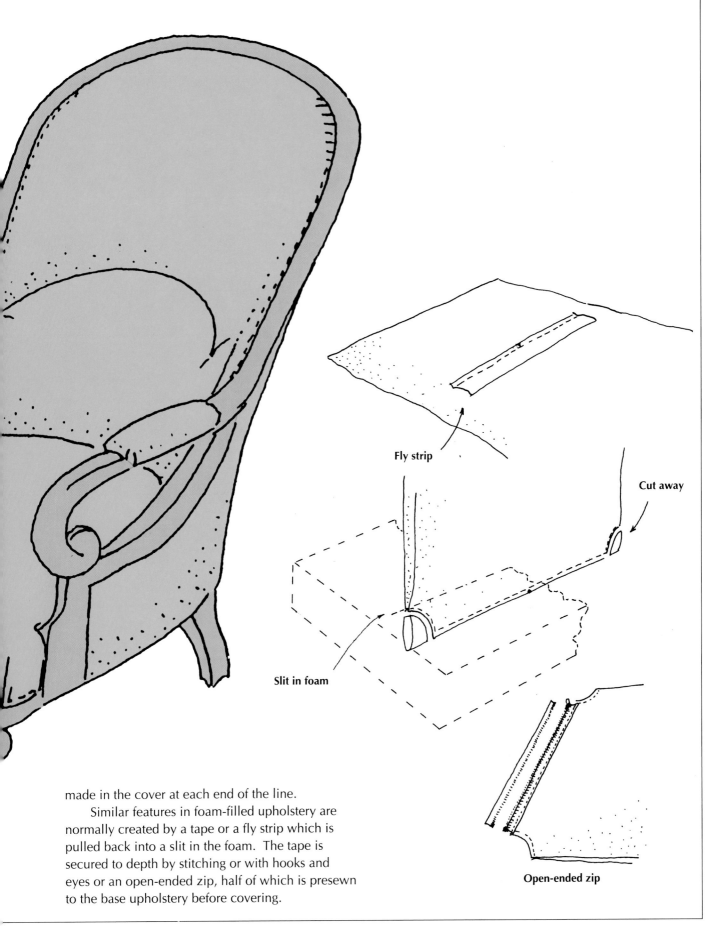

Fly strip

Cut away

Slit in foam

Open-ended zip

made in the cover at each end of the line.

Similar features in foam-filled upholstery are normally created by a tape or a fly strip which is pulled back into a slit in the foam. The tape is secured to depth by stitching or with hooks and eyes or an open-ended zip, half of which is presewn to the base upholstery before covering.

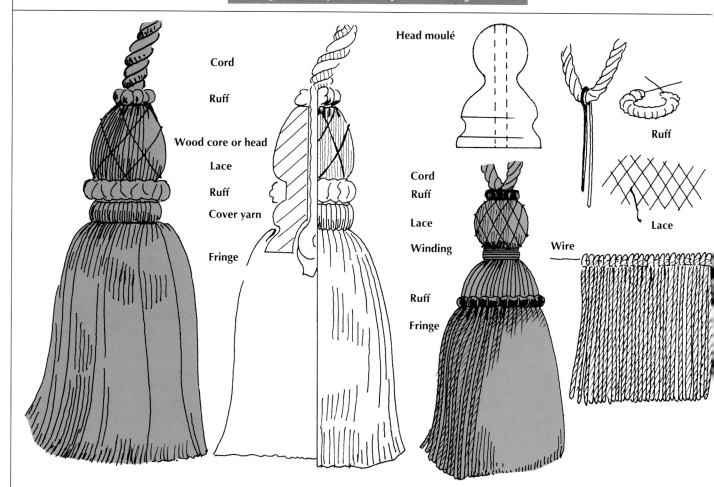

Cord

Ruff

Wood core or head

Lace

Ruff

Cover yarn

Fringe

Head moulé

Ruff

Cord
Ruff

Lace

Winding

Ruff

Fringe

Lace

Wire

Fig 11.5   The tassel has a long and fascinating history and has been used as an embellishment in furnishings for several centuries. The type used in furnishing has a turned wooden core or moulé (French for tassel head) which forms the basis of the tassel head and its shape. The head may be overwound vertically or horizontally with fine yarn and a winding used if there is a waisted shape. Glues and wires are then used to hold and finish the various parts in place.

A simplified version of the tassel can be made using a length of upholstery cord, a wooden bead and several metres of embroidery thread or coloured cotton yarn. The yarns are tied very tightly above the bead with two thirds of the yarns length above the tie.

The yarns are arranged evenly around the bead and then pulled into a waisted tassel shape under the bead. The waist is held and fixed with a horizontal winding to a good depth and knotted off.

Contrasting coloured yarn may be added in by stitching with a needle both in the fringe and as a lace on to the head. Several yarns can be plaited to produce a ruff which can also be added to the head and the waist.

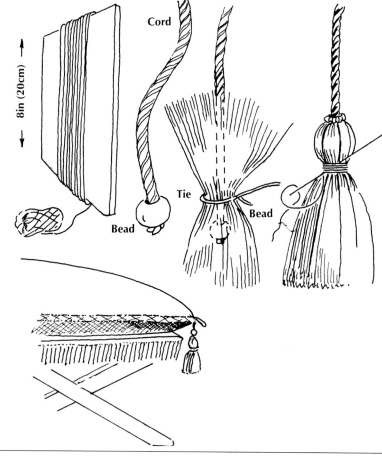

8in (20cm)

Cord

Bead

Tie

Bead

98

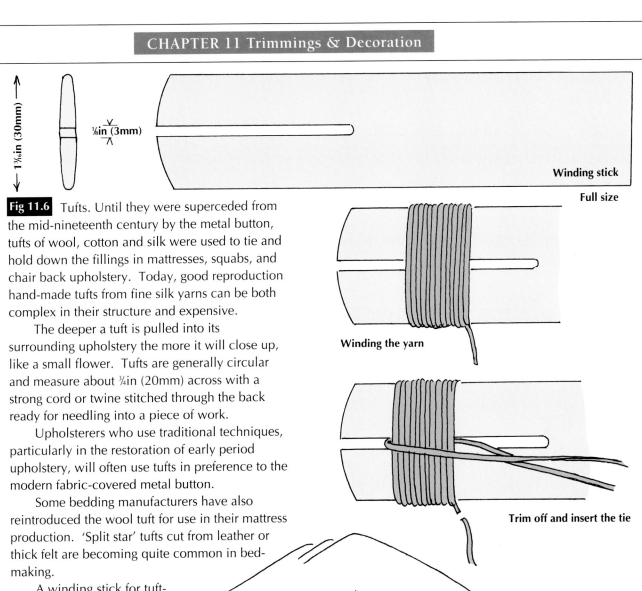

1³⁄₁₆in (30mm)

¹⁄₈in (3mm)

Winding stick

Full size

Winding the yarn

Trim off and insert the tie

Make the slip knot and draw off the winding

Fig 11.6 Tufts. Until they were superceded from the mid-nineteenth century by the metal button, tufts of wool, cotton and silk were used to tie and hold down the fillings in mattresses, squabs, and chair back upholstery. Today, good reproduction hand-made tufts from fine silk yarns can be both complex in their structure and expensive.

The deeper a tuft is pulled into its surrounding upholstery the more it will close up, like a small flower. Tufts are generally circular and measure about ¾in (20mm) across with a strong cord or twine stitched through the back ready for needling into a piece of work.

Upholsterers who use traditional techniques, particularly in the restoration of early period upholstery, will often use tufts in preference to the modern fabric-covered metal button.

Some bedding manufacturers have also reintroduced the wool tuft for use in their mattress production. 'Split star' tufts cut from leather or thick felt are becoming quite common in bed-making.

A winding stick for tuft-making is a simple tool made from ¼in (6mm) thick hardwood with curved faces, softly rounded edges and a saw cut or groove. The stick is well sanded and smooth to the touch, and may be lightly waxed. Twenty complete turns will produce a good thick tuft which is pulled in and knotted at its centre. The tighter the centre tie is tied the more rounded and splayed the tuft yarns will become. A fine strong mattress twine can be needled into the back of the tuft for tying into the work.

A and **B** show an end and a face view of the completed tuft, while **C** shows how the tuft is slightly reduced in size and closed up when pulled tightly into place; **D** is a square-shaped tuft made from cotton cord and drawn from an original, taken from a chair which was designed and made in the late nineteenth century. The drawing is approximately life size.

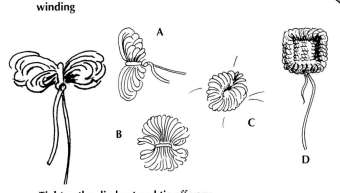

A

B

C

D

Tighten the slip knot and tie off very tight

Chapter 12
Creative Work
with Fabrics

The upholsterer enjoys the freedom to work with fabrics and coverings in both a functional and a decorative way. Techniques such as pleating, ruching and buttoning are widely used and have become recognized work methods. Each in its way produces the surface detail and design that gives a piece of upholstered furniture its distinct style or finish.

Many of these techniques are simply fine details and may not necessarily be very obvious, while others, particularly tufting, buttoning and fluting are quite overt upholstery design treatments. They are chosen and used at the discretion of the craftsman as expressions of the craft. He is influenced in his use of these techniques by the origin of a chair or, quite often, by a desire to simplify or enhance an original style.

Although much of the work that we do is concerned with chairs and seating of various kinds, the opportunity is always there to use other techniques. Wall coverings, upholstered screens, ottomans and bed upholstery are good examples of how inventive fabric work can produce fascinating results.

Fig 12.1   Gathering, ruching and pleating. Ruching or gathering a length of fabric can be used on borders and facings to produce depth of texture and colour. Pinched fabric techniques work well with silks and velours on flat boards, a traditional method used to line small boxes.

The running stitch worked with a curved or a straight needle produces a gathered fabric panel. Fullness can be varied but is effective around 100% to 150%. A gathered length will therefore be between one-third to one-half of its original length. Ends are knotted or tied and the gather evenly spread before being fixed in place by machine sewing to a length of India tape or a piping.

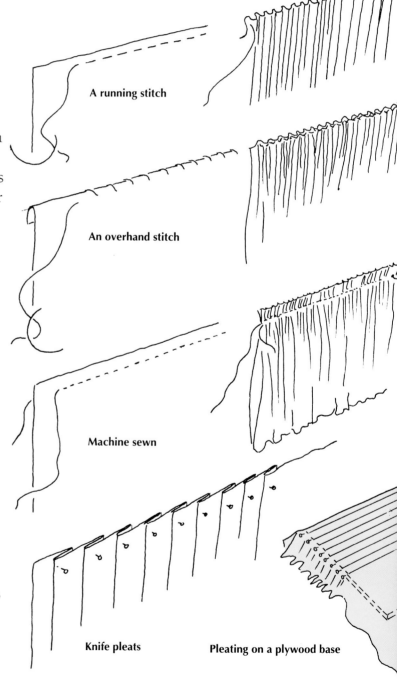

A running stitch

An overhand stitch

Machine sewn

Knife pleats

Pleating on a plywood base

The overhand stitch is used along a folded edge to produce a similar gathered length. This technique is often preferred when a ruched effect is made for an upholstered border. The ruched length is pinned in place around a seat side and the free edge is ruched in by hand and tacked down to complete the border.

Fine gathering can be produced on the sewing machine by using the largest stitch length possible and unwinding the needle thread tension screw. This will produce a loose loop stitch on the reverse side. When the cover is removed from the machine it can then be drawn up and gathered along the bobbin thread to give a fine gathered edge.

When a length of elastic is stretched to about twice its original length and sewn to a panel edge while still stretched, the resulting gather will be even and permanently set. This technique can be used in cushion-making or, for example, where short lengths of gather are to be resewn into corners. The elasticated method is a fast and convenient method for short lengths.

Fine knife pleats can be produced on a flat board by folding, stretching and tacking at each end. Patience will be needed to keep the grain of the cloth smooth and the pleats straight so that an even effect is achieved. It may be necessary to set the pleats by heat, pressing with a moderate iron. Fine woven lightweight fabrics respond best to this type of work.

Dimensions are of course variable but ½in (13mm) pleats will give a fully pleated effect. A good tension is needed, end to end, to set the folds flat and straight. Needlework boxes, cupboard linings and glazed door panels were often decorated with fabrics in this way from the middle of the last century.

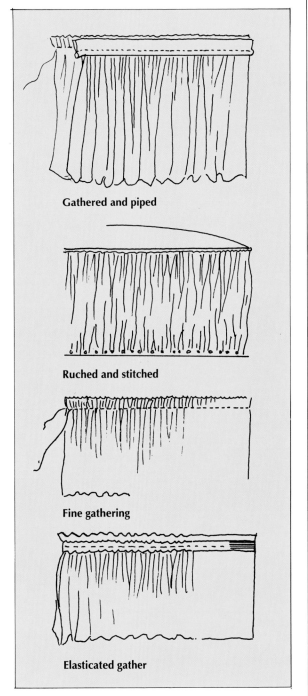

Gathered and piped

Ruched and stitched

Fine gathering

Elasticated gather

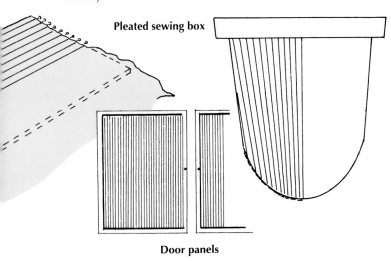

Pleated sewing box

Door panels

Cabbages and rosettes

These decorative pieces of upholstery are used traditionally at the junctions and centres of furnishings and drapes and also to enhance and finish cushions and bolsters. As large versions they are used as focal points, smaller coin size pieces simply decorate the end of a bolster or the corner of a drape.

Almost any type of fabric can be used but, for the best effect, plain, slightly shiny resilient fabrics give the most interesting results. Cabbages and rosettes are simply gathered circular pieces of fabric, shaped and stitched to produce cabbage- or rose-like features. They are fixed in place by hand stitching or with velcro fasteners.

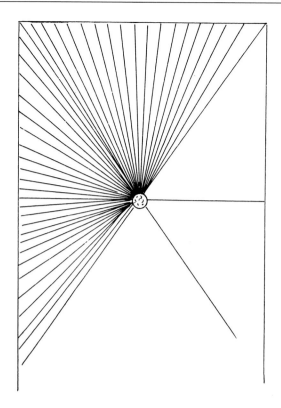

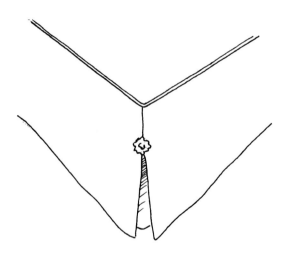

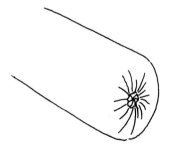

Fig 12.2(a)   Three typical applications of cabbages and rosettes. In the top example the cabbage appears as a centre piece on the pleated ceiling of a four-poster bed, neatly concealing the wires on to which the drapery has been pleated.

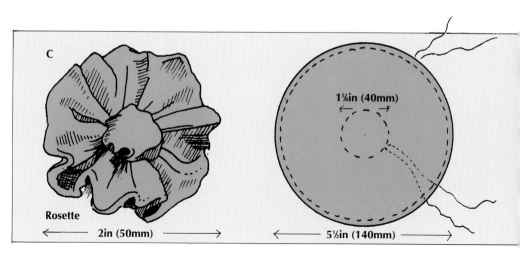

C

Rosette

← 2in (50mm) →

1⅝in (40mm)

← 5½in (140mm) →

Cabbages

A

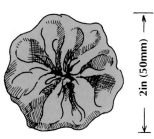

2in (50mm)

B

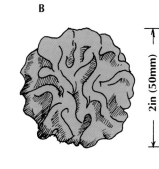

2in (50mm)

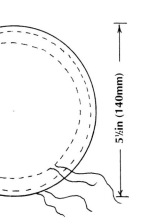

5½in (140mm)

Fig 12.2(b) Dimensions for making up two kinds of cabbage and a rosette to a finished size of approximately 2in (50mm). **A** has two rows of running stitches worked by hand. The outer and inner stitches are drawn up and gathered at the same time. The cabbage is then flattened and the outer cords tied off. The raw edges of the fabric are then turned in as the inner cords are tightened to hold the centre very tightly together. A few tiny holding stitches can be sewn and stabbed right through at the centre to bind the face and reverse sides together. It is important to centralize the gathering before stitching through.

B is the most difficult of the three types to make up. Once gathered into the centre, tied off and flattened the top surfaces of the cabbage are rolled into the centre with fingers and thumb. Stab stitches are placed at random to hold and secure the surface random fold pattern. Each finely sewn stitch is sewn through with matching thread as the thumb is used to move and create the folds. Stitching through is continuous until a circular shape is formed.

The rosette marked **C** is relatively simple to make and relies on careful gathering of the outer edges before tying off and pressing the piece central and flat with the fingers. The inner pair of threads can then be needled through to the reverse side and lightly drawn up until the rosette centre is formed. This should be just enough to create a centre and a petal effect.

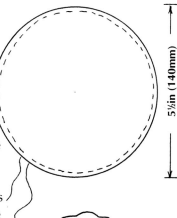

5½in (140mm)

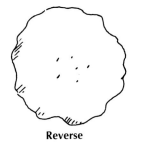

Reverse

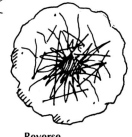

Reverse

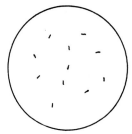

Face stitches

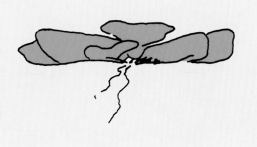

Reverse

Pinched and quilted effects

These effects, produced with fine velours and silks, give a raised and textured surface. Both techniques can be developed and experimented with by using fine stitches or glues on cardboard or thin plywood panels. They can be used for effect and can be contrasted alongside plain-covered panels to create colour and texture on small pieces of furniture such as the interiors of boxes and small cabinets.

Panels of thick cardboard, buckram, or thin plywood can serve as a working base which has to be cut to a reduced size to allow for cover thickness all round. The allowance will usually be about ³⁄₃₂in (2.5mm) all round a base panel or a little more for cotton velours.

A pinched and glued fabric is worked with a wet glue spread lightly on both surfaces. The technique has no regular pattern and is simply a random pinching and raising of the surface with the tips of the fingers while the glue is sticky. No tools are required to create the surface, but producing the effect relies on working the fabric in and to a height of approximately ³⁄₈in (10mm). The panel is then left to set before the edges are trimmed and the corners cut across, so that a small amount of fabric can be glued under the edge of the base. Corners can be trimmed to within ¹⁄₁₆in (2mm), turned and mitred (*see* Fig 12.3(a)).

Fig 12.3(a)   The pinched effect.

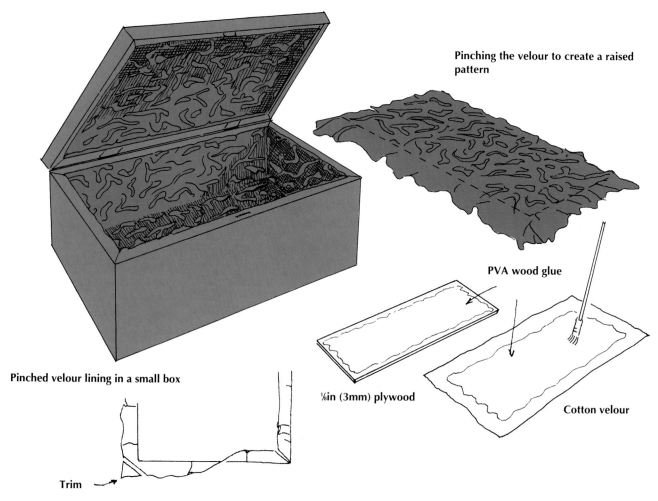

Pinching the velour to create a raised pattern

PVA wood glue

⅛in (3mm) plywood

Cotton velour

Pinched velour lining in a small box

Trim

Fig 12.3(b)   The quilted effect.

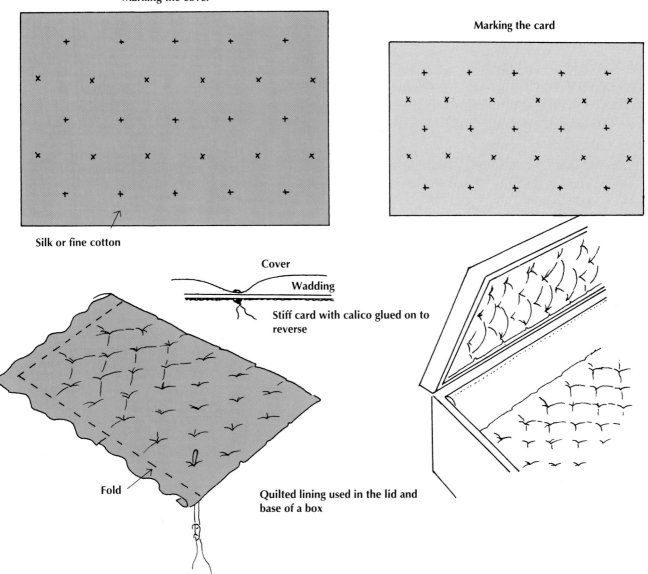

Marking the cover

Marking the card

Silk or fine cotton

Cover

Wadding

Stiff card with calico glued on to reverse

Fold

Quilted lining used in the lid and base of a box

Square or diamond quilted panels are produced on a cardboard base with calico backing glued to the underside. The chosen pattern is marked out on to the underside or reverse side of the panel. An enlarged version of the pattern is then marked on to the reverse side of the fabric (see Fig 12.3(b)). The increase in pattern size on the fabric is about 20%, but this can be varied to suit different applications and fabrics.

Two or three layers of cotton or polyester wadding are cut and laid over the face side of the panel. With a straight or curved needle and some fine matching thread the cover is then stitched down at the marked points through the card base. The thread can run continuously along the reverse of the panel, with a knot at each point. Each stitch is pulled down tightly, catching the fabric at the marked points to show a fine stitch of about $\frac{1}{16}$in (2mm) on the surface of the fabric. To finish the work excess fabric is trimmed away to leave enough for gluing under and mitring the corners.

Valances

A valance is a short curtain or trim which is hung as a matching drape above windows and bedsteads. A valance may be plain, gathered, pleated, broken or continuous. When it is used as a finish on loose covers or fixed on to upholstered work it is commonly called a skirt. In this form it provides the base line on settees and chairs and makes a skirted edging between the floor and a chosen point below the seat. Valances for beds, chairs and settees may be lined, unlined or a double thickness of fabric and sewn to a head tape or a piping. Plain valances which are often stopped or broken at the corners and centres of settees, are usually stiffened which helps the drape and holds them in place.

A gathered valance being hand stitched in place.

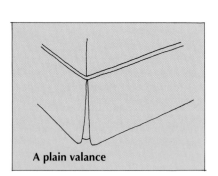

A plain valance

Fig 12.4(a) Shown here are some variations of the plain valance or skirt and its general construction. Dimensioning needs to be precise so that the position and fit are good. The depth of the valance is usually in proportion to the whole piece and the height is set at 1in (25mm) above the floor line when the chair or bed is standing on a firm floor. This allows for a very small amount of drop and for the depth of carpeting etc. When viewed from a normal eye level the gap between flooring and skirt will appear as a fine shadow line and still leave space for the skirt to hang well.

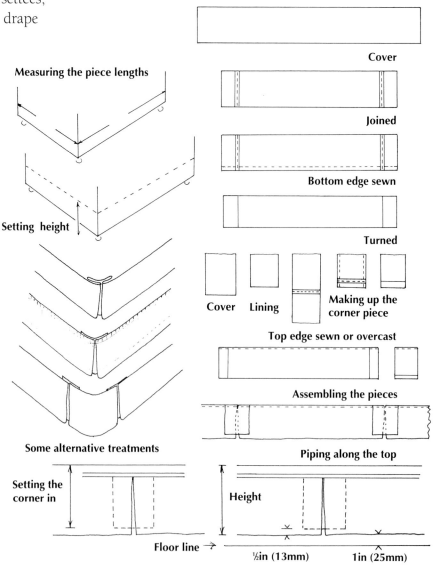

Measuring the piece lengths

Setting height

Some alternative treatments

Setting the corner in

Floor line →

Lining

Cover

Joined

Bottom edge sewn

Turned

Cover   Lining   Making up the corner piece

Top edge sewn or overcast

Assembling the pieces

Piping along the top

Height

½in (13mm)   1in (25mm)

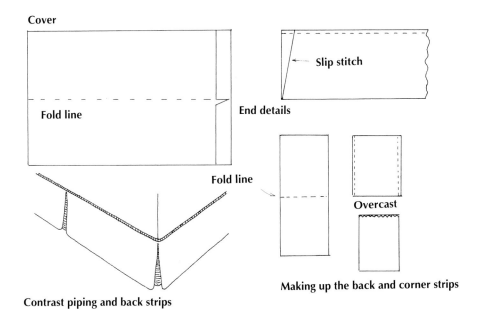

Cover

Fold line

Slip stitch

End details

Fold line

Overcast

Making up the back and corner strips

Contrast piping and back strips

Fig 12.4(b) A plain valance is shown above made up from a single cut of fabric which is folded in half to form the depth required. Ends are snipped and the inner ply folded in and set back and slip stitched at approximately 70°. The top edges are sewn or overcast with a zigzag stitch. Corner inserts are made up if required and used as necessary.

Fig 12.4(c) Illustrated below are some interesting variations showing valances that have been gathered, box pleated or box pleated with space. The technique of fold back corners is often used in industrial upholstery as this allows for the making up of skirting strips in quantity, which can then be set to varying lengths as they are assembled either on to a piping or back-tacked directly on to a chair.

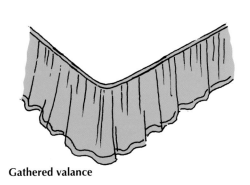

Gathered valance

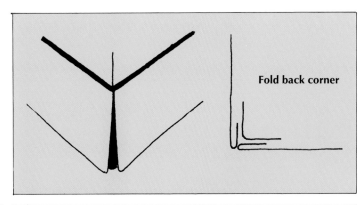

Fold back corner

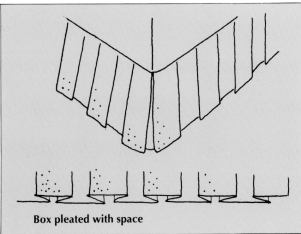

Box pleated with space

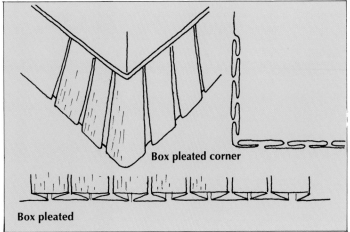

Box pleated corner

Box pleated

Chapter 13
Trade Calculations

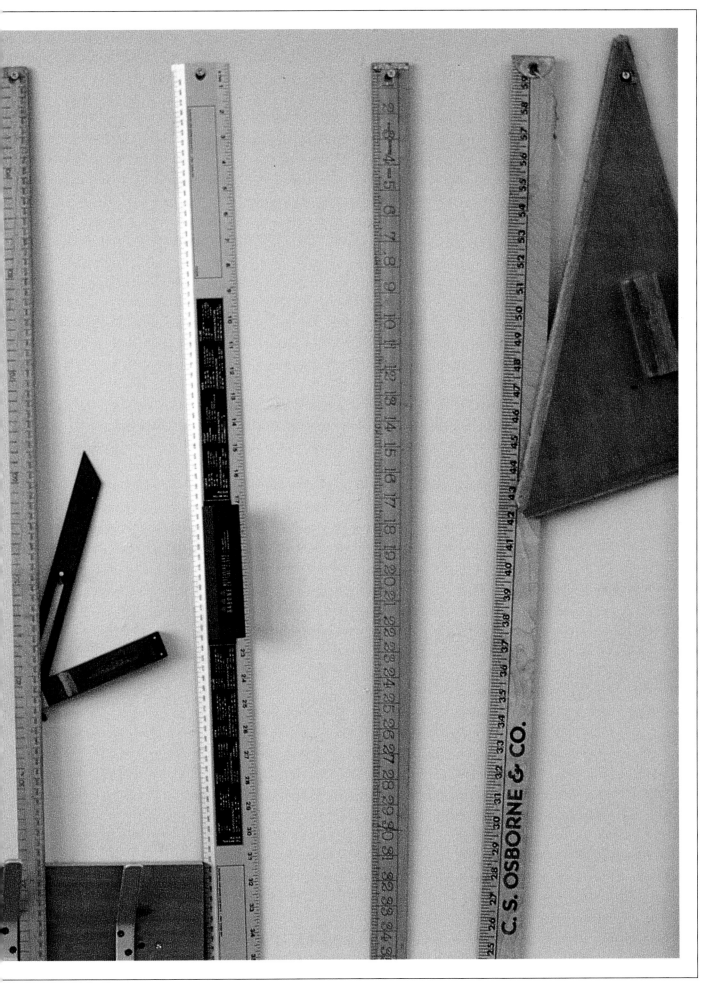

Measuring, costing, calculating and buying are all part of the upholsterer's daily routine. When so many different materials are to be brought together into one piece of work, there has to be some control over size, cost and possible waste. The calculations are quite similar whether one is working for pleasure or to make a living. All types of upholstery involve taking measurements, planning, totalling amounts and specifying exactly what is needed.

It is a good idea to record the requirements for each job in a notebook. The costs can then be worked out on paper before expensive commitments are made. Your day book or job book can thus serve as a valuable diary for future reference and as a source of information for current work.

Measuring

Linear measurement

In upholstery and reupholstery, the length or linear measurement is the most important dimension to be established when working out quantities for the planning and cutting of materials. Because material and fabric widths are set sizes it is the length which must be worked out and planned for.

The term 'up the roll' or 'along the roll' is common in the craft when we speak of a length direction. Generally speaking, almost all woven materials such as scrim, lining or upholstery cover, are rolled up and received with the face side innermost, so when a roll of fabric is laid on to a table and unrolled the face or upper side will be revealed.

It is good practice to check and measure

the width of any material before any other measuring or marking is done (*see* Table 13.1).

Table 13.1

Some typical upholstery materials and their common widths

	inches	millimetres
rubber webbings	1½, 2	37, 50
woven webbings	2	50
India tape	½, 1	13, 25
hessians	36, 54, 72	900, 1350, 1800
canvases	36, 39	900, 1000
cambric	48, 72	1200, 1800
ticking	82	2080
linings	48, 54	1200, 1350
scrims	36, 72	900, 1800
calico	36, 72	900, 1800
upholstery fabrics	48, 50, 54	1200, 1270, 1350

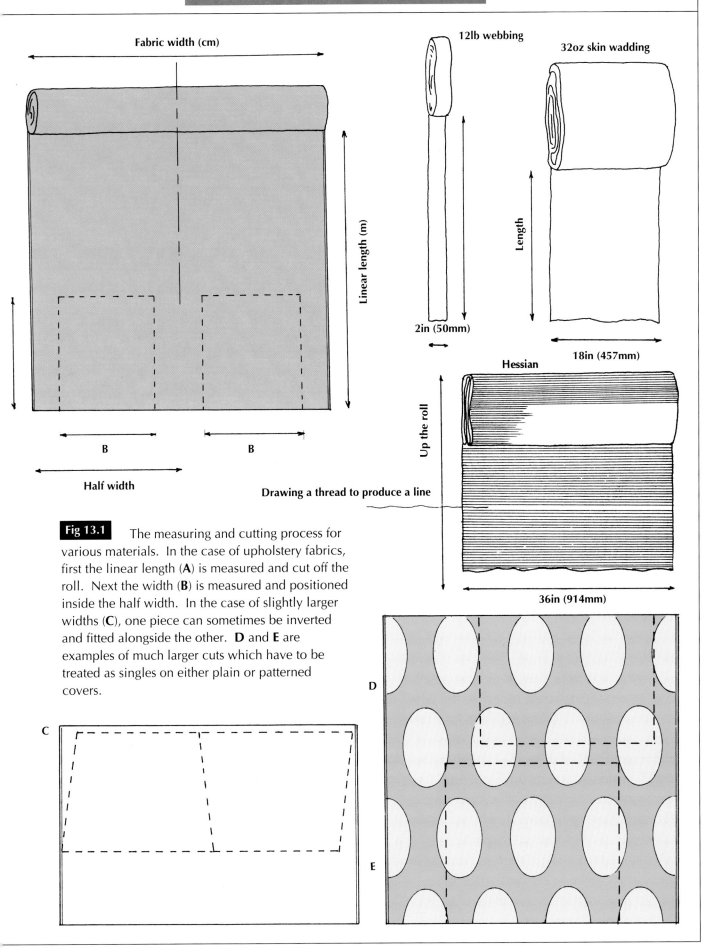

Fabric width (cm)

Linear length (m)

12lb webbing

2in (50mm)

32oz skin wadding

Length

18in (457mm)

Hessian

Up the roll

Drawing a thread to produce a line

36in (914mm)

B

B

Half width

Fig 13.1 The measuring and cutting process for various materials. In the case of upholstery fabrics, first the linear length (**A**) is measured and cut off the roll. Next the width (**B**) is measured and positioned inside the half width. In the case of slightly larger widths (**C**), one piece can sometimes be inverted and fitted alongside the other. **D** and **E** are examples of much larger cuts which have to be treated as singles on either plain or patterned covers.

C

D

E

Imperial measurements are still in wide use in upholstery, although there has been a partial change to metric. Upholstery covers and fabrics, for example, are made and sold in centimetre widths, whereas most of the other materials in Table 13.1 are still sold in inch widths. Lengths, however, are cut and bought in metres. The minimum amount sold is normally one metre (39⅜in). The piece length of an upholstery fabric can be as much as 60m (197ft) and the piece length of linings, hessians and calicos etc. will often be around 100m (328ft). The cost per metre of piece lengths is always less than the per metre price of a cut length.

Material widths in upholstery are mostly set and are the parameters within which the work has to be done. The range may be anything from 1in (25mm) to about 80in (2m).

There is very little waste with narrow materials such as webbings, tapes and borders, unlike wider woven materials where planned measuring and careful marking out is essential. Widths can be extended whenever needed by adding extra strips or half widths or whole widths. On top covers and fabrics the position of joins should be carefully considered so that they are placed unobtrusively and well away from areas of high wear and tear.

Areas

Square feet and square metre measurements occur in upholstery when hides and leathers are being bought or calculated, and, to a lesser extent, when board materials and foams are being costed. All of these are bought and used as sheet materials and their quality is in direct proportion to their weight over a given area. Paper, for instance, is measured by its weight in grams over a square metre (gsm). Millboard, which is used in upholstered chairs as a stiffener and a lining for frames, is measured in square feet and manufactured in sheet and half sheet sizes.

Table 13.2

Metric and imperial comparisons which are used all the time

millimetres	inches	inches	millimetres
6	¼	¼	6.35
10	⅜	⅜	9.525
13	½	½	12.7
25	1	1	25.4
50	2	2	50.8
100	4	4	101.6
300	12	12	305
900	36	36	914
1000	39⅜	39	990.6

nominal sizes which are used in the workshop.

conversion when more precise sizes are needed.

However, of all these items, hide or leather in its different forms and thicknesses is the most familiar to the upholsterer, and will no doubt remain one of the principal traditional covering materials for both modern and period work.

Hides for upholstery are mainly cow because of their availability and their good size. Like all hides they are measured and costed in square feet and they range in size from 40 sq ft (3.75 sq m) to 60sq ft (5.5 sq m), although the average cow hide measures approximately 48 sq ft (4.5 sq m). Dimensions are variable but lengths are usually in the region of 7½ft (2.29m) and the widths around 6½ft (1.98m), giving an area of 48¾ft (4.53 sq m). The waste factor with upholstery leathers is similar to that with solid timber, usually between 25 and 30%. A waste figure as high as this has to be taken into

Fig 13.2 Measuring for small seats.

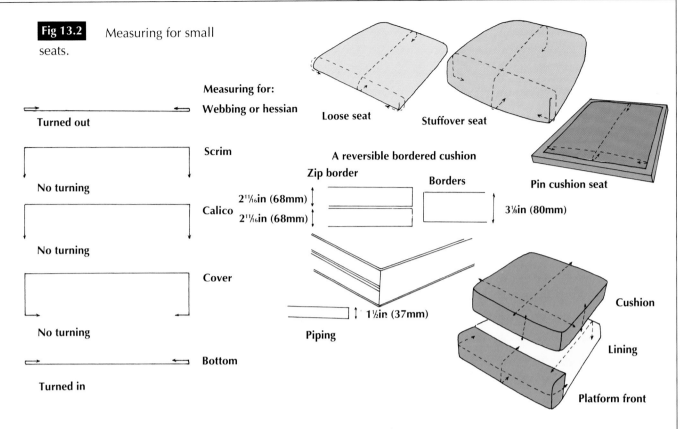

Measuring for:

Webbing or hessian — Turned out

Scrim — No turning

Calico — No turning

Cover — No turning

Bottom — Turned in

Loose seat

Stuffover seat

Pin cushion seat

A reversible bordered cushion

Zip border — 2¹¹⁄₁₆in (68mm), 2¹¹⁄₁₆in (68mm)

Borders — 3⅛in (80mm)

Piping — 1½in (37mm)

Cushion

Lining

Platform front

account when estimating and calculating quantities.

Measuring for hide

The skins used for upholstery leather are specially selected for size and are as free from natural blemishes as possible. They are manufactured to British standard BS 6608, and are fire retardant to BS 5852 Part 1.

When calculating the amount of hide needed for a particular job, first measure the job in linear metres. The area per metre is found by multiplying the required width - say 1.32m (52in) - by 1m, giving an area of 1.32 sq m. For buying purposes this is then converted to square feet by multiplying by 10.7639 (the number of square feet in a square metre) to give a total of 17.76 sq ft, which can be rounded up to 18 sq ft.

The same estimated area can be arrived at by using imperial measurements: a fabric width of 52in is multiplied by the length of 39½in to give 14.263 sq ft which is increased by 25% for waste giving a total of just under

18 sq ft. This gives a useful formula: every metre of cover needed is equal to 18 sq ft of leather.

Example

A chair requiring 4.5m of 129cm-wide cover (14¾ft of 51in-wide cover) will need a nominal figure of 7.5 sq m (80 sq ft).

4.5m by 1.29m	=	5.80 sq m
plus 25% waste	=	1.45 sq m
Total	=	**7.26 sq m**

Rounded up to 7.5 sq m

Or:

14¾ft by 4¼ft	=	62¾ sq ft
plus 25% waste	=	15¾ sq ft
Total	=	**78¼ sq ft**

Rounded up to 80 sq ft

Nominal figures are used in the workshop to make calculating and estimating less complicated. These are mostly rounded up for convenience to the nearest half or whole figure.

Fig 13.3 Approximate dimensions of a cow hide (average size: 50 sq ft).

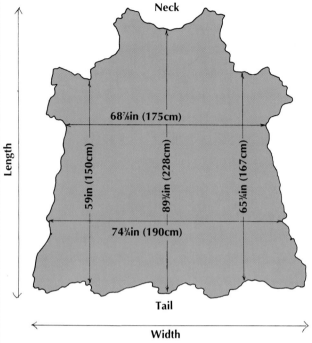

Neck

Length

68⅞in (175cm)

59in (150cm)

89¾in (228cm)

65¾in (167cm)

74¾in (190cm)

Tail

Width

4.674 sq metres
50.3 sq feet

The reason for the very high waste factor in upholstery leather is that every skin is a different shape and their dimensions are taken along their maximum length and width which includes all the protruding neck and leg areas. These are odd shaped and often unusable, but are all part of the skin (*see* Fig 13.3).

The average thickness of leather produced for upholstery is ¹⁄₁₆in (1.5mm).

Measuring foams

Foam fillings for upholstery are produced in large blocks or slabs known as slab stock which are converted on cutting machinery into components or sheets of foam. Foam is measured in cubic metres. A new block measures approximately 2.3m by 2m by 1.1m high (90½in x 78¾in x 43⁵⁄₁₆in). A block of foam will therefore contain about 4.5 cubic metres (159 cu ft).

The outer skin has to be removed from all the faces of a new block before conversion and cutting can begin. Sheets of foam of any required thickness will therefore measure a little less than the area of a new block. The nominal area of a sheet is about 92in x 75in (233cm x 190cm). The sheet size of reconstituted chip foams is, in most cases, slightly smaller than that of standard foams, because chip foams are manufactured using a different process which involves compressing the block to produce firmness and density.

A sheet of foam contains a usable area of 47 sq ft (4.4 sq m). Sheet thickness is specified and bought as required, but minimum thickness is about ¼in (6mm) and maximum thickness for average use is around 6in (150mm). However, if requirement demands,

Table 13.3

To convert square feet to square metres or square metres to square feet		
square feet		**square metres**
10.764	1	0.093
21.528	2	0.186
32.292	3	0.279
43.056	4	0.372
53.820	5	0.465
64.584	6	0.557
75.347	7	0.650
86.111	8	0.743
96.875	9	0.836
107.64	10	0.93

The centre column gives the key figures and can be read as either the imperial measurement or metric measure. Example: one square metre is equal to 10.764 square feet, or one square foot is equal to 0.093 square metres.

the thickness of a sheet is only limited by the height of a block, i.e. 43⁵⁄₁₆in (1.1m) (*see* Fig 13.4).

There is quite a high waste factor to be built in to any calculation of the amount of foam required. Waste in the form of offcuts after conversion and shaping is about 33%, so for every three new blocks used one will be waste. This seems at first to be quite profligate, however, almost all foam offcuts and waste are recycled to be reproduced as chipfoam.

It is possible to calculate how many of a required component - a cushion, for example - one can cut from a block of foam (*see* Fig 13.5). If the cushion's dimensions are 600mm x 500mm x 110mm (23⅝in x 19¹¹⁄₁₆in x 4⁵⁄₁₆in), then the volume used is 0.033 cu m (0.043 cu yd). The volume of the block is 5.117 cu m (6.692 cu yd). 5.117 cu m divided by 0.033 cu m equals 155 potential cushions.

Fig 13.5 Calculating how many cushions can be cut from a block of foam.

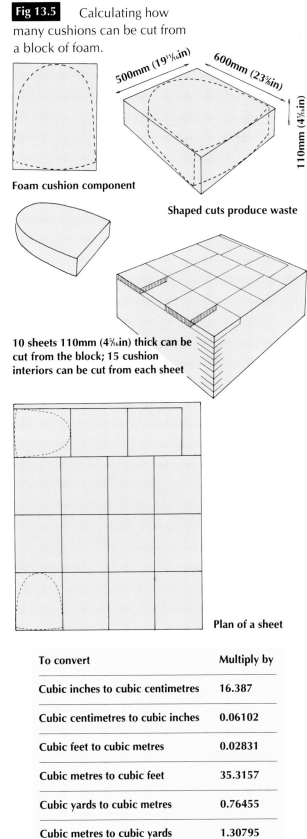

Foam cushion component

Shaped cuts produce waste

10 sheets 110mm (4⁵⁄₁₆in) thick can be cut from the block; 15 cushion interiors can be cut from each sheet

Plan of a sheet

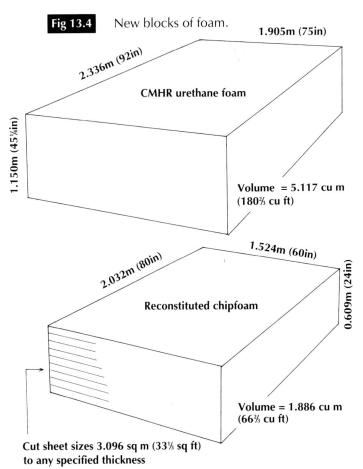

Fig 13.4 New blocks of foam.

1.905m (75in)
2.336m (92in)
CMHR urethane foam
1.150m (45¹⁄₄in)
Volume = 5.117 cu m (180⅔ cu ft)

1.524m (60in)
2.032m (80in)
Reconstituted chipfoam
0.609m (24in)
Volume = 1.886 cu m (66⅔ cu ft)

Cut sheet sizes 3.096 sq m (33⅓ sq ft) to any specified thickness

To convert	Multiply by
Cubic inches to cubic centimetres	16.387
Cubic centimetres to cubic inches	0.06102
Cubic feet to cubic metres	0.02831
Cubic metres to cubic feet	35.3157
Cubic yards to cubic metres	0.76455
Cubic metres to cubic yards	1.30795

However, in practical terms only 150 of these cushions can be cut from the foam block. As shown in Fig 13.5, 15 cushions can be cut from one sheet 110mm (4⁵⁄₁₆in) thick, and ten sheets can be cut from the block, so producing 150 cushions.

This illustrates the very practical nature of cutting foam and shows why each different component has to be measured, cut and shaped before being accurately costed.

A practical approach

For ease of working, it is best to adopt a practical approach to calculations in upholstery. It is particularly advantageous to be able to judge size and quantity with speed and a fair degree of accuracy. For this purpose, the eye may be as useful as any measuring device.

Weights and amounts of filling are often judged by feel in the workshop so that, for example, the density and firmness of an upholstered edge is consistent and even. Thus the body can be used as a measuring tool to assess quickly an approximate length, or to proportion an equal amount. A gradient, an angle or a rake can be drawn by eye initially to see if it looks right and then checked by measuring for accuracy. Fig 13.6 shows ways in which the body can be used to make approximate measurements.

However, for accurate marking and for checking dimensions, measuring tools such as a linen tape measure, a metre stick and a two metre straight edge are essential. A set square, an adjustable bevel and a carpenter's roofing square are also necessary for the accurate marking of materials.

There are many useful tools without which

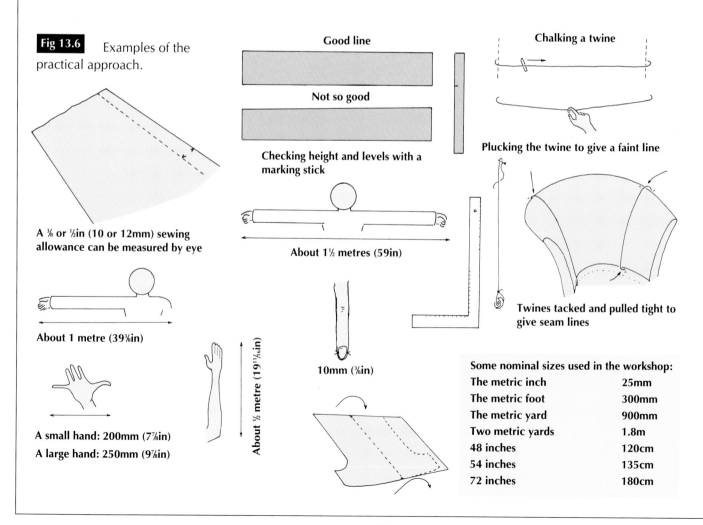

Fig 13.6 Examples of the practical approach.

A ⅜ or ½in (10 or 12mm) sewing allowance can be measured by eye

About 1 metre (39⅜in)

A small hand: 200mm (7⅞in)
A large hand: 250mm (9⅞in)

About ½ metre (19¹¹⁄₁₆in)

Good line

Not so good

Checking height and levels with a marking stick

About 1½ metres (59in)

10mm (⅜in)

Chalking a twine

Plucking the twine to give a faint line

Twines tacked and pulled tight to give seam lines

Some nominal sizes used in the workshop:	
The metric inch	25mm
The metric foot	300mm
The metric yard	900mm
Two metric yards	1.8m
48 inches	120cm
54 inches	135cm
72 inches	180cm

Measuring seat length for cover.

no upholsterer's workshop is complete. The spring balance is used to check material weights, especially large amounts of hair and fibre fillings. Patterns, templates and marking sticks are commonly employed to ensure good fit and allow for repeating when quantities of cover parts or foam parts are needed.

There are, however, several very practical techniques one can adopt in the workshop without having to resort to the purchasing of expensive tools. A length of twine and a stick of chalk, for example, will produce fairly accurate lines which can easily be rubbed off when marking is complete. A length of twine can also be used as a temporary line by fixing

it tightly end to end over upholstered areas while cover is being fitted. A weight suspended on a piece of twine will give an accurate plumb line to check uprights and vertical lines.

Centring and checking for square are frequent requirements in upholstery. Fabrics can be folded in half and notched with scissors at their edge to give a true centre. From a centre mark or line, a shape or curve can be drawn directly on to covers or to produce a template. Components and paper patterns are easily checked for symmetry by folding them at a centre and trimming to fit or match the opposing edge.

Specifying upholstery materials

The following pages represent a typical upholstery warehouseman's catalogue. It is presented in alphabetical order; descriptions are as accurate as possible, but prices are indicative and are given for exercise purposes only.

Code		Unit Price		
	ADHESIVES			
	Aerosol adhesive			
j01	Flam. Heavy duty spray adhesive in 400ml cans`	12 cans	£1.65	
		under 12 cans	£1.80 per can	
	Copydex adhesive	4 or more	1-3	
j02	½ litre (includes brush)	£5.50	£5.80	
j03	1 litre	£7.50	£7.90	
	Foam building adhesive			
	Dunlop	5 litre	1 litre	
j04	SN 1501 (non flam sprayable)	£29.00 per can	£4.80 per can	
	Hot melt adhesive			
j05	Clear hot melt glue sticks	£4.85 per kilo		
	Thinners			
	Dunlop	2½ litres		
j06	TN 1239 Thinners (non flam)	£10.75 per can		
	BAIZE			
	Good quality 100% wool felt baize			
	72in width 30m rolls			
j07	Green, black, red, blue, brown	30m	£5.70 per metre	
		Cut lengths	£6.20 per metre	
	BEESWAX (for waxing thread and sealing needle holes)			
j08	1oz blocks	£0.76 per block		
j09	4oz blocks	£2.80 per block		
	BLACK LINING CLOTHS			
	Cotton cloths	100-500m	Cut lengths	
j10	48in (4oz)	£0.95	£1.05	
j11	31in (5oz)	£0.78	£0.95	
	Fibertex (non woven)	4 rolls	1-3 rolls	
j12	76cm (70g)	£0.34	£0.36	
j13	90cm (70g)	£0.40	£0.42	
	BUCKRAM			
	Woven (starched hessian)	Roll price	Cut lengths	
j14	18in single starched	£0.58	£0.64 per metre	
j15	36in double starched	£2.85	£3.00 per metre	

BUTTON MOULDS
Size 24-36 boxed 2000, prices per box

		24	26	30	36	45
j16	Wire loop	£11.54	£12.94	£11.25	£16.16	£11.24 (box 1000)
j17	Tape			£9.50	£12.64	£11.40 (box 1000)
j18	Serrated nail			£24.14		£26.04

CALICO
Loomstate

		80-100m pieces	Cut lengths
j19	2 ½oz muslin weight 54in	£0.65	£0.70
j20	5oz medium weight 72in	£1.40	£1.55
j21	5oz medium (flame retardant, permanent)	£2.65	£2.92

N.B. These permanently flame retardant calicos also meet the requirements for Permanent Covers, Schedule 5 part 1 and can be used when upholstered furniture is covered only in calico.

CAMBRIC
Downproof waxed cambrics Non-durable flame retardant

j22	48in width FR	100-500m £1.35	Cut lengths £1.55 per metre

CANVAS
Loomstate cotton duck 10oz

j23	72in in 50m rolls	1-4 rolls £3.95 per metre	Cut lengths £4.35
j24	36in 15oz	100m £2.95 per metre	Cut lengths £3.20

CARDBOARD SHEETS
Cardboard 2mm 30in x 40in sheets

j25	30 sheets £0.85 per sheet	1-29 sheets £0.95 per sheet

Millboard 2mm 44in x 49in

j26	30 sheets £2.60 per sheet	1-29 sheets £2.80 per sheet

CHALK
Boxes of 100 pieces; mixed colours

		5 boxes	1-4 boxes
j27	Tailor's chalk (triangular)	£11.85	£12.50
j28	Laypowder (1½ kilo boxes)	£7.25	£7.55
j29	Vanishing chalk (50 pieces per box)	£15.85	£16.45

CUSHION PADS

		Feather	Polyester	Comforel
j30	12in x 12in	£1.50	£1.25	
j31	16in x 16in	£1.75	£1.60	£3.70
j32	18in x 18in	£2.35	£2.00	£4.80

ELASTIC

j33	½in Braid elastic on 150m reels (wht)	£11.50 per reel
j34	½in Braid elastic on 150m reels (blk)	£12.75 per reel
j35	1in Braid elastic on 25m rolls (blk)	£4.85 per roll

EYELETS
Brass - 144 per box

	Hole size	Box (144)
j36	6mm	£3.75
j37	10mm	£7.25
j38	12mm	£11.85
j39	13mm	£14.65

FABRIC PROTECTOR

Fabguard Gives good oil and water repellancy on most types of upholstery fabric

j40	16oz cans (12 cans per box)	12 cans	£2.00 per can
		1-11 cans	£2.20 per can

FACING FIXINGS

Heavy duty push-fit plastic fixings For all types of arm facings where concealed fixing is required

j41	555	£6.90 per 100
j42	666	£8.60 per 100
j43	777	£5.60 per 100

FILLINGS

All fillings supplied meet the Furniture and Furnishings (Fire) (Safety) Regulations 1988

	Cotton felt F.R. treated	Roll weight	3-10 rolls	1-2 rolls
j44	27in x 2½oz 16 yard rolls	17lb	£10.70	£11.30
j45	27in x 4oz 10 yard rolls	17lb	£11.20	£11.90

	Feathers	per sack	per bag
j46	Curled upholstery feathers in 44lb sacks and 1 kilo bags	£30.00	£2.50
j47	Feather/down mixture in 33lb sacks or 1 kilo bag	£105.00	£9.40

	Fibre	28lb bag	7lb bag
j48	Brown curlfil fibre (F.R. treated)	£22.00	£7.50
j49	Black dyed curled fibre	£25.90	£8.50

	Hair (85% hog 15% cow tail)	per sack	per bag
j50	28lb sacks or 7lb bags	£54.00	£16.00

	Rubberized hair Flame retardant sheets 72in x 36in	10 sheets	1-9 sheets
j51	1in medium density (36oz)	£9.50	£10.50
j52	2in medium density (36oz)	£19.00	£20.00

	Polyester loose carded fibre	
j53	Hollow fibre 1 kilo bags	£4.90 per bag
j54	Carded polyester 5 kilo bags	£16.30 per bag

	Polyester wadding	10 rolls	3-9 rolls	1-2 rolls
j55	27in x 2 ½oz 50m rolls	£12.70	£13.30	£14.00 per roll
j56	36in x 4oz 40m rolls	£19.40	£20.40	£21.50 per roll
j57	27in x 7oz 20m rolls	£12.80	£26.00	£28.00 per roll

FOAM

	Cushion, pincore latex		
j58	22in x 20in x 4in	30 cushions £17.50	Singles £18.90 each

	Sheets, pincore latex (grade 65 med CM)	
j59	2in 79in x 59in	£94.95 per sheet
j60	3in 79in x 59in	£142.90 per sheet
j61	4in 79in x 59in	£180.90 per sheet

	5lb cu ft (CMHR) Chipfoam	
j62	1in 78in x 54in	£14.00 per sheet
j63	2in 78in x 54in	£28.00 per sheet

	6lb cu ft	
j64	1in 78in x 54in	£16.00 per sheet
j65	2in 78in x 54in	£30.00 per sheet

Polyurethane foam (conforms to Ign source 5)

		CMHR 30H	CMHR 35H	CMHR 40	CMHR 25
j66	½in	£5.75	£7.50	£6.90	£5.50 per sheet
j67	1in	£11.45	£15.00	£13.75	£10.00 per sheet
j68	2in	£22.90	£29.00	£27.40	£19.00 per sheet
j69	3in	£34.50	£43.50	£41.15	£30.75 per sheet
j70	4in	£45.75	£57.96	£54.86	£41.20 per sheet

Specification for use:

CMHR 30 H - for arms and paddings
CMHR 35 H - for seats
CMHR 40   - for firm seats
CMHR 25   - for soft backs

Explanation of grading:

CM = Combustion modified
HR = High resilience
30 = Hardness in kilograms
H = Hard F = Firm S = Soft

Vilux 2 polyester cushions

| j71 | 16in x 16in | £1.27 each | (50 and over) £1.20 each |
| j72 | 18in x 18in | £1.50 each | (50 and over) £1.30 each |

Loose crumb foam (Polycrumble)

| j73 | 1 kilo bags | £1.10 per bag |
| j74 | Large bags approx 9 kilo | £1.50 per bag |

Polystyrene beads for bean bags (F.R.)

| j75 | 6 cu ft poly bags | £12.00 per bag |

GIMPINS

Available in nine colours: black, brown, blue, grey, fawn, red, yellow, white.

| j76 | 500g boxes | 10mm (⅜in) | £1.40 per box |
| j77 | 500g boxes | 13mm (½in) | £1.30 per box |

HESSIAN

Prices per metre		5 rolls	1-4 rolls	Cut lengths
j78	36in x 7 ½oz 100m rolls	£0.20	£0.23	
j79	36in x 10oz	£0.25	£0.31	
j80	54in x 10oz 50m rolls	£0.39	£0.45	£0.55
j81	72in x 10oz	£0.47	£0.52	£0.65
j82	72in x 12oz	£1.50	£1.60	£1.80

HESSIAN SCRIM

Fine jute scrim

| j83 | 72in x 6oz 50m rolls | £1.20 | £1.26 | £1.39 |
| j84 | 72in x 9oz 50m rolls | £1.30 | £1.34 | £1.45 |

Linen scrim

| j85 | 36in x 50m rolls | £1.51 | £1.60 | £1.69 |

INTERLINER

Permanently flame retardant interliner (schedule 3)

| J86 | 54in heavyweight calico | £2.95 per metre | Cut lengths £3.35 |

LAIDCORD

500g balls (6 balls per packet)

| j87 | 6 balls £1.85 per ball | Singles £2.20 per ball | 2 ½ kilo cops £9.00 |

Polypropylene lashing twine 500g spools

| j88 | 6 spools £4.00 | Singles £4.50 per spool |

MATTRESS TICKING
100% black and white rail stripe - 82in wide 70m rolls

j89	Non-durable F.R.	Roll £4.25 per metre	Cut lengths £4.72
j90	Proban permaflam	Roll £6.00 per metre	Cut lengths £6.80

PIPING CORD

Cotton twist natural

		24 cops	3-23 cops	Singles
j91	thin 250m	£3.50	£3.75	£3.90
j92	medium 180m	£3.50	£3.75	£3.90
j93	thick 140m	£3.50	£3.75	£3.90

Cotton braided (bleached) Soft washable cord gives smooth piping with fine fabrics

j94	4mm	500m reels	£22.40 per reel
j95	5mm	400m reels	£20.50 per reel
j96	6mm	250m reels	£18.00 per reel

Twisted paper cord

j97	4mm	500m reels	£14.75 per reel

PLATFORM CLOTHS

Cotton

		500m	100-400m	Cut lengths
j98	5oz black or brown 48in	£1.00	£1.05	£1.10 per metre
j99	6 ½oz brown only 54in	£1.50	£1.60	£1.75 per metre

SEWING MACHINE NEEDLES

j100	Domestic machine needles size 10, 12, 14, 16, 18 £15.00 box of 100
j101	Industrial machine needles size 16, 18, 19, 20, 21 £15.00 box of 100 £2.00 per box of 10

SKIN WADDING (flame retardant)

		10 rolls	3-9 rolls	1-2 rolls
j102	32oz 20m rolls	£6.45	£6.75	£7.05
j103	52oz 10m rolls	£4.85	£5.05	£5.25

SPRINGS
Double cone upholstery springs (per bundle of 50)

		8½ gauge	9 gauge	9 ½ gauge	10 gauge	10 ½ gauge	11 gauge	12 gauge	13 gauge	14 gauge
j104	3in				£8.70	£7.76	£7.25	£6.50	£5.60	£4.90
j105	4in		£11.84	£10.54	£9.50	£8.68	£7.78	£6.92	£5.10	
j106	5in		£13.21	£11.63	£10.54	£9.60	£8.84	£7.56	£6.08	
j107	6in		£14.00	£13.30	£11.62	£10.34	£9.68	£8.40	£6.60	£5.95
j108	7in		£15.35	£14.20	£12.68	£11.38	£10.56	£9.20		
j109	8in	£18.94	£17.06							
j110	9in	£20.62	£18.42							
j111	10in	£22.08	£19.92							
j112	11in	£23.80								
j113	12in	£25.75								

Mesh top spring units

		Front	Back	Depth	
j114	Chair	19in	17in	2in	£7.00
j115	2 seater settee	43in	42in	22in	£14.50
j116	3 seater settee	57in	56in	22in	£18.50

Tension springs ½in x 14swg plastic coated or braided

j117	14in £4.50 per 10		18in £5.50 per 10
j118	15in £4.60 per 10		19in £5.70 per 10

j119	16in £4.90 per 10		20in £6.00 per 10		

j120   Side plates 17in £53.00 per 100

Zigzag springs (in 100ft rolls)

		3 coils	1-2 coils
j121	9 gauge (seat quality)	£7.90	£8.40
j122	10 gauge (seat/back quality)	£6.90	£8.00
j123	11 gauge (back quality)	£5.80	£7.30

Finished springs

j124	Nailing clips	£10.00 per 1000	£1.50 per 100
j125	Stapling clips	£10.80 per 1000	£1.60 per 100

SPRING EDGE CANE
8/10mm Red Pahang untreated canes Approximately 14ft long

j126   10 canes £1.00 each   1-9 canes £1.20 each

STAPLES
Upholstery staples Prices per box of 10,000

		Carton (20 box)	Box (1 box)
j127	10mm (⅜in)	£2.00 per box	£2.15 per box
j128	10mm (⅜in) black	£2.20	£2.32
j129	6mm (¼in)	£1.80	£1.90
j130	3mm (⅛in)	£1.80	£1.90

STOCKINETTE
Rayon stockinette For cushions on 5 or 2 kilo rolls

j131   £3.50 per kilo

STUDS
Press studs Four part (boxes of 500)

Top parts		Box	Per 100
j132	Brass top	£20.00	£5.00
j133	Spring socket	£16.00	£4.00

Back parts		Box	Per 100
j134	Stud	£10.00	£2.50
j135	Stud fastener	£7.50	£2.00

TACKS
Cut steel

		10 kilo	2½ kilo	500g
j136	6mm (¼in) Fine			£1.50
j137	10mm (⅜in) Fine and improved	£19.00	£5.00	£1.30
j138	13mm (½in) Fine and improved	£16.50	£4.50	£1.25
j139	16mm (⅝in) Fine and improved	£16.50	£4.50	£1.25
j140	20mm (¾in) Fine and improved			£1.27
j141	25mm (1in) Fine and improved			£1.27

TACK ROLL (DUG ROLL)
Paper tack roll flanged

j142	½in	100m coils	£20.70 per coil
j143	¾in	100m coils	£27.50 per coil
j144	1in	50m coils	£19.00 per coil

TACKING STRIP
Blind seam profile

j145   100m and 300m rolls   £28.50 per 100m

Cardboard strips

j146   ½in x 40in (10 kilo bundles) £12.50 per bundle

Fibre tacking strips (tack inserts)

j147   ½in x 24in   500 per box   £50.00 per box

j148   ½in x 30in   500 per box   £62.00 per box

Flextrim

Flexible metal strip zinc coated   (100ft coils)

j149   20 coils £4.00 per coil   5 coils £4.40   Singles £5.00

Pligrip

Flexible metal tacking strip electro tin plated   (100ft coils)

j150   10 coils £4.50 per coil   1-9 coils £4.90 per coil

Presspahn

⅛in cardboard tacking strip on 1 kilo (100m coil)

j151   12 coils £2.90 per kilo   Singles £3.20 per kilo

TEE NUTS

		Barrel length	Inside thread	Per 1000
j152	Tee nut	⅜in (10mm)	³⁄₁₆in (4mm)	£28.00
j153	Tee nut	½in (13mm)	¼in (6mm)	£16.00
j154	Tee nut	⅝in (16mm)	⁵⁄₁₆in (7.5mm)	£23.00

THREADS

Machine sewing threads

Metric 36 thread (upholstery weight)

4000m spools

j155   White/natural   Box of 10 £10.20 per spool   Singles £10.80

j156   Colours   Box of 10 £12.00 per spool   Singles £12.50

Coats Koban 36 soft 2500m cones

j157   White/natural   Box of 10 £4.85 per cone   Singles £5.10

j158   Colours   Box of 10 £6.30 per cone   Singles £6.60

Metric 50 thread (curtain weight)

Barbours Terko 50 soft (4000m spools)

j159   Natural   Box of 8 £8.30 per spool   Singles £8.75

Metric 75 thread (curtain weight)

Coats Koban 75 soft 5000m cones, 10 cones per box

j160   White/natural   Box of 10 £6.80 per cone   Singles £7.10

Slipping threads

Barbours 18/4 linen thread (250g cops) black, brown and drab

j161   Box price   £10.90 per cop   Singles £11.45

Barbours 18/3 linen thread on 50g skeins (mixed colours)

j162   10 skeins   £2.35 per skein   Singles £2.45 per skein

TWINES

Stitching

Barbours best quality 1,2,3,4, mattress twine (250g balls)

j163   6 balls £4.95 per ball   1-5 balls £5.20 per ball

Buttoning

Barbours best quality nylon twine on 250g & 1 kilo cops

j164   250g cops   12 cops £4.05 per cop   Singles £4.30 per cop

j165   1 kilo cops   4 cops £15.00 per cop   1-3 cops £15.75

UPHOLSTERY NAILS

	Fisco nails (boxes 1000)	25 boxes	12 boxes	1-11 boxes
j166	1660 Brassed Steel	£3.61	£3.80	£4.25
j167	1660 Polished Brass	£8.60	£9.03	£9.90
j168	1660 Antique Steel	£4.16	£4.38	£4.80
j169	1660 Antique Brass	£9.57	£10.04	£11.00
j170	1660 Bronze Renaissance	£5.67	£5.95	£6.55
j171	1660 French Natural	£4.26	£4.38	£4.80

VELCRO

Hook and loop fastener Stocked in black, white, ecru on 10m and 25m rolls

		15mm	20mm	30mm	50mm
j172	10m hook or loop	£2.50	£3.30	£4.40	£5.65
j173	25m hook or loop	£5.50	£7.25	£9.90	£13.15
j174	10m self adhesive hook or loop	£3.90	£4.60	£6.40	£8.45

Mushroom fastener (Cric-crac) Black or white on 25m rolls

		20mm	30mm	50mm
j175	Cric (mushroom)	£6.50	£8.50	£13.25
j176	Crac (soft velour)	£3.76	£5.99	£7.75

VENTILATORS

Brass

j177	¼ in	£18.50 per gross
j178	1in	£30.15 per gross

Plastic Plastic cushion ventilators with clips (box 8000)

j179 £17.40 per 1000   £3.80 per pack 100

WEBBING

Black and white English webbing 2in wide – 18 yard rolls

		16 rolls	1-15 rolls
j180	Grade 2	£3.70 per roll	£4.00 per roll
j181	Grade 1	£4.30 per roll	£4.60 per roll

Brown and white webbing 2in wide – 18 yard rolls (15% stronger than black and white)

j182 £4.20 per roll (16 rolls)   £4.40 per roll (1-15 rolls)

Jute webbing 2in wide – 36 yard rolls (24 rolls per bale)

		24 rolls	1-23 rolls
j183	2in x 9lb	£1.30 per roll	£1.60 per roll
j184	2in x 10lb	£1.40 per roll	£1.70 per roll
j185	2in x 11lb	£1.50 per roll	£1.80 per roll
j186	2in x 12lb	£1.60 per roll	£1.90 per roll

Polypropylene webbing bedding quality 2in x 200m rolls (20 rolls per bale)

j187 £5.10 per roll (20 rolls)   £5.50 per roll (1-19 rolls)

Rubber webbing Pirelli webbing on 50m rolls

j188	38mm standard beige		£17.99 per roll	
j189	51mm standard beige or black		£22.75 per roll	
j190	1½in Pirelli clips	£3.30 per 100	Wire hooks	£3.60 per 100
j191	2in Pirelli clips	£43.00 per 100	Wire hooks	£3.55 per 100
j192	2in Mortice clips	£5.40 per 100	Plates	£1.75 per 100
j193			Staples	£1.05 per 100

Seat webbing Jumbo Elastic
10% stretch as for standard Pirelli webbing. High tensile strength, and does not narrow under stretch.

j194	2in wide	10 rolls £17.20 per roll	1-9 rolls £18.35 per roll

Jumbo webbing available in cut straps with standard clip at each end.
To obtain correct size of strap, measure distance between grooves, deduct 10% and add 1in for clips.

		per 100	per 10
j195	18in	£35.55	£3.88
j196	19in	£36.45	£4.10
j197	20in	£37.55	£4.15
j198	21in	£38.45	£4.25
j199	22in	£39.40	£4.50
j200	23in	£39.80	£4.60

ZIPS

YKK lightweight nylon. Continuous chain on 100m rolls (fawn)

j201	£30.35 per 100m
j202	YKK no 3 sliders fawn enamel self lock £3.90 per 100

Optilon medium weight no. 5 polyester chain

j203	Fawn and cream on 150m reels	£40.00 per 100m
j204	Optilon no. 5 sliders	£5.45 per 100

Open end zips Price per 100

		No. 5 alloy	No. 6 nylon
j205	15in	£40.55	£62.65
j206	18in	£44.65	£69.05
j207	20in	£47.25	£73.10
j208	22in	£49.85	£77.10
j209	24in	£52.30	£81.10

The upholsterer's warehouseman is always a mine of information and will help the buyer to specify and select the materials, tools and equipment he requires. New products and product information, plus discounts for quantity are always on offer.

A check should always be made on items delivered and the quantities. When an item is not in stock or only a part order is received, the delivery note, which normally has to be signed by the recipient, will state that certain items are to follow or are not available.

A catalogue offers the upholsterer a wealth of information and also useful tips on the use and application of materials, hardware and equipment. Good work begins with good materials and the wise craftsman buys the best that can be afforded.

Estimating and costing materials

Three Worked Examples

The following examples of upholstery work have been broken down into their constituent materials; the quantities required have been estimated, and the materials then costed from the catalogue on pp 120-8. Amounts are totalled and 10% added for sundries, such as twines, staples and tacks etc. The sundries figure may also include handling and the inevitable wastage of small materials.

The upholsterer normally adds an on-cost or mark-up to all materials used. This can vary a great deal and is calculated as a percentage of the wholesale cost of all the materials used in the workshop to produce upholstered work. The percentage added to materials may be as low as 25% or as high as 100%, often depending on the nature and the size of the business.

1. Four traditional loose seats for dining chairs

a. Webbing 2in (51mm) black and white	9ft 10in (3m)	£0.77
b Hessian 10oz 36in (91mm)	39in (1m)	£0.25
c Curled hair	4lb	£7.72
d. Calico 72in (183cm)	39in (1m)	£2.65
e Skin wadding 32oz	79in (2m)	£0.68
f. Black bottom lining	39in (1m)	£0.95
g. Sundries (tacks, twine, staples etc.)	10%	£1.30
h. On cost of 50%	50%	£7.16
	Total	£21.48

2. Two sprung, stuffover dining-chair seats

a. Webbing 2in (51mm) black and white	23ft (7m)	£1.79
b. Springs 5in (127mm) x 9½ gauge	8	£1.86
c. Hessian 12oz 36in (91cm)	19½in (½m)	£0.13
d. Fibre for first stuffing	4lb	£3.16
e. Scrim 72in (183cm)	23½in (600m)	£0.81
f. Curled hair	½lb	£2.90
g. Cotton felt 2½oz	39in (1m)	£0.67
h Calico 72in (183cm)	23½in (600mm)	£1.56
i Black lining cloth	19½in (½m)	£0.50
j. Sundries	10%	£1.34
k. On cost of 50%	50%	£7.36
	Total	£22.08

3. Twenty plywood seats for a set of boardroom chairs

a. Recon chipfoam 6lb x ⅞in (22mm) thick	53.82 sq ft (5 sq m)	£32.00
b Foam CMHR 35 10mm (⅜in) thick	53.82 sq ft (5 sq m)	£15.00
c. Polyester wadding 4oz	9ft 10in (3m)	£2.70
d Calico 72in (183cm)	11ft 6in (3.5m)	£9.28
e. Black lining 48in (122cm)	16ft 5in (5m)	£2.50
f. Sundries	10%	£6.15
g. On cost	50%	£33.81
	Total	£101.44

Estimating for piping
– cuts and amounts

Fig 13.7 There are three different ways to cut piping strips from a fabric or cover: across the width, along the length or on the bias. Each produces a slightly different kind of piping and each behaves differently when it is made up and in use. Grain, weave and direction of cut all affect its feel and its flexibility.

Ways of Cutting

Piping strips 1½in (38mm)

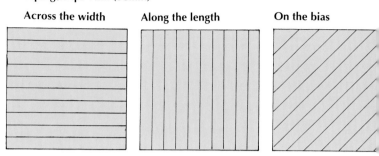

Across the width | Along the length | On the bias

Table 13.4

Metreage chart for piping lengths

Fabric amount	Cut/direction	Amount of piping	Strip width
Half metre (19⅝in)	Bias cut	19m (62ft 4in)	1½in (38mm)
One metre (39⅜ in)	Bias cut	38m (124ft 8in)	1½in (38mm)
One and quarter metres (49¼in)	Bias cut	47.5m (155ft 10in)	1½in (38mm)
Half metre (19⅝in)	Along length	16m (52ft 6in)	1½in (38mm)
One metre (39⅜ in)	Along length	32m (105ft)	1½in (38mm)
One and quarter metres (49¼in)	Along length	40m (131ft 3in)	1½in (38mm)
Half metre (19⅝in)	Across width	16m (52ft 6in)	1½in (38mm)
One metre (39⅜ in)	Across width	32m (105ft)	1½in (38mm)
One and quarter metres (49¼in)	Across width	40m (131ft 3in)	1½in (38mm)

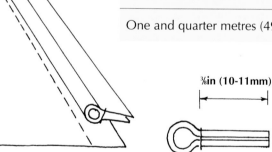

⅜in (10-11mm)

Fig 13.8 The width of piping or welt strip is 1½in (38mm). This is a good average width and is suitable for making up with piping cords of ³⁄₁₆in, ¼in and ⁵⁄₁₆in (4mm, 6mm and 7.5mm). When piping thicknesses go beyond these sizes then a little more width in the strip will be needed.

When a piping of average size is made up and sewn from a 1½in (38mm) fabric strip, the flange width measured from the sewing line out to the raw edge will be approximately ⅜in (10 to 11mm). This is provided of course that in the making up the fabric strip is folded exactly along its centre and the raw edges are running together. This measurement becomes critical when the piping is eventually sewn on to a panel. As thicknesses of cover are added to the piping the groove in the piping foot which is a set size, will move the stitch line over a fraction to form a tightened joint against the cord.

During assembly, the second and third sewings will take up the ⅜in (10 to 11mm) sewing allowance automatically, on a panel or a border to which the piping is being sewn.

- Length and width of material required
- Where joins will occur
- Visual display of all the parts
- Visual check on shapes and any waste areas
- A check on the essential pieces needed
- Use of extensions
- Use of fly pieces for economy
- Notching and centring especially for sewn parts
- Amounts and lengths of piping strips needed
- Centring and alignment of design or pattern
- Exact shape of curves and facings

Estimating for covering materials

Working out the amount of covering material that will be needed for a particular job begins with the measuring tape and a cutting plan. The value of a cutting plan, even if it is only a rough sketch, can be appreciated as soon as the dimensions taken and listed, are committed to paper. It gives a clear picture of the piece parts to be cut within the limits of the cover type and its width. It also offers scope for adjustment and replanning to obtain the best cutting arrangement, allowing an economical use of materials.

When repetition of the work is likely, then it is worth making an accurate plan or layout; this can be used as a working drawing to be interpreted by others who may be involved in the work. A plan is also of advantage when design and pattern are important so that matching and alignment of a cover design or motif is accurate and acceptable. A large or complex pattern on a cover can influence the amount of material that will eventually be required. Once the layout is drawn up and the amounts totalled then changes can easily be made to the original or an alternative and more advantageous plan can be produced.

Cover-cutting layouts are basically dimensioned drawings or sketches and they should give the following information:

Chairs should preferably be measured for their cover either before they are stripped or at the calico stage. The vertical or length measurements taken from a chair are particularly important because it is these that, when added up, give the length of cover to be bought. Almost all chairs and settees have some left and right hand parts which are mirrored on the layout. One length measurement will therefore give the amount needed for both these parts, provided they fit within the cover width. If not, then each has to be placed separately along the cover length and the waste used up for some other smaller parts.

It is good practice to try to arrange for as many parts to pair as possible. This may sometimes mean using flies sewn to the sides of the inside back and to the inner ends of the inside arms etc. A cutting list is written out with measurements recorded at the widest and the longest points of each part. The length measurements are taken first followed by the widths and the number of each part required. Table 13.5 shows the cutting list for the armchair in Fig 13.9.

Fig 13.9   A typical cover cutting plan on plain upholstery cover which shows all the parts required for an armchair.

Table 13.5

Cutting list

Part		Length	Width	No.
IB	inside back	38%⁄₁₆in (980mm)	27%⁄₁₆in (700mm)	1
OB	outside back	34⅝in (880mm)	23⅝in (600mm)	1
IA	inside arm	25¹⁹⁄₃₂in (650mm)	25¹⁹⁄₃₂in (650mm)	2
OA	outside arm	21²¹⁄₃₂in (550mm)	23⅝in (600mm)	2
S	seat	29½in (750mm)	31½in (800mm)	1
SB	seat border	11¹³⁄₁₆in (300mm)	24⅝in (625mm)	1
AF	arm facing	26in (660mm)	7⅞in (200mm)	2
P	piping	19¹¹⁄₁₆in (500mm)	33ft 7½in (10.25m)	

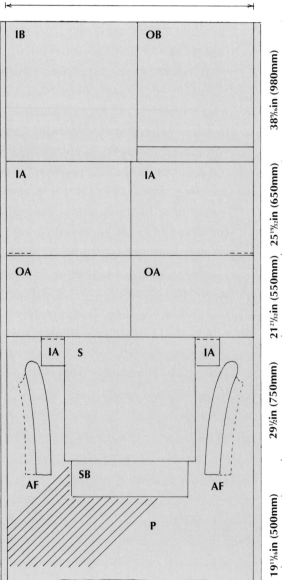

Table 13.6

Metreage chart for common-sized pieces of upholstery furniture

Pinstuffed seats or backs	19¾in (500mm) for 1 or 2
Loose seat	23⅝in (600mm) for 1 or 2
Library chair (seat and back)	6ft 6in (2m)
Stuffover seat (dining chair)	25⅝in (650mm)
Prie-dieu (prayer chair)	4ft 3in (1.3m)
Desk chair (swivel)	4ft 11in (1.5m)
Ottoman (box only)	3ft 11in (1.2m)
(with end)	6ft 6in (2m)
Stool	29½in (750mm)
Sewing chair	4ft 11in (1.5m)
Fireside chair	8ft 2½in (2.5m)
Small arm chair	11ft 10in (3.6m)
Large easy chair (with seat cushion)	15ft 7in (4.75m)
Wing arm chair (plain)	17ft 3in (5.25m)
(patterned)	19ft 8½in (6m)
Single-end *chaise-longue*	11ft 6in (3.5m)
Chaise-longue (with end and back)	16ft 5in (5m)
(with buttoned end and back)	18ft (5.5m)
Double-ended chaise longue	23ft (7m)
Two-seater settee (fixed back)	19ft (5.8m)
Two-seater settee (cushion back)	24ft 7½in (7.5m)
Three-seater settee (fixed back)	25ft 11in (7.9m)
Three-seater settee (cushion back)	31ft 2in (9.5m)
Chesterfield (plain)	23ft (7m)
(patterned)	27ft 11in (8.5m)

Upholstered chair design and the requirements

The dimensions and proportions used in seating design have to be based principally on the provision of comfort for the user. This involves the study of anthropometric data, which in this case can be defined as the measurement of the human body, taking into account the varying proportions of people of different sizes and different ages.

The healthiness of the sitter's posture is important but this has to be related to the likely user and the specific uses of different types of chair. Seats are generally produced for use either as easy chairs for relaxing, or as occasional chairs for short period use, or as chairs for dining, working and general use.

The upholsterer is unlikely to be deeply involved in the design of chairs and seating until the work has to be built, either as a prototype or as a piece of reupholstery. Nevertheless, an awareness of the requirements of proportion, shape and the basic dimensions of comfort is a definite advantage (*see* Fig 13.10). Depths and angles that are produced with suspension and fillings can so easily be wrongly set, particularly in stuffover work using modern or traditional materials.

Furthermore, a frame may not give sufficient guidance as to the layout and design of the upholstery needed. The outline of a chair frame is generally set by its designer but the inner surfaces are not always so specific, particularly in development work and antique restoration. The slope of a seat or the angle of a back support or the height of an arm rest will often be governed by the choice and thickness of the materials used; thus the upholsterer quite often has the responsibility

Fig 13.10 The requirements of proportion, shape and comfort in seating.

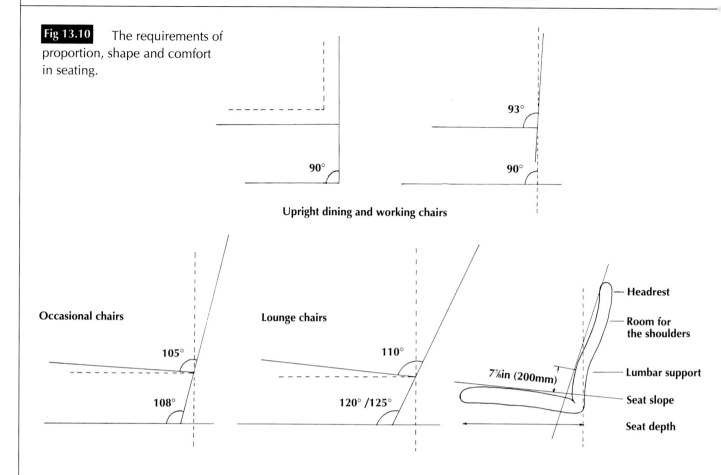

of providing the final sitting position and the support to suit both the end use and the potential user.

Wherever possible the client should be consulted and the requirements outlined so that the work is – at least to some extent – client orientated. If there is no particular customer involved then the upholstery work can be based purely on the design and the proportions dictated by the type of frame, its age or period.

The following guidelines and general requirements are based on published standards (*see* Furniture Industry Research Association Technical Report Nos. 22 and 41), and the experience gained by those working in the industry.

Average dimensions for different types of chair

Dining and general seating

1. Seat height	15³⁄₈in-16¹⁄₈in (390mm-410mm)
2. Seat depth	16¹⁷⁄₃₂in (420mm)
3. Seat width	15¾in (400mm)
4. Slope of seat	3°
5. Height of back above seat	16¾in (425mm) (min)
6. Overall height	31½in (800mm) (min)
7. Angle between back rest and seat	93° - 95°

Occasional seating

1. Seat height $14^{15}/_{16}$in-$16^{1}/_{8}$in (380mm-410m)
2. Seat depth $16^{15}/_{16}$in-$19^{11}/_{16}$in (430mm-500mm)
3. Seat width $19^{11}/_{16}$in-$20^{7}/_{8}$in (500mm-530mm)
4. Slope of seat $4°$ - $5°$
5. Height of back above seat $17^{23}/_{32}$in (450mm) (min)
6. Overall height $27^{9}/_{16}$in (700mm) (min)
7. Angle between back rest and seat $105°$ - $110°$

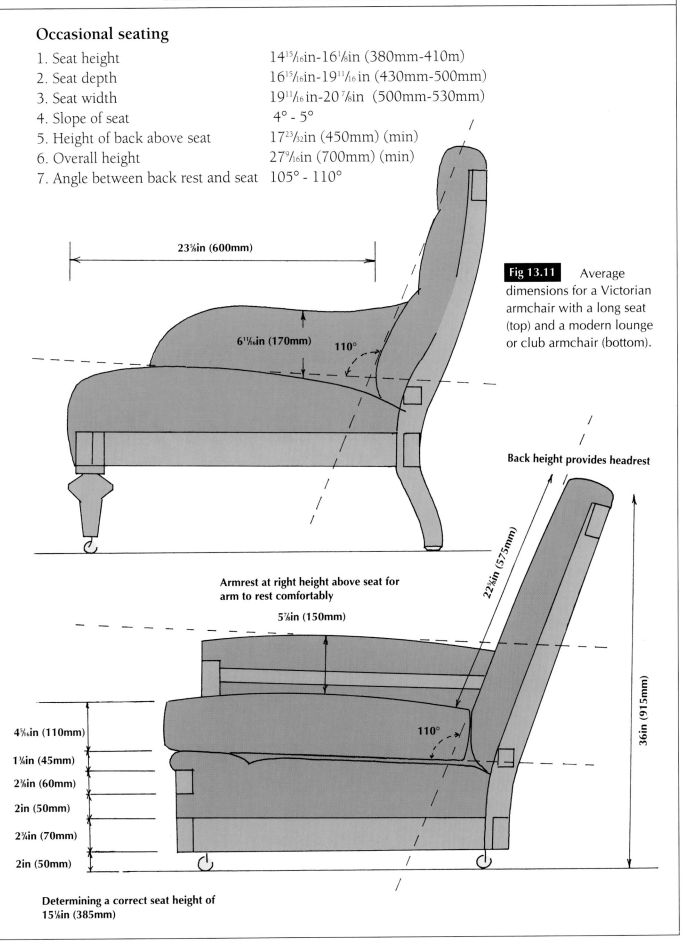

Fig 13.11   Average dimensions for a Victorian armchair with a long seat (top) and a modern lounge or club armchair (bottom).

23⅝in (600mm)

6¹¹⁄₁₆in (170mm)

110°

Back height provides headrest

22⅝in (575mm)

Armrest at right height above seat for arm to rest comfortably

5⅞in (150mm)

110°

36in (915mm)

4⁵⁄₁₆in (110mm)

1¾in (45mm)

2⅜in (60mm)

2in (50mm)

2¾in (70mm)

2in (50mm)

Determining a correct seat height of
15⅛in (385mm)

Lounge seating

1. Seat height $\qquad$ 13¾in-16¹⁷⁄₃₂in (350mm-420mm)
2. Seat depth $\qquad$ 19⁵⁄₁₆in-19¹¹⁄₁₆in (490mm-500mm)
3. Seat width $\qquad$ 19¹¹⁄₁₆in-21²¹⁄₃₂in (500mm-550mm)
4. Slope of seat $\qquad$ 4° - 6°
5. Height of back above seat $\qquad$ 22⁵⁄₈in (575mm) (min)
6. Overall height $\qquad$ 33³⁄₈in (850mm) (min)
7. Angle between back rest and seat $\qquad$ 110°
8. Height of armrest above seat $\qquad$ 6¹¹⁄₁₆in (170mm)

Fig 13.12 Top: How the shape of upholstery changes when a chair is occupied. Bottom: Foam thicknesses.

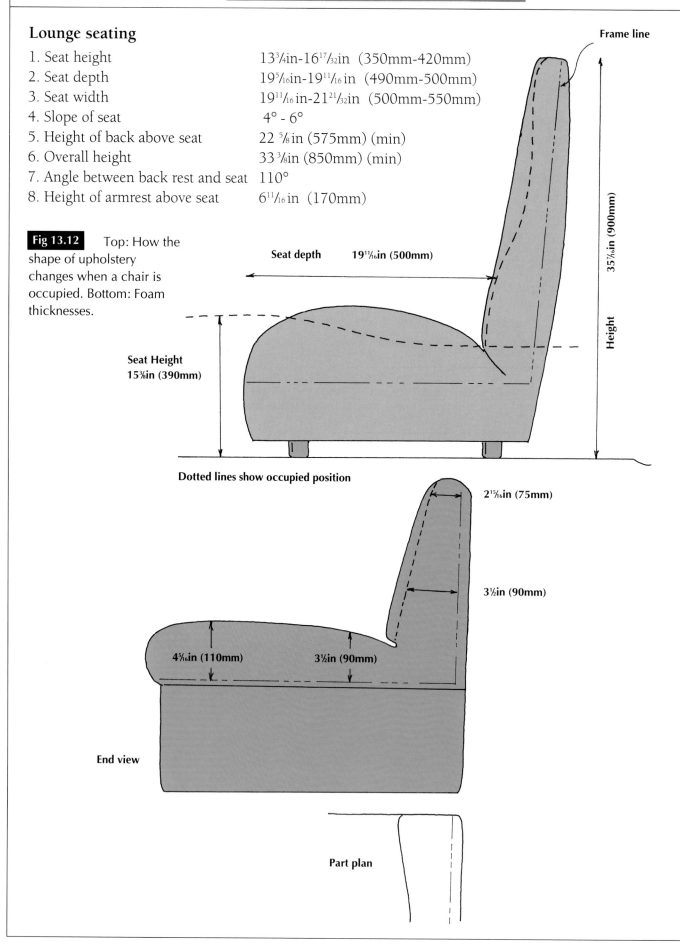

Frame line

Seat depth 19¹¹⁄₁₆in (500mm)

35⁷⁄₁₆in (900mm)

Height

Seat Height 15⅜in (390mm)

Dotted lines show occupied position

2¹⁵⁄₁₆in (75mm)

3½in (90mm)

4⁵⁄₁₆in (110mm)

3½in (90mm)

End view

Part plan

136

Needles and threads for upholstery sewing

The upholsterer cuts and sews a very wide range of covers and fabrics, from soft cotton prints for cushion making at the lighter end of the range, to leathers, plastics and canvases for modern upholstery at the heavier end. The majority of work in upholstery and reupholstery falls somewhere between these two extremes. Medium-weight upholstery coverings are mainly soft, woven fabrics for house furnishings and the contract seating market. These include tapestries, brocades, wool weaves and velvets.

size and cover all compatible, to produce a strong and balanced seam.

Added to these basic requirements for good sewing is the choice of thread type. There are three: glacé thread, which is polished; soft thread, which has a matt surface; and monofilament, which may be nylon or polyester. All of these are suitable for upholstery sewing but the glacé core-spun threads are generally the most common in use.

Fig 13.13 Stitch density for upholstery sewing.

Table 13.7

Choosing the appropriate needle and thread for upholstery sewing

	Lightweight upholstery	Medium upholstery	Heavy upholstery
Needle size	18 Singer 110 Metric	19 Singer 120 Metric	21 Singer 130 Metric
Thread size	75	50/36	36

Sewing machine threads and needles are chosen by upholsterers according to the weight of material they are working with - generally classified as light, medium or heavy. Matching a needle and thread ensures that the hole size made by the needle is suitable for the thread passing through it, and a good loop formation is achieved when the stitch is made. Equally, the thread and needle chosen should suit the weight and the type of cover being sewn. To get the best results the relationship has to be a threesome, with thread size, needle

Finally, the length of stitch has to be chosen to suit the particular application and the cover type. Generally speaking, the heavier materials should have the lower number of stitches per inch to avoid excessive perforation, while finer fabrics can be sewn with more stitches per length of seam. Stitch length is measured by the number of stitches per inch or per centimetre (see Fig 13.13). Table 13.7 gives some equivalents and some recommended needle and thread relationships.

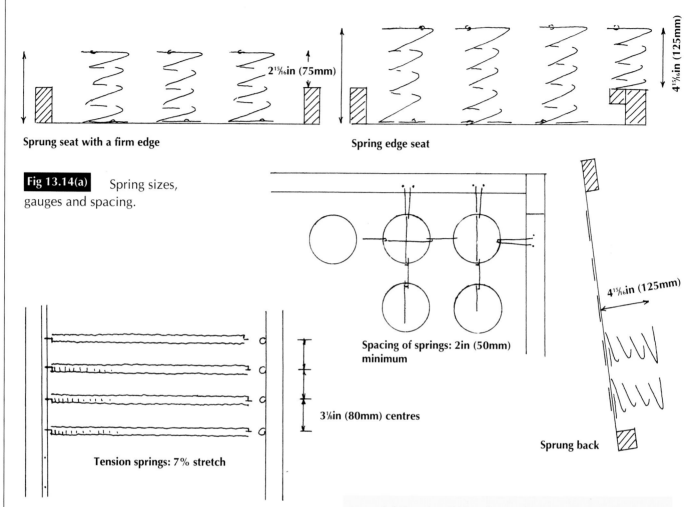

Sprung seat with a firm edge

2¹⁵⁄₁₆in (75mm)

Spring edge seat

4¹⁵⁄₁₆in (125mm)

Fig 13.14(a) Spring sizes, gauges and spacing.

Spacing of springs: 2in (50mm) minimum

4¹⁵⁄₁₆in (125mm)

Sprung back

Tension springs: 7% stretch

3⅛in (80mm) centres

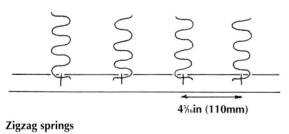

4⁵⁄₁₆in (110mm)

Zigzag springs

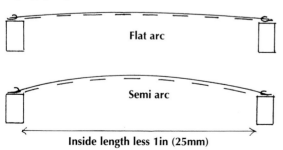

Flat arc

Semi arc

Inside length less 1in (25mm)

Imperial Standard Wire Gauge Sizes				
Standard wire gauge	**inches**	**nearest fraction of an inch**		**nearest metric gauge**
7	0.176	³⁄₁₆	0.187	4.5
8	0.160	⁵⁄₃₂	0.156	4.0
9	0.144			3.6
10	0.128	⅛	0.125	3.3
11	0.116			3.0
12	0.104			2.7
13	0.092	³⁄₃₂	0.093	2.4
14	0.080			2.1
15	0.072			1.9
16	0.064	¹⁄₁₆	0.062	1.65
17	0.056			1.45
18	0.048			1.25
19	0.040			1.05
20	0.036			0.95
21	0.032			0.85
22	0.028	¹⁄₃₂	0.031	0.72

Checking a gauge on a sinuous wire spring.

Fig 13.14(b) Resilient webbings.

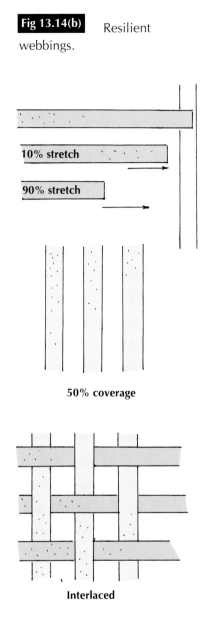

50% coverage

Interlaced

Keeping accounts

No matter how skilled a craftsman and his workforce may be, the whole enterprise can fall apart if accurate accounts are not kept. Apart from the legal aspect of preparing accounts for the taxman, records of materials purchased and sales achieved provides a reference that can be consulted if comparisons need to be made, or if you need to know how much a certain job has cost.

It is not necessary to have a detailed knowledge of business accounts, but it is essential that this aspect of the business is kept up to date and all transactions recorded.

Basically the paperwork can be summarized as follows:

1. Purchase ledger; this is divided into
    a. Purchase invoices
    b. Purchase payments
2. Sales ledger; this is divided into
    a. Sales invoices
    b. Sales payments received

Any purchases, whether materials for jobs or running expenses (e.g. telephone bills), should be entered in a ledger, and invoices retained. As items are not always paid for immediately, a separate ledger sheet is kept for payments made.

When a job has been completed a sales invoice should be written and the details entered in the sales ledger; the top copy of the invoice is given to the customer and a copy is filed. On receiving payment, the amount and the reference number of the original invoice are entered in a separate ledger sheet.

A current account for the business should be opened at the bank and all sales payments received should be paid into the account via a paying-in book. This gives a further check on transactions and when a bank statement is received, it is a simple matter to reconcile.

One of the problems of running a workshop is to know how much to charge for a particular job. Of course an estimate should always be given (*see* Fig 13.15), but while the job is in progress a record of how much the work is actually costing should be kept. This is done by entering the cost of all materials and labour on a job card. This provides a useful reference if similar projects are taken on in the future.

If an accountant is to complete the yearly accounts these are the records that he or she will want to see:

- Purchase ledger (2 sheets)
- Sales ledger (2 sheets)
- Copies of purchase and sales invoices
- Paying-in books
- Cheque books used
- Bank statements

From these records the accountant will prepare detailed accounts (*see* Fig 13.16) and will send copies to the Inland Revenue who will ascertain how much (if any) tax has to be paid. It can be appreciated that if records have been neatly and accurately kept, the accountant's job will be made easier and his or her charge to you reasonable, as most accountants charge hourly rates.

There is one important cost that should never be underestimated, and that is overheads. These are items that would have to

Fig 13.15 A typical estimate form.

Job estimate

Customer	Date	
Job		Costing
The Frame condition		
repairs		
restoration	estimate	£
The Cover type		
design		
width		
length repeat		
		£
Upholstery condition	materials	
replace		
labour	hours at £	
trimmings	amounts	£
		£
Total		£
Estimate: Actual:		

Fig 13.16 A peep into the trading accounts of a small company will show most of the essential items to be considered during one year.

Trading and profit and loss account for the year end

	31.3.1994	31.3.1995
Invoiced amounts receivable		
Cost of sales		
Materials		
Cost of restoration/outwork		
Ancillary expenses		
Gross profit		
Interest receivable		
Less overheads		
Salaries and wages, nat ins.		
Motor running expenses		
Repairs and renewals		
Telephone, fax, postage		
Entertaining		
Printing and stationary		
Advertising		
Travelling		
Heating and lighting		
Insurances		
Rent and rates		
Leasing and charges		
Technical publications		
Bank charges		
Staff welfare		
Legal and professional fees		
Cleaning		
Subscriptions		
Donations		
Accountancy fees		
Directors' remuneration		
Directors' pension scheme		
Directors' national ins.		
Auditors' remuneration		
Depreciation		
Sundry expenses		
Total		
Profit for the year		

be paid even if no jobs were actually done. For example:

- Rent
- Heating
- Insurance
- Vehicle running expenses
- Telephone bills
- Stationery

When starting a business, a detailed estimate of these items for the coming year should be worked out and the labour charge should reflect these costs.

In business today, cash flow has become of paramount importance. It is fairly obvious that a commission cannot be undertaken if the money to buy materials and to pay the bills is not readily available. A cash flow projection gives an idea of how one's bank balance is going to fluctuate over a given period, indicating when purchases can be made. This is particularly important if a major purchase e.g. a new delivery van, is necessary.

A cash flow analysis begins with the current bank balance; to this is added sales payments expected during the coming month and from this figure payments that have to be made are subtracted. The resultant figure is the new bank balance carried forward to the next month's forecast. Most businesses should do a cash flow projection for about three to four months; this will give a pretty good idea of any problems that might occur. If a bank loan is required, the manager will almost certainly ask for such a record to be produced.

The most important advice that can be given to anyone wishing to start business is not to neglect keeping accounts as it could mean the difference between success and failure. All stationers stock ledger sheets specifically designed for keeping accounts and it is well worth setting aside a couple of hours each week for paperwork. The rewards will almost certainly be reflected in the bank balance at the year end.

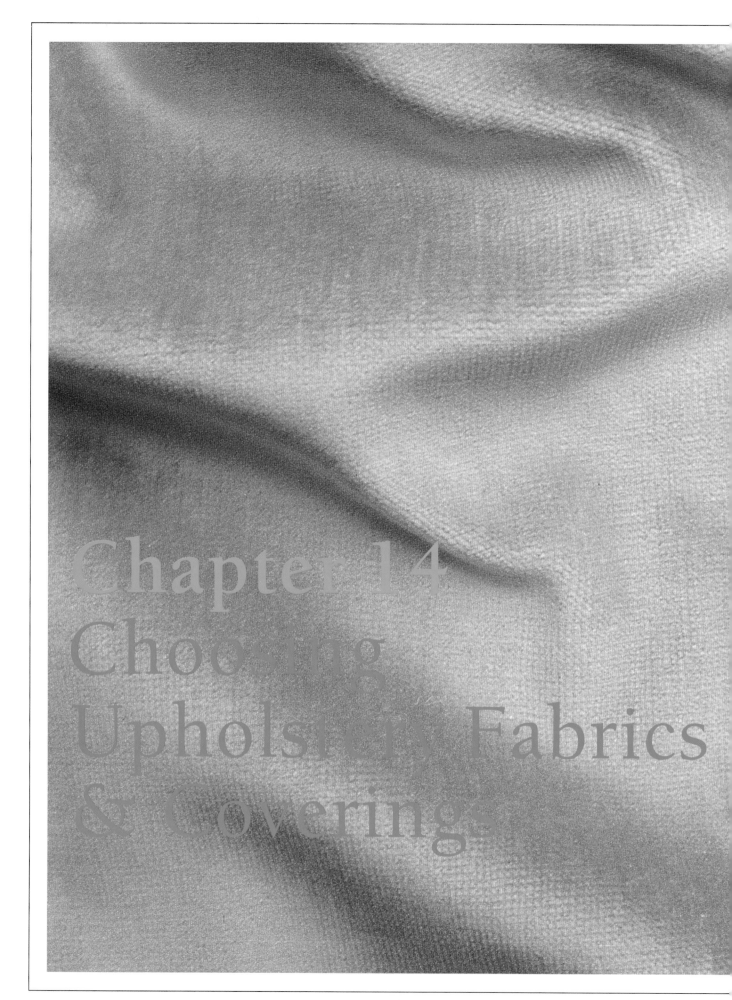

Chapter 14
Choosing
Upholstery Fabrics
& Coverings

Anyone engaged in upholstering or restoring a chair will at some point need to choose a covering, either for themselves or on behalf of a client. When reaching a decision it is important, first of all, to establish the preferences and tastes of the client, and the surroundings into which the chair will be placed once it is completed.

Once the basis for choice is reached then the sample book should be allowed to take over. Visualizing a finished piece from a small sample of fabric is very difficult even for the experienced buyer. The larger the swatch or sample, the easier it will be to assess, and to arrive at a short list. Making the final choice can be quite a challenge but is nevertheless an exciting part of the upholstery process.

The following are the most likely situations that the upholsterer will face when selecting a cover:

● The chair must suit an existing room and its scheme.

● The chair cover is being chosen as part of a newly furnished and decorated interior.

● The chair cover must reflect or repeat the chair's original style and period.

The last of these may not necessarily refer to a very old piece. Indeed, even a 25-year-old piece of furniture deserves to be covered in a fabric that suits its era.

Another factor which must be considered when choosing a covering is its suitability for its intended purpose. The purpose is usually defined by the kind of chair being covered and the type of use that it will get. An occasional chair, for example, which will stand in the corner of a bedroom for much of its life, can be contrasted with a large armchair in a prominent position in a family lounge. For

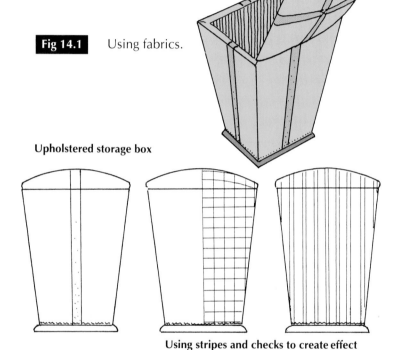

Fig 14.1   Using fabrics.

Upholstered storage box

Using stripes and checks to create effect

the armchair, the best and most expensive fabric that can be afforded should be chosen. Its level of use will be very high and the new covering should have most of the following properties:

● Flexibility and strength

● Good draping

● Retention of shape and size

● Softness and absorbency

● Good dye fastness to light and water

● Easy cleaning and good strength for stitching and sewing

● Should conform to current fire safety legislation (*see* pages 153-4).

Traditional upholstery covers

Over the long history of upholstered furniture the pile fabric has been considered one of the most practical and durable of coverings. It has drifted in and out of fashion at various times but remains a favourite whenever a plain, hard-wearing cover is required. Early fine velvets were mainly silk and cotton pile but, more recently, a whole variety of natural and synthetic fibres have been used for the fine soft surface of velvets and velours: linen, wool, mercerized cotton, mohair, nylon and Dralon have all been used with enduring success.

Today, most of these are available with variable pile lengths and surface effects that give design and added texture to what are otherwise plain-colour fabrics. Texture can be added by crushing, figuring or embossing.

Apart from the more recently developed knitted fabrics, most covers have a long and chequered history in upholstery. They have all been used, modified and reintroduced in a multitude of ways. However, the basic structures remain and can be recognized by their make up, their feel and general appearance. A close analysis is possible by unravelling warp and weft threads carefully to examine an exact structure. Tensioning a sample with the fingers, in the warp, weft and bias directions will indicate how a fabric will react to pressure and stretch. The upholstery process itself can be very demanding and will test a fabric long before it ever gets sat upon.

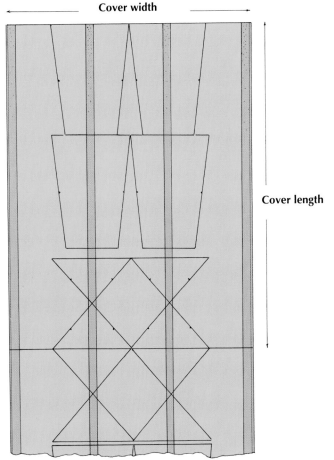

A cutting plan for the box, with balance marks used to line up the parts for sewing

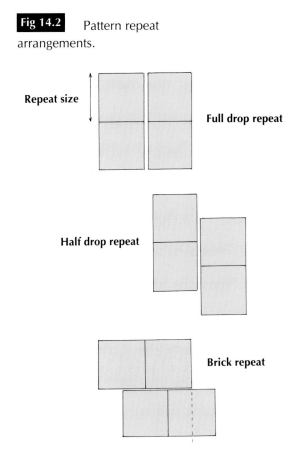

Fig 14.2 Pattern repeat arrangements.

Repeat size

Full drop repeat

Half drop repeat

Brick repeat

The following is a list of upholstery coverings from the 17th century to the 20th century:

1600-1650	Turkey work; Indian cotton; oriental silks; plain wool cloths; hides.
1650-1700	Velvet; silk brocade; leather; wool worsted.
1700-1750	Embroidery work; silk velvet; damask; printed cotton chintz; painted silks.
1750-1800	French and English tapestry; satin; casement; silk damask; genoa velvets; haircloth.
1800-1850	Needlework; striped brocade; cut and patterned velour; haircloth; wool plush; embroidery; printed cotton.
1850-1900	Embossed leather; striped brocade; printed and painted cottons; machine-made tapestries; distinct jacquard patterns; velvet.
1900-1950	Stylized tapestry; floral unions and chintz; leather; wool velvet and plush; moquette; leathercloth.
1950-today	Soft wool moquette; cut pile moquette; vinyl and polyurethane coated fabrics; plain tweeds; synthetic velvets; tapestries and jacquards; printed cottons and unions; damasks and dobby weaves.

Recommendations for use

Furnishing fabrics for upholstery are generally grouped into three categories: curtaining, loose covers, and fixed upholstery. In some cases these will overlap. Certain loosely woven fabrics may, for example, be perfect for drapes or curtains, but would not be considered at all for use as loose covers, or in fixed upholstery. Any fabric which snags easily should be avoided for fixed or loose upholstery. One such fabric is satin-faced cloth. This makes an excellent curtain material and is usually printed with a surface sheen, but the weft floats which sit tightly on the surface are soon raised by the slightest abrasion.

There are however a vast range of light, medium and heavy coverings which are eminently suitable for upholstery work. A large percentage of these contain natural fibres which are frequently blended with synthetics, to create the properties required for the job. Wool, cotton and linen are very often blended with rayon, nylon or acrylics to give the best of both worlds.

Silk is a good example of a fine natural fibre which needs the support of other fibres when being woven for upholstery purposes. It blends well with wool or cotton for surface yarns, with the structural support of cotton or rayon to add strength and stability to the fabric. Composition is therefore important along with a weave structure which is close and reliable.

Cotton repp, with a fine rib weft. 53% cotton, 47% viscose; 55½in (140cm) wide.

Glazed chintz, plain weave, furnishing weight. 100% cotton; 55⅛in (140cm) wide.

Labelling

Today we demand clear information about the products that we buy and fabrics are no exception. A ticket or label should give most, if not all, of the following information:

- Fibre content
- Width of the cloth in centimetres
- Its suitability for use
- The colourways available
- The pattern repeat size if any
- The price

In some cases a colour coding system is used with fabrics suitable for upholstery, marked with tickets of a certain colour, another colour indicating fabrics for loose covers and a third for curtaining and linens etc. Labels on upholstery fabrics also always include a code to indicate its level of fire retardancy.

Abrasion test results in the form of rub counts are also sometimes included to give an indication of a fabric's ability to stand up to hard wear and tear. This figure should only be taken as an indication and not as a guarantee that a fabric is good or not.

Manufacturers and retail houses are keen to see that the buyer has all this information, which helps when a cover is being chosen.

Structure and type

Ingredients alone will not necessarily produce a good upholstery covering. The structure, whether woven, knitted or laminated, is of equal importance. The following list gives some of the most common upholstery fabrics, grouped according to structure. Also included are fabrics which are not woven, but which are used in upholstery particularly.

Plain Weaves

Chintz	A fine, close-weave, 100% cotton fabric; plain or patterned and glazed or semi-glazed.
Cretonne	A strong, close-weave cotton or rayon fabric, usually with printed patterns; heavier than chintz and sometimes twill woven.
Duck	A heavy cotton or linen canvas with natural or plain-dyed colours.
Repp	A plain wool or cotton fabric with a pronounced weft rib effect; strong and of good weight.
Shantung	This can be made in furnishing weight from silk or cotton with a rough-textured surface. Its natural colour is brown when made from rough silk.
Tweed	Blends of wool cotton and rayon are used for furnishing tweeds which are finished with a smooth surface; hard-wearing, pliable and warm.
Unions	This is made from a combination of two main natural fibres such as cotton and linen, although today synthetics may be added;

Modern printed cretonne.
100% cotton; 24⅜in (62cm) repeat;
52¹⁵⁄₁₆in (137cm) wide.

Printed union cloth.
60% linen, 22% cotton,
18% viscose; 24⅜in (62cm) repeat;
52¹⁵⁄₁₆in (137cm) wide.

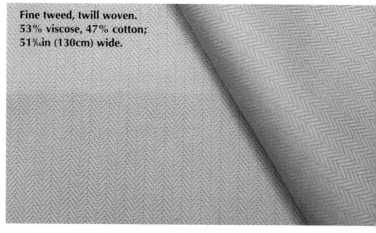

Fine tweed, twill woven.
53% viscose, 47% cotton;
51³⁄₁₆in (130cm) wide.

strong and durable and will wash easily; usually printed.

Twill Weaves

Denim A tough, close-weave fabric, produced in plain colours and made from 100% cotton.

Tartan Check designs woven for furnishings from wool and blends of man-made fibres.

Ticking A good upholstery and cushion fabric with a stiff feel; may be cotton or linen; woven stripes are typical, either in black and white or colours.

Tweed A strong woollen fabric with diagonal and herringbone weave patterns; the simple and coarse weaves make a resilient medium-weight cloth.

Unions Printed and plain-colour cloths with strong, close-twill weaves; a good upholstery and loose cover material.

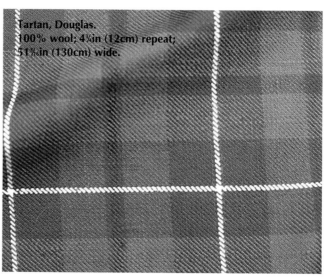

Tartan, Douglas.
100% wool; 4¾in (12cm) repeat;
51³⁄₁₆in (130cm) wide.

Jacquard Weaves

Damask The combination of weaves defines the pattern, which may be one or two colours. Wool, cotton, silk and synthetics are also combined to give matt and lustre effects. Generally the warp forms the background with a sateen weave pattern.

Brocade A colourful, richly patterned fabric traditionally made from silk with embroidery effects. It is made in a variety of yarns today with the colours running in a stripe formation in the back of the fabric.

Damask, large two colour pattern. 100% silk; 11¹³⁄₁₆in (30cm) repeat; 51³⁄₁₆in (130cm) wide.

Brocatelle A heavy and durable upholstery fabric with a raised or padded pattern surface. It is made from strong mercerized cotton combined with silk or rayon; jute may also added for stability and weight.

Tapestry Developed from needlework tapestries and woven on the jacquard loom with pictorial designs and motifs. The structures can be complex and heavy from cotton, worsted and rayon yarns.

Matelasse A traditional upholstery cloth construction with a raised surface texture. Cotton and viscose rayon are the typical fibre composition, making a hard-wearing and stable fabric.

Pile fabrics

Velour A smooth short pile fabric made from mercerized cotton with warp yarns forming the pile surface. This is a serviceable upholstery covering

Tapestry. 62% viscose, 38% modacrylic; 11⅜in (29cm) repeat; 55⅛in (140cm) wide.

with a distinct look of luxury, and shaded effects created by the brush of the fine pile.

Velvet   A warp pile fabric generally heavier than a velour and made with a variety of different pile yarns. Silk, linen, mohair and Dralon are all widely used to produce a good hard-wearing upholstery cover. Velvets may be plain, figured or embossed and sometimes printed. Genoa and Utrecht are two types.

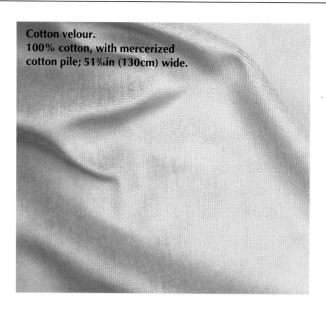

Cotton velour.
100% cotton, with mercerized cotton pile; 51¾in (130cm) wide.

Cut and uncut moquette.
68% wool, 20% cotton, 12% viscose; 7¾in (20cm) repeat; 55⅛in (140cm) wide.

Mohair plush.
76% mohair, 24% cotton (100% mohair pile); 51¾in (130cm) wide.

Corduroy   Cords run through the length of this fabric and may be fine or heavy. It is made from 100% cotton with a plain or twill-weave foundation. It is a strong and covering with a distinct nap or lay of pile. Corduroy is not normally chosen for traditional upholstery work.

Plush   A heavy, long-pile upholstery fabric which may have a pile of wool, mohair, cotton or synthetics. The pile is often coarse and is not laid. It is durable and easy to clean.

Moquette   The pile of moquette may be looped, cut, or a combination of the two. Warp yarns form the pile which can be wool, rayon or synthetic, making a very hard-wearing upholstery fabric used today mainly for commercial interiors.

Chenille   A medium to heavyweight fabric made with a special weft yarn prewoven to produce a thick pile yarn. A heavily textured fabric, chenille is often made from wool and cotton for furnishing use. Not a true pile fabric but similar in texture and feel.

A selection of vinyl-coated fabrics (with knitted and plain backings). 52¹⁵⁄₁₆in (137cm) wide

Embossed and striped velvet.
60% silk, 28% cotton, 12% viscose
(100% silk pile); 11¹³⁄₁₆in (30cm)
repeat; 51³⁄₁₆in (130cm) wide.

Warp knitted jersey.
100% rayon; 59in (150cm) wide.

Knitted Fabrics

Warp knits   Two-bar knit fabrics are produced for furnishing purposes and can be laminated to make stable cloths with good stretch. Raised-loop velours are produced on this knitting system, as are Raschel velvets; these make good upholstery cloths and have an extra pile yarn knitted in and cut as knitting progresses. Base cloths for vinyl-coated fabrics are mainly knitted construction.

Coated Fabrics

Vinyls and expanded vinyls   Embossed grain, printed pattern and matt effects are all used to produce attractive vinyl cloths which are robust and very resilient upholstery materials. An expanded vinyl may be up to ¹⁄₁₆in (1.5mm) thick with good surface resilience and wear properties. They are generally practical, washable and clean looking for use on contract and public service furniture. Vinyl and expanded vinyl coatings have knitted or woven base cloths.

Leathers

Cow hide This by far the most popular leather covering for upholstery purposes, and fashionable for both contract and domestic furniture. Cow skins are large and have an average thickness of 1½mm to 2mm thickness. A tough, warm and flexible covering which is produced in a range of both traditional and modern colours. Upholstery hide is always good value and compares in cost with a good woven cloth. The distinct look and feel of leather improves with age as its attractive character blends with almost any interior.

Cow hides, red and blue, showing face side and suede side.

Suede The reverse or flesh side of a hide is as distinct as leather itself. It has all the good properties of a hide with the addition of a soft, smoothly shaved surface. Available in a variety of colours and tones suede is sometimes laminated to produce heavier more stable coverings.

Oxhide and pigskin are also used as upholstery coverings.

Taking care of coverings

While work is in progress it pays to take good care of fabrics, hides and vinyls so that the possibility of damage or soiling is kept to the absolute minimum. A large sheet of calico makes a good dust cover when a piece of work is to be left unattended or overnight.

Storage of covers is important both before and after cutting. Rolls of cover of any kind, but particularly velvet and vinyls, should never be left standing on end for very long. Very few covers will take kindly to being folded for any length of time. Crease and crush lines on hides, vinyls and pile fabrics particularly, can result in permanent lines or marks, usually in all the wrong places. Cut cover parts are seldom stored for very long but are best rolled loosely or laid flat on a large shelf or a side table.

The fabric on a piece of upholstered

Cow hide with an antique rub-off colour.

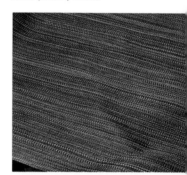

Unusual upholstery fabrics: Hair cloth made from horse hair strands and a cotton warp. 21in (53cm) wide.

Needlework tapestry on a canvas base.

furniture is usually the most expensive part and may often exceed the labour charge. Once a job is finished the motto has to be 'cover it up and then deliver it as soon as possible'.

Advising the customer

Most people will appreciate any advice to be offered regarding their newly upholstered furniture. This can form part of the good relations act and be given in printed form or verbally. The following is a summary of the sort of advice that might be appropriate:

Regular soft brushing or vacuum cleaning will keep covers in good condition. Fabrics are weakened by dust and grit. Most fabric suppliers grade their range of covers for wear. The wearing qualities of upholstery fabrics vary enormously depending on the strength of the yarn and the weaving technique. Pile fabrics such as velvet may flatten when people sit on them. This is mostly inevitable and does not affect the durability of the fabric. Leather will age and crease attractively but will need cleaning from time to time. A leather manufacturer's instruction sheet is recommended.

Wherever possible removable cushions should be plumped and rotated to keep furniture looking good and to spread the wear. Fabrics are damaged by direct heat and strong sunlight which weakens fibres and fades the colours. Loose threads should never be pulled or cut but carefully threaded and needled back into the upholstery.

Spillages and stains should be dealt with quickly but don't use anything wetter than a damp cloth. Soaking an upholstery cloth can leave a permanent mark or cause puckering or damage to the interior. Professional cleaning is recommended.

Fire safety regulations for upholstery fabrics and upholstered furniture

A free booklet is available from Local Authority Trading Standards Departments entitled, *A Guide to the Furniture and Furnishings (Fire) (Safety) Regulations*. This invaluable guide to the safety regulations should be read by all suppliers, manufacturers, upholsterers, reupholsterers, and retailers.

The guide explains the new updated requirements in general terms, but does not cover all the details. For a full statement of the requirements refer to a copy of the regulations which can be obtained from H.M. Stationery Office, HMSO Publications Centre, P.O. Box 276, London SW8 5DT, or through HMSO bookshops.

The guide explains the following:

1   **The product ranges covered.**

2   **The suppliers affected by the regulations; for example:**
● Persons who supply filling materials and fabrics to the furniture industry or direct to consumers.
● Persons who supply furniture, furnishings or reupholstery services.

3   **Exemptions; for example:**
● Exports of furniture.
● Furniture made before 1950.
● Reupholstery of furniture made before 1950.
● Furniture in secondhand caravans.

4   **Action dates (dates on which new regulations come into force).**

5 **What suppliers need to do, for example:**

● Ensure that foam fillings and non-foam fillings pass the appropriate tests.

● Ensure that fabrics supplied to provide or replace permanent covers on furniture pass the appropriate match test.

● Determine whether fabrics supplied are to be used to provide a visible or non-visible part of the upholstery.

6 **What the regulations include in their definition of furniture and furnishings; for example:**

● All upholstered seating furniture.

● Upholstered articles such as music stools, foot stools, pouffes, bean bags, and floor cushions, which are intended for use in a private dwelling.

● Domestic upholstered furniture (whether complete or ordered with the customer's own choice of cover fabric).

● Visible and non-visible platform cloths and dust covers on the underside of furniture.

7 **Parts of the furniture that are not subject to the requirements of the regulations:**

● Braids and trimmings.

● Scrims or stockinet for foams and other fillings.

● Springs.

8 **The regulations relating to nursery furniture, beds and bedding; for example, loose covers and stretch covers. These are covers that are supplied separately from the furniture.**

Loose covers for upholstered furniture must be match resistant when tested over standard polyurethane foam.

9 **The regulations relating to the upholstery of furniture (only that made after 1st January 1950). All filling material and cover fabric used in reupholstering such furniture must meet the new levels of fire resistance.**

However, when only re-covering is requested by the customer, the reupholsterer is not obliged to replace non-conforming filling material which the furniture may contain. It is recommended though, that in such circumstances, the reupholsterer should draw the fire risk to the customer's attention. Any filling which the reupholsterer adds to the existing filling must, of course, meet the new requirements. In ordering upholstery materials the reupholsterer should seek advice from his supplier about their suitability for use in furniture.

10 **The regulations applying to secondhand furniture sold in the course of trade, including auction. From 1st March 1993, secondhand furniture made from 1st January 1950 onwards and sold in the course of trade must meet the requirements of the regulations.**

11 **The regulations applying to labelling. For new and second-hand furniture sold between 1st March 1990 and 28 February 1993, the regulations do not require the following items to carry a display label:**

● Mattresses and bed bases.

● Pillows, scatter cushions and seat pads.

● Loose covers and stretch covers for furniture.

Copies of the guide may be obtained from: The Consumer Safety Unit, Department of Trade & Industry, Room 302, 10 to 18 Victoria Street, London SW1H ONN. Enquiries about the specific contents of the guide should be made to your local county trading standards department.

Part Two

Chapter 15
Projects

1. A Knole style settee

One of the earliest upholstered settees, the Knole settee dates from about 1660. The original can still be seen at Knole House in Kent. Its high back and adjustable ends give it the distinctive style which has been reproduced many times since the mid-nineteenth century.

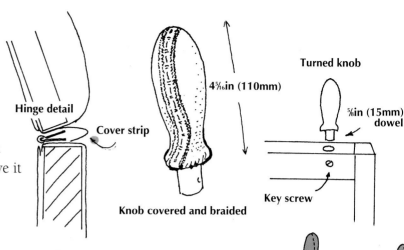

Hinge detail

Cover strip

4⁵⁄₁₆in (110mm)

Knob covered and braided

Turned knob

⁵⁄₈in (15mm) dowel

Key screw

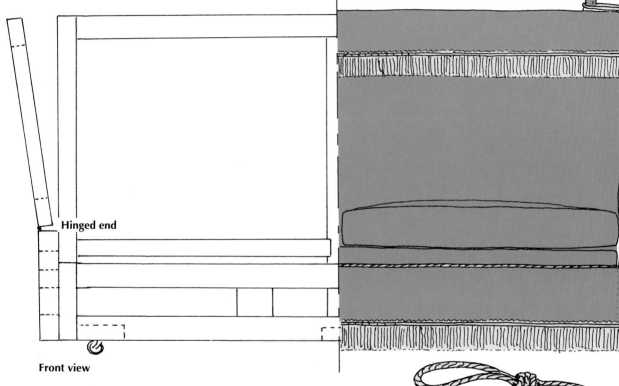

Hinged end

Front view

Section to show frame

End cords

Notes

The seat is firm edge with a sprung platform supporting two feather-filled cushions, to give a general seat height of 15in (380mm). The adjustable ends are unsprung. Eight hourglass springs - 5in (127mm) x 13swg - are used in the back which is webbed on the outside. Castors are 1⁷⁄₁₆in (37mm) in diameter.

Cover cutting plan

Cover width | **54in (135cm)**

IB		— 35⁷⁄₁₆in (900mm)
OB		
IA		— 39³⁄₈in (1m)
OA		
PL/T		— 31½in (800mm)
SB		— 29¹⁵⁄₁₆in (760mm)
SEI	SEI	— 9⅞in (250mm)
SEO	SEO	— 9⅞in (250mm)
C	C	— 13¾in (350mm)
C	C	— 11¹³⁄₁₆in (300mm)
		— 21²¹⁄₃₂in (550mm)
		— 21²¹⁄₃₂in (550mm)

Total cover length required in unpatterned fabric is 23ft 6in (7.51m). 39³⁄₈in (1m) has been allowed for extension pieces to seat platform, inside back, outside back, inside arms and outside arms.

Key to cover parts on project cutting plans

AF	arm facing	FL	flies	SB	seat border
AT	arm top	GB	gathered border	SC	seat cushion
BB	black bottom	IA	inside arm	SCR	scroll
BC	back cushion	IB	inside back	SEI	seat end inside
C	cushion	IW	inside wing	SEO	seat end outside
CB	cushion border	OA	outside arm	SF	seat facing
CF	cross frame	OB	outside back	SI	sides
DF	disc facing	OW	outside wing	SI/B	side border
E	ends	P	panel	S/PL	seat platform
EB	end border	PF	plain facing	SS	seat side
ER	edge roll	PL	platform	UF	underframe
EXT	extensions	PL/T	platform top	ZB	zip border
F	facing	S	seat		

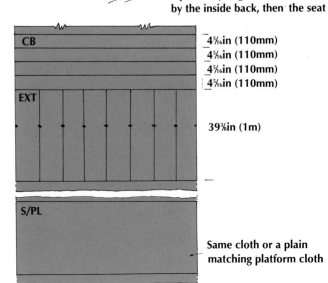

Cover Calico Tack roll

Cover fitted and fixed to seat end rails

Upholstery begins here, followed by the inside back, then the seat

CB	4⁵⁄₁₆in (110mm)
	4⁵⁄₁₆in (110mm)
	4⁵⁄₁₆in (110mm)
	4⁵⁄₁₆in (110mm)
EXT	39³⁄₈in (1m)
S/PL	

Same cloth or a plain matching platform cloth

2. An 'X' frame fold stool c. 1600

There were many variations of the 'X' frame construction in seventeenth-century furniture. Folding stools were typical of French and English seating and were completely upholstered in leathers, velvets or wool cloths. Some had wool-stuffed cushions which were often covered in needlework, trimmed with braided edging and a tassel hung at each corner.

Frame covered in velvet; cushion covered in tapestry

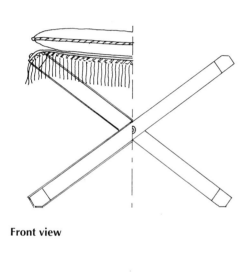

Front view

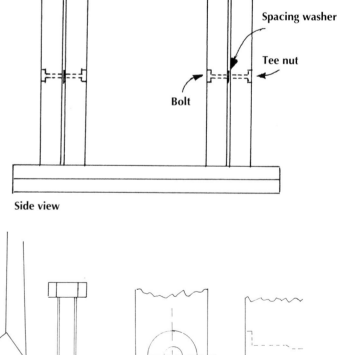

Side view

Spacing washer

Tee nut

Bolt

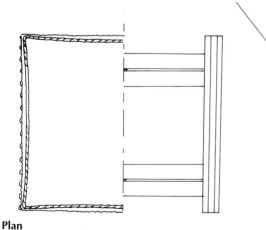

Plan

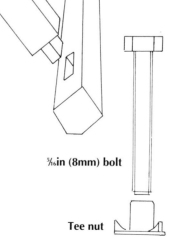

⁵⁄₁₆in (8mm) bolt

Tee nut

Drilling for the tee nuts

Cover cutting plan

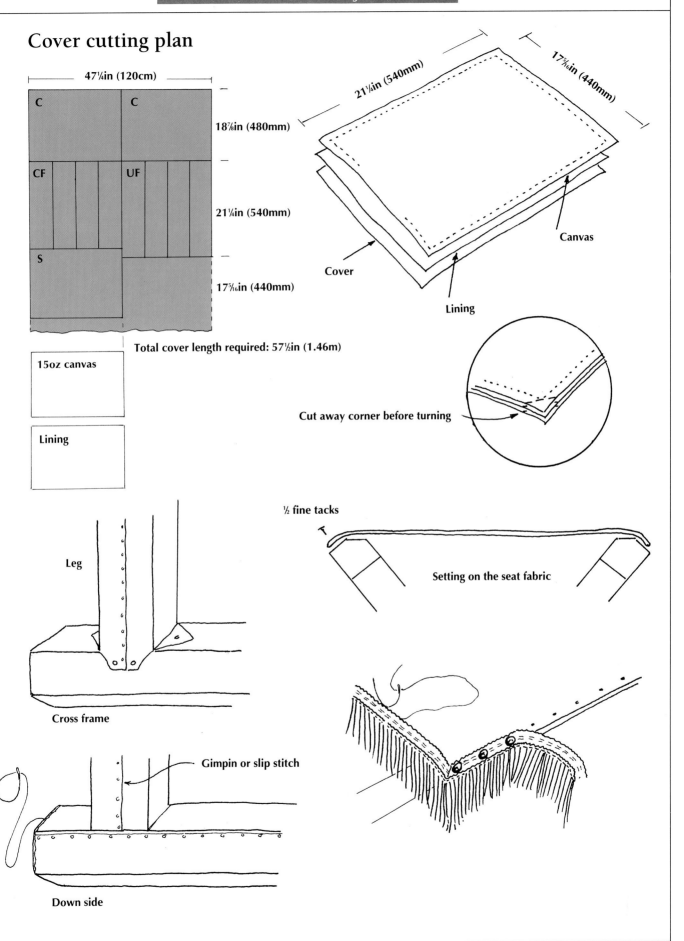

47¼in (120cm)

C

C

18⅞in (480mm)

CF

UF

21¼in (540mm)

S

17⅝in (440mm)

Total cover length required: 57½in (1.46m)

15oz canvas

Lining

21¼in (540mm)

17⅝in (440mm)

Canvas

Cover

Lining

Cut away corner before turning

½ fine tacks

Leg

Setting on the seat fabric

Cross frame

Gimpin or slip stitch

Down side

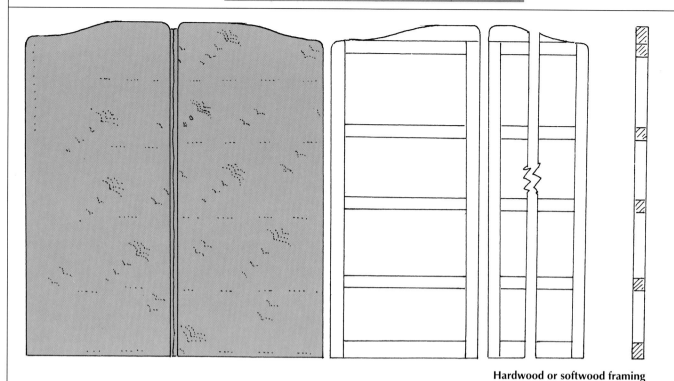

Hardwood or softwood framing

3. An upholstered four fold screen

For some three centuries the screen has been a feature in both small and large houses. Two fold, three fold or four fold varieties provide a mobile dividing wall which can be both functional and decorative.

Details drawn below show **A** the inner covering, **B** the cover strip, **C** the webbing hinge, **D** the outer cover, and **E** the border or edging.

Outer

Inner

Two panels forming a V

Covered and hinged panels

Alternative hinging

Four panels forming a W

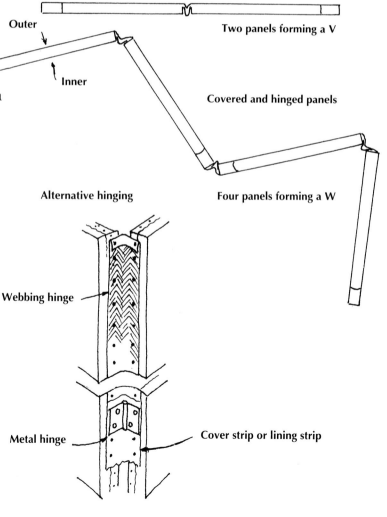

Webbing hinge

Metal hinge

Cover strip or lining strip

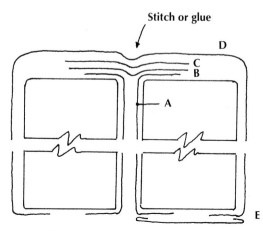

Stitch or glue

D
C
B
A
E

Details of covering

Cover cutting plan

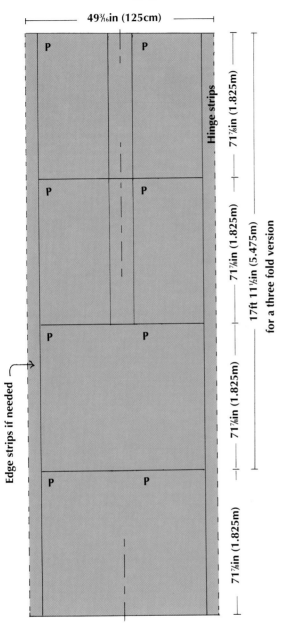

49⁷⁄₁₆in (125cm)

P   P

P   P

P   P

P   P

Edge strips if needed

Hinge strips

71⅞in (1.825m)

71⅞in (1.825m)

71⅞in (1.825m)

71⅞in (1.825m)

17ft 11½in (5.475m) for a three fold version

Total cover length required: 23ft 11in (7.3m)

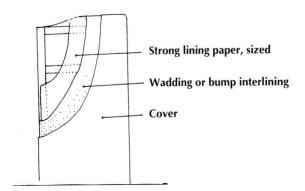

Strong lining paper, sized

Wadding or bump interlining

Cover

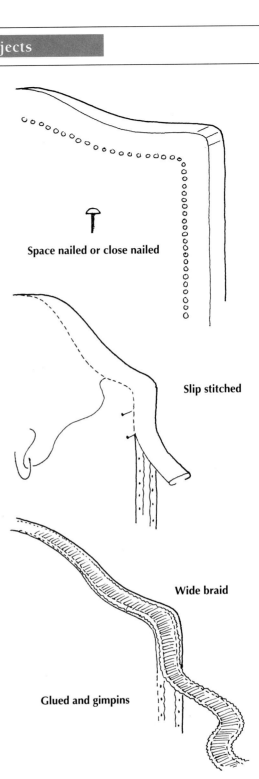

Space nailed or close nailed

Slip stitched

Wide braid

Glued and gimpins

Notes

Sequence of working: the panels are covered in pairs or, in the case of a three fold screen, in a pair and a single.

A Each inner face
B Cover strip
C Hinge
D Double width outer
E Border edge strip after linking the panels together

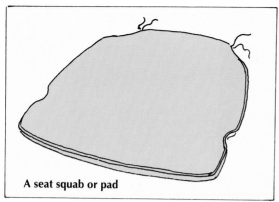

A seat squab or pad

16in x 15in wide x 1¼in thick (406mm x 381mm x 32mm)

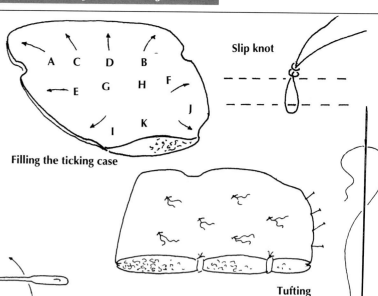

Filling the ticking case

Slip knot

Tufting

4. Squabs and cushions

The hair-filled, bordered cushion is tufted, has mattress-stitched edges and a first and second stuffing, typical of cushions made from the mid-eighteenth to the mid-nineteenth century.

The squab is hair and cotton filled and is unbordered. Edges are lightly stitched with a running top stitch. This provided comfort on hard seating such as window seats and Windsor chairs.

The feather cushion with a sectioned cambric case and a filling of feather and down mixture, is still produced in large quantities today. It has remained popular over the last century as a warm, resilient filling which lends itself well to both formal and informal seating.

Running top stitch secures the edge after regulating

A bordered, hair-filled cushion

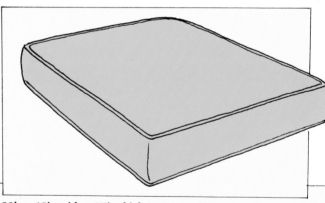

20in x 18in wide x 3½in thick (500mm x 450mm x 87mm)

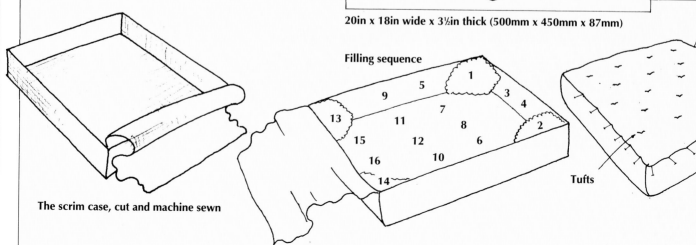

The scrim case, cut and machine sewn

Filling sequence

Tufts

Cover cutting plan for squab

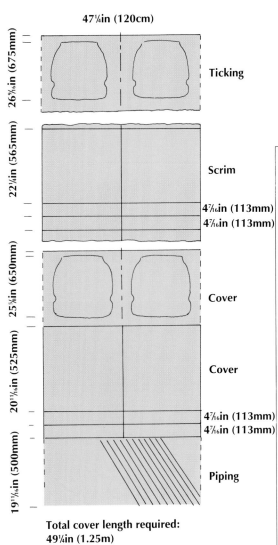

47¼in (120cm)

26⁹⁄₁₆in (675mm) — Ticking

22¼in (565mm) — Scrim

4⁷⁄₁₆in (113mm)
4⁷⁄₁₆in (113mm)

25⁵⁄₈in (650mm) — Cover

20¹¹⁄₁₆in (525mm) — Cover

4⁷⁄₁₆in (113mm)
4⁷⁄₁₆in (113mm)

19¹¹⁄₁₆in (500mm) — Piping

Total cover length required:
49¼in (1.25m)

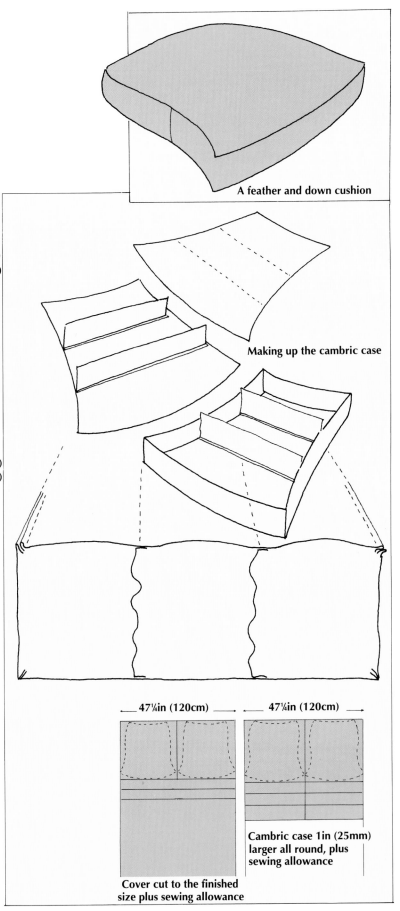

A feather and down cushion

Making up the cambric case

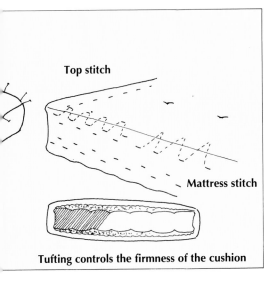

Top stitch

Mattress stitch

Tufting controls the firmness of the cushion

47¼in (120cm)   47¼in (120cm)

Cambric case 1in (25mm)
larger all round, plus
sewing allowance

Cover cut to the finished
size plus sewing allowance

5. A Cromwellian-style side chair or dining chair

A chair with a strong Jacobean influence, related to those made in large numbers in the north of England in the mid-seventeenth century. The simple, firm upholstery, often covered in hide or wool cloth, was tacked and nailed on to oak frames.

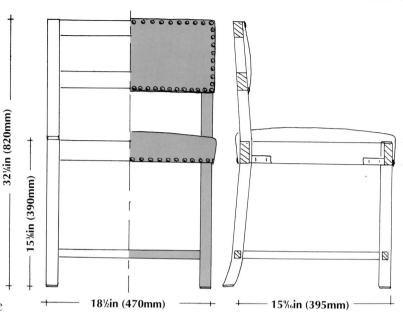

32¼in (820mm)

15¼in (390mm)

18½in (470mm)

15⅝in (395mm)

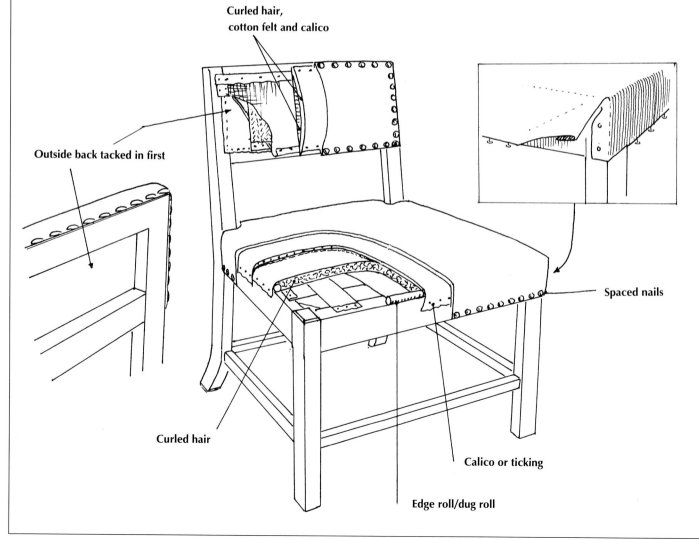

Curled hair, cotton felt and calico

Outside back tacked in first

Curled hair

Calico or ticking

Edge roll/dug roll

Spaced nails

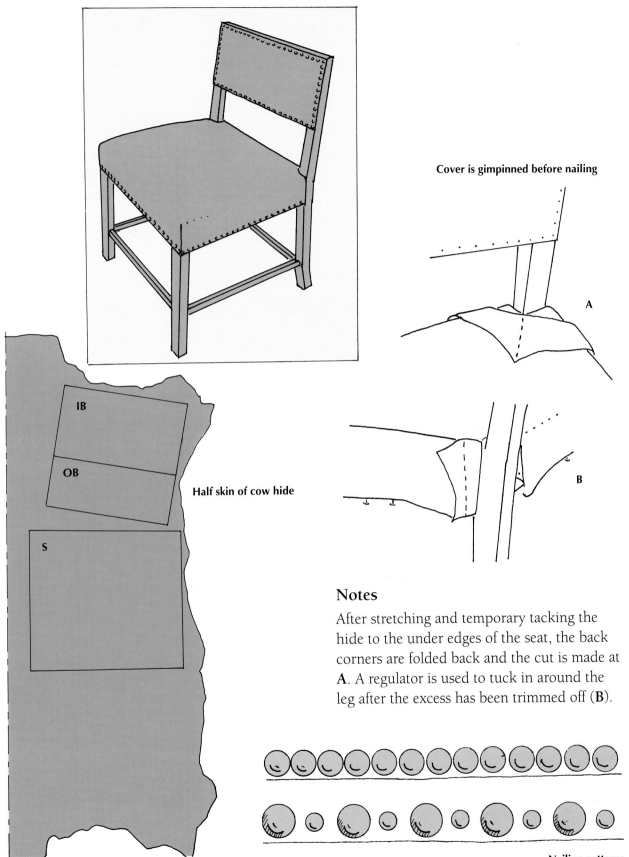

Cover is gimpinned before nailing

A

Half skin of cow hide

B

Notes

After stretching and temporary tacking the hide to the under edges of the seat, the back corners are folded back and the cut is made at **A**. A regulator is used to tuck in around the leg after the excess has been trimmed off (**B**).

Nailing patterns

Half hide measuring approx. 21 sq ft (1.95 sq m). Quantity used: 9 sq ft (0.84 sq m), plus 25% wastage.

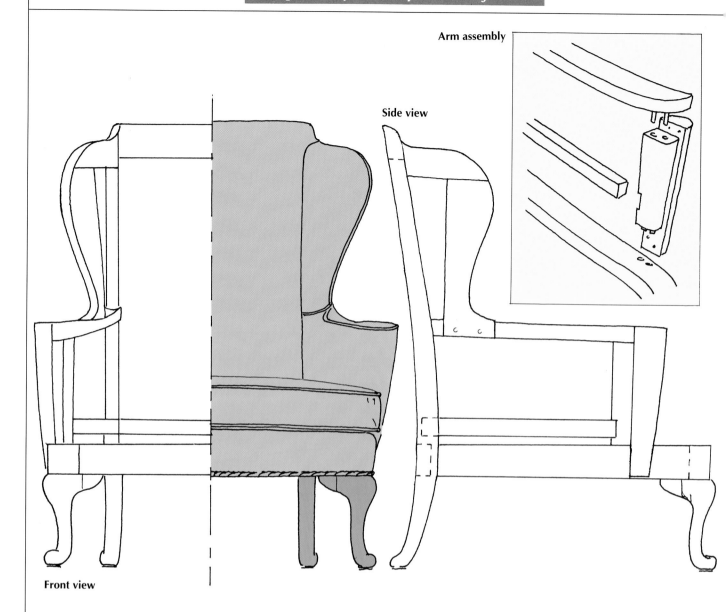

Arm assembly

Side view

Front view

6. A Georgian wing armchair

It is said that the early Georgian wing armchair was one of the most comfortable chairs produced in the history of furniture. Its elegant lines and wide seat have been reproduced time after time. Many fine upholstered examples originated from New England, USA, in the late eighteenth century.

Making up sequence for the piped and bordered cushion:

(a) Centre the cushion panels and the 3^{15}⁄$_{16}$in (100mm) wide border strip.

(b) Sew the made up piping around each cushion panel.

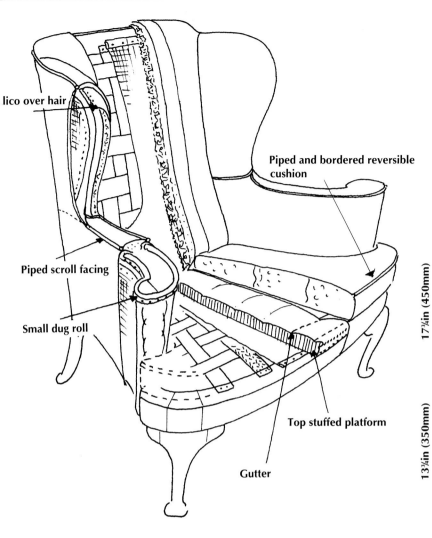

lico over hair

Piped scroll facing

Small dug roll

Piped and bordered reversible cushion

Top stuffed platform

Gutter

Cover cutting plan

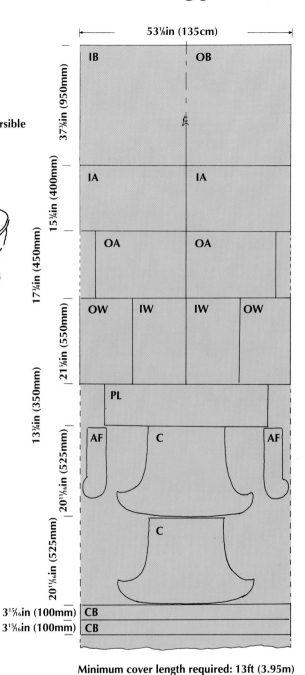

53⅛in (135cm)

37⅜in (950mm)

15¾in (400mm)

17¾in (450mm)

21⅝in (550mm)

13¾in (350mm)

20¹¹⁄₁₆in (525mm)

20¹¹⁄₁₆in (525mm)

IB   OB

IA   IA

OA   OA

OW   IW   IW   OW

PL

AF   C   AF

C

3¹⁵⁄₁₆in (100mm) CB
3¹⁵⁄₁₆in (100mm) CB

Minimum cover length required: 13ft (3.95m)

(c) Select one of the cushion panels to be the cushion top and sew on the cushion border all round. If the border is carefully notched and centred, joins with the second border will fall on each side of the cushion.

(d) Finally, sew on the second panel, leaving most of the rear edge open for filling

Fly pieces may be used where needed. Joins on OA and OW may be machine sewn or slip stitched.

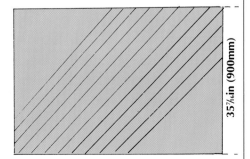

35⅜in (900mm)

Approx 33ft (10m) of piping cut from 1⁹⁄₁₆in (40mm) strips on the bias; all the piping strips are joined and made up in one continuous length and used as required.

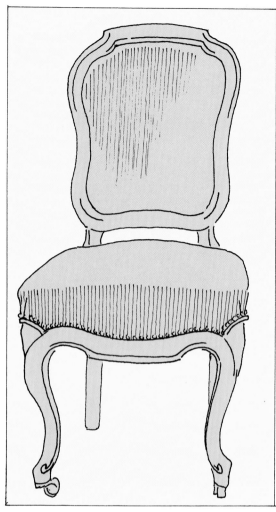

Panel back and sprung seat

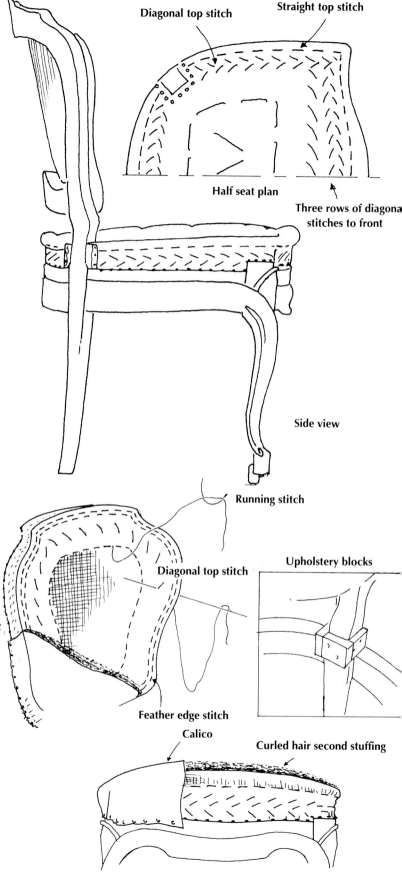

Diagonal top stitch

Straight top stitch

Half seat plan

Three rows of diagonal stitches to front

Side view

Running stitch

Diagonal top stitch

Upholstery blocks

Feather edge stitch

Calico

Curled hair second stuffing

7. A French side chair c. 1900

A plain version of a Louis XV panel-back side chair, made at the turn of the century. Armchairs and side chairs of this type are common in French houses today.

The spring seat is heavily stitched with a variety of top stitches, but no blind stitching. The panel back is feather edged and follows the show-wood outline particularly well. It is usually covered in plain silk or wool tapestry.

Typical decoration on French chairs

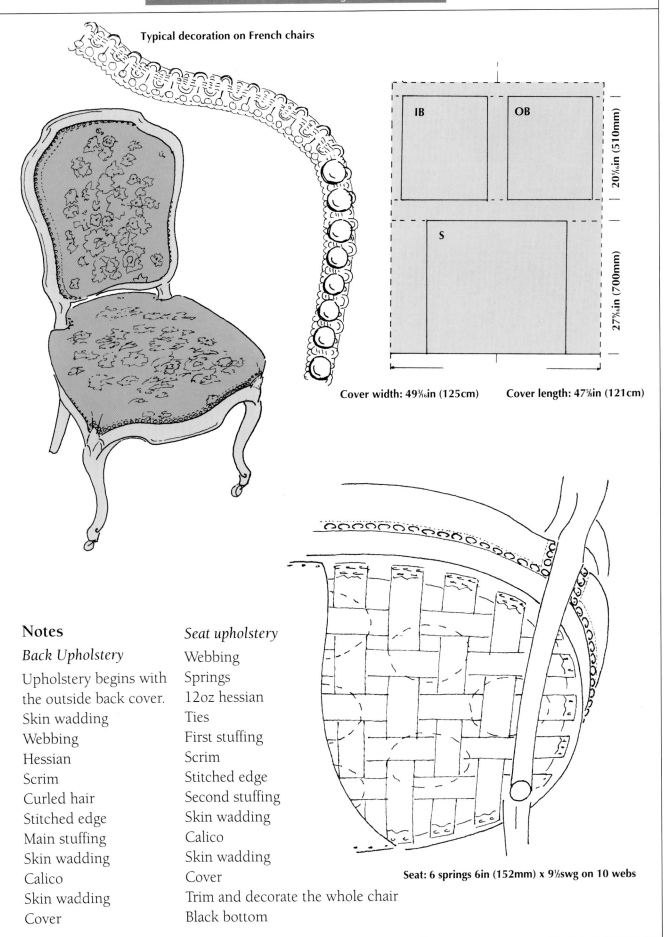

Cover width: 49³⁄₁₆in (125cm)   Cover length: 47⅝in (121cm)

20¹⁄₁₆in (510mm)

27%in (700mm)

IB   OB   S

Seat: 6 springs 6in (152mm) x 9½swg on 10 webs

Notes

Back Upholstery

Upholstery begins with the outside back cover.

Skin wadding
Webbing
Hessian
Scrim
Curled hair
Stitched edge
Main stuffing
Skin wadding
Calico
Skin wadding
Cover

Seat upholstery

Webbing
Springs
12oz hessian
Ties
First stuffing
Scrim
Stitched edge
Second stuffing
Skin wadding
Calico
Skin wadding
Cover
Trim and decorate the whole chair
Black bottom

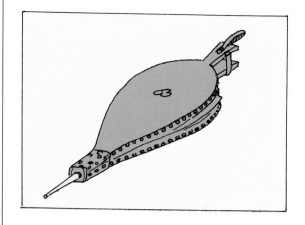

8. A pair of bellows in oak and hide

½in (12mm) oak boards provide the foundation for traditional fire bellows. The air inlet valve is made up from a strip of hide, a small wood block and some twine and tacks. Brass nailing may be close or spaced with banding. **A**, **B** and **C** show the sequence of trapping the nozzle.

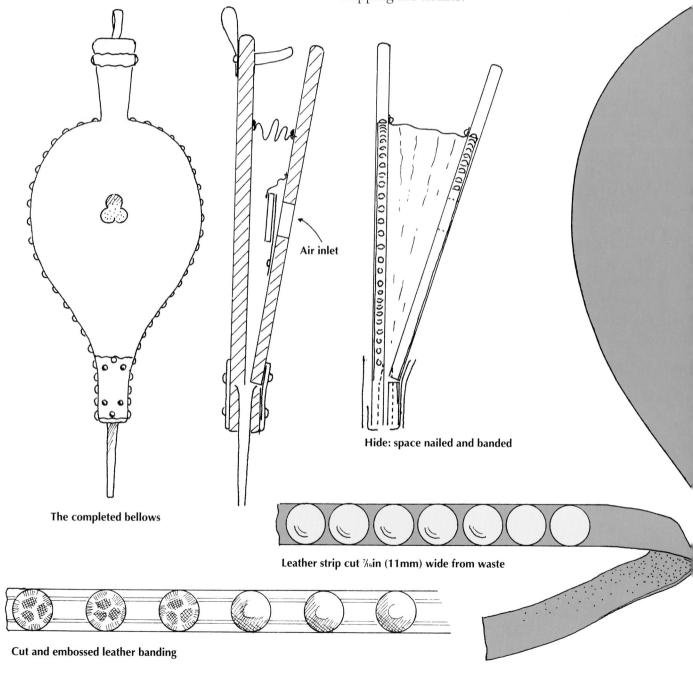

Air inlet

The completed bellows

Hide: space nailed and banded

Leather strip cut ⁷⁄₁₆in (11mm) wide from waste

Cut and embossed leather banding

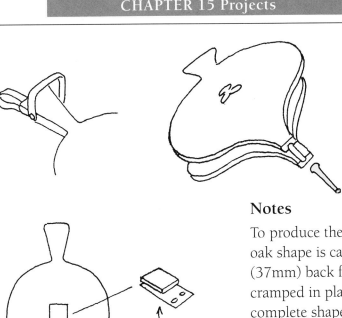

Hammered brass tube

Notes

To produce the hinge, the end of the bellows oak shape is carefully sawn through 1½in (37mm) back from its point. The piece is then cramped in place on to the end of the complete shape. A ½in (13mm) hole is then drilled down the centre to a depth of just beyond 1½in (37mm). The hole is then chiselled out to form a scribed channel to house the tube.

Breather hole

Hide glued to wood block suede side

A Sandwich the brass nozzle in place and glue and cramp together. Fit and gimpin the leather hinge end piece.

Hide shape

Banding strip

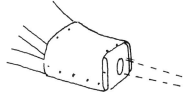

B Wrap the whole end tightly with hide and gimpin in place.

Cuts around handles

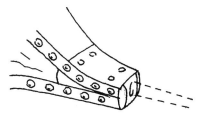

C The bellows hide is then fitted and pinned before the banding strips are applied and finished with spaced upholstery nails. (Three square feet (0.279 sq m) of hide is required.)

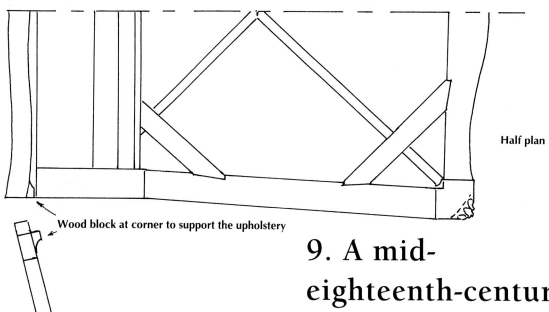

Half plan

Wood block at corner to support the upholstery

Housed back frame

9. A mid-eighteenth-century Chippendale side chair

These chairs were often produced in large sets with pierced underframing and carved front legs. The originals show a fascinating glimpse of upholstery stuffing and stitching techniques used in the late eighteenth century. Canvas, scrim and webbings - all made from linen - were typical of the period. Flax fibre was also used for the seat edge fillings. The restoration of such original pieces provides the upholsterer with an interesting challenge.

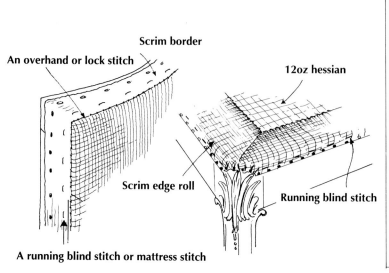

Scrim border

An overhand or lock stitch

12oz hessian

Scrim edge roll

Running blind stitch

A running blind stitch or mattress stitch

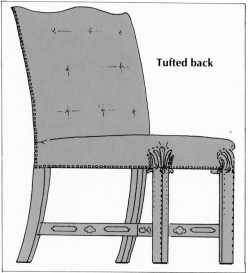

Tufted back

Cover cutting plan

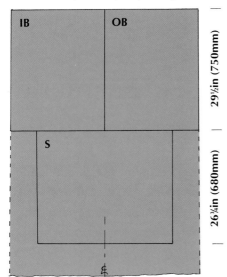

← Cover width: 49⁵⁄₁₆in (125cm) →

IB	OB
S	

29½in (750mm)

26¼in (680mm)

Total cover length required: 4ft 8¼in (1.43m)

Set of eight: 37½ft (11.44m)

A set of eight chairs would require 206 sq ft (19.137 sq m) of hide (which includes 25% wastage).

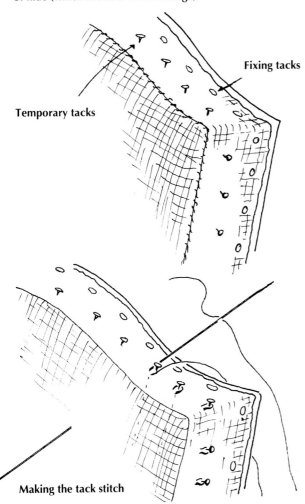

Temporary tacks

Fixing tacks

Making the tack stitch

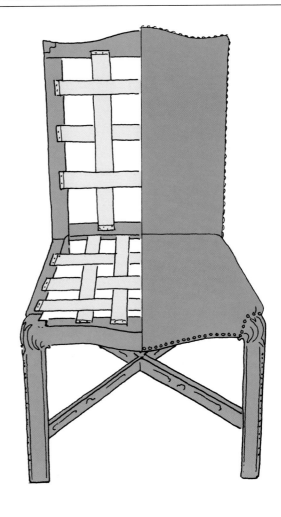

Notes

Linen canvases and scrims were used extensively for upholstery during the eighteenth century. Coarse grasses and horse hair provided the main fillings. Today we would restore such chairs by using coir fibre, black fibre and hog or cow hair. The upholstery techniques, however, we can reuse.

In this project the first stuffing has been covered in linen scrim, the back is bordered and over sewn, tack stitched and tufted. The seat has a shallow roll edge to form a well and is mattress stitched. Cotton waddings and cotton calico completes the basic work.

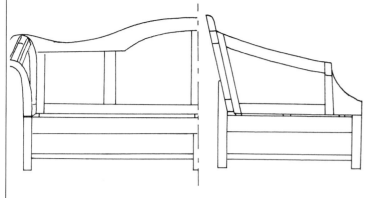

10. A Chippendale-style settee c. 1790

Many such pieces were reproduced during the early part of the twentieth century and this style of settee, constructed on a mahogany seat frame with detachable arm and back supports, remains popular today.

Stitched edge work was minimal but tufting of the back and the seat squab was common practice. Settees of this kind were placed around the walls of large rooms such as drawing rooms, music rooms and galleries.

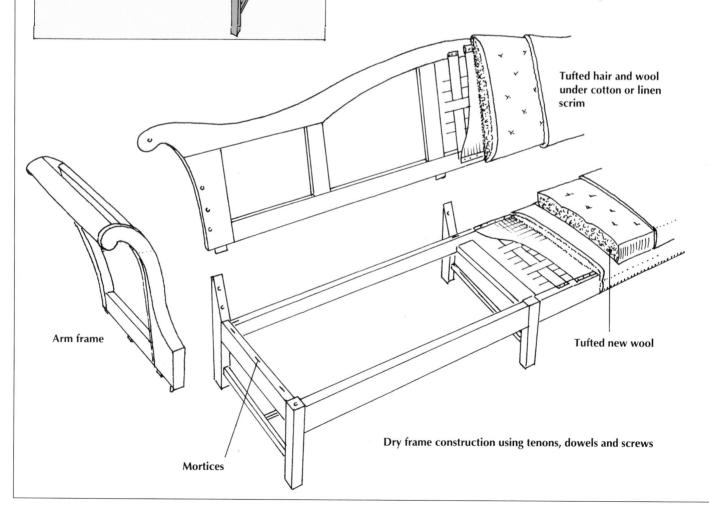

Tufted hair and wool under cotton or linen scrim

Tufted new wool

Arm frame

Mortices

Dry frame construction using tenons, dowels and screws

Cover cutting plan

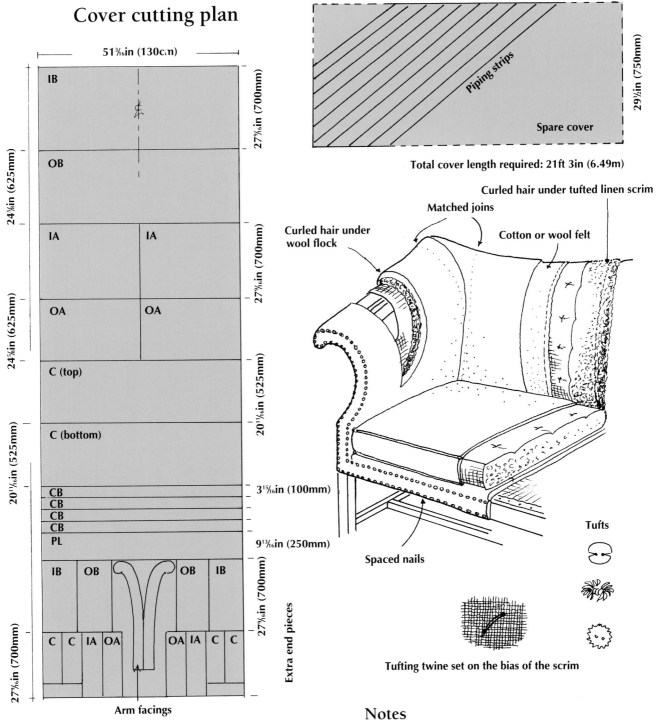

51³⁄₁₆in (130cm)

27⁹⁄₁₆in (700mm)

24⅝in (625mm)

IB

OB

IA   IA

24⅝in (625mm)

OA   OA

27⁹⁄₁₆in (700mm)

C (top)

C (bottom)

20¹¹⁄₁₆in (525mm)

20¹¹⁄₁₆in (525mm)

CB
CB
CB
CB
PL

3¹⁵⁄₁₆in (100mm)

9¹³⁄₁₆in (250mm)

IB   OB   OB   IB

C   C   IA   OA   OA   IA   C   C

27⁹⁄₁₆in (700mm)

27⁹⁄₁₆in (700mm)

Extra end pieces

Arm facings

Piping strips

Spare cover

29½in (750mm)

Total cover length required: 21ft 3in (6.49m)

Curled hair under tufted linen scrim

Matched joins

Curled hair under wool flock

Cotton or wool felt

Spaced nails

Tufts

Tufting twine set on the bias of the scrim

Notes

A cover length of 4ft 7in (1.4m) is allowed for extension pieces where required.

The long tufted seat cushion may be hair or wool filled in the traditional manner, to a thickness of 4in (102mm). Where feather fillings are preferred, the cushion should be made to a minimum of 5in (127mm).

11. A William IV day bed

A couch of ample proportions which was fully upholstered, deep buttoned and heavily trimmed with cording, tassels and a deep cotton and wool fringe of almost 5 inches (125mm). Lounging and day bed furniture of this kind became very common around the middle part of the nineteenth century. During a period often referred to as the age of the upholsterer, the spring edge seat exhibited the leading kind of handmade work, providing the ultimate in luxury seating.

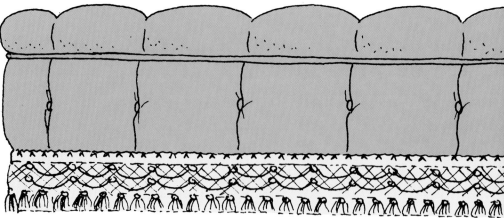

End con

Elevation from 'D' end

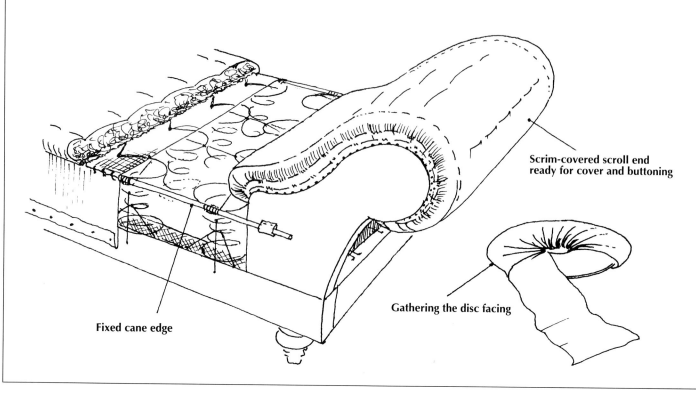

Scrim-covered scroll end ready for cover and buttoning

Gathering the disc facing

Fixed cane edge

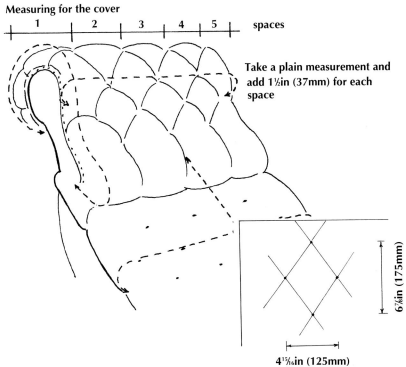

Measuring for the cover

1 2 3 4 5 | spaces

Take a plain measurement and add 1½in (37mm) for each space

6⅞in (175mm)

4¹⁵⁄₁₆in (125mm)

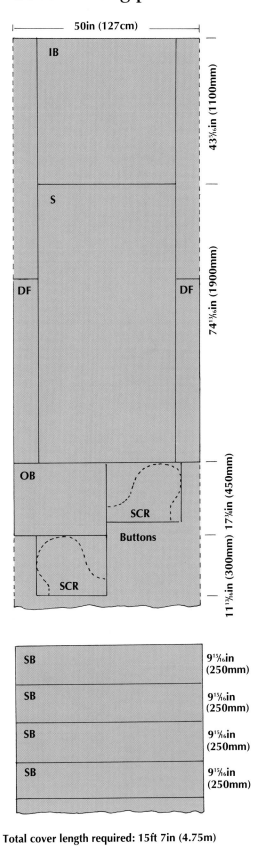

Cover cutting plan

50in (127cm)

IB

43¾₆in (1100mm)

S

74¹¹⁄₁₆in (1900mm)

DF   DF

OB

SCR

Buttons

SCR

11¹³⁄₁₆in (300mm) 17¾in (450mm)

SB   9¹⁵⁄₁₆in (250mm)

SB   9¹⁵⁄₁₆in (250mm)

SB   9¹⁵⁄₁₆in (250mm)

SB   9¹⁵⁄₁₆in (250mm)

Total cover length required: 15ft 7in (4.75m)

179

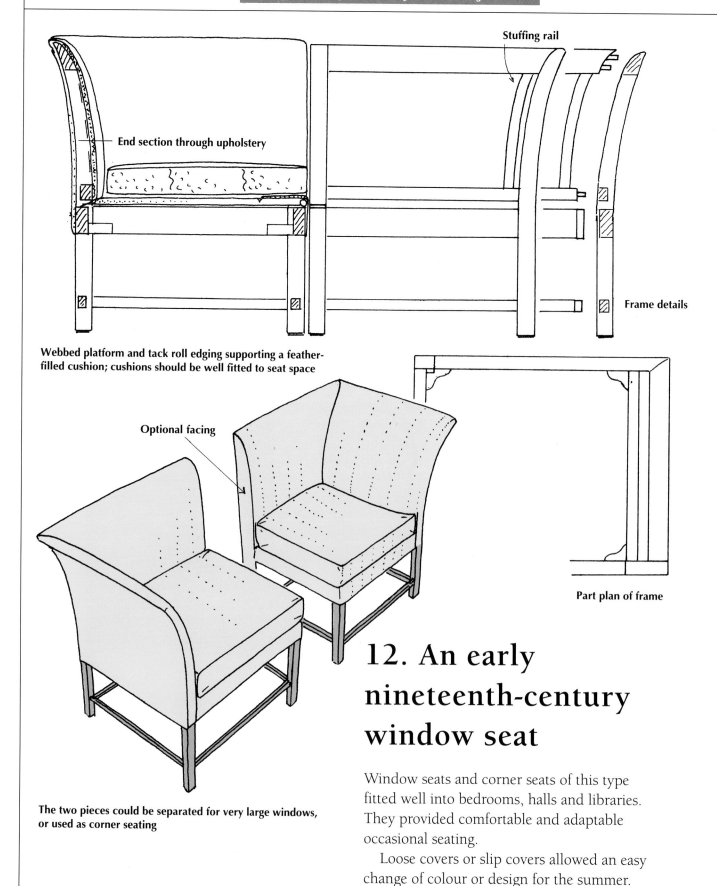

Stuffing rail

End section through upholstery

Frame details

Webbed platform and tack roll edging supporting a feather-filled cushion; cushions should be well fitted to seat space

Optional facing

Part plan of frame

The two pieces could be separated for very large windows, or used as corner seating

12. An early nineteenth-century window seat

Window seats and corner seats of this type fitted well into bedrooms, halls and libraries. They provided comfortable and adaptable occasional seating.

Loose covers or slip covers allowed an easy change of colour or design for the summer. Upholstery was slim and modest, reflecting the Regency style.

Cover cutting plan for single seat

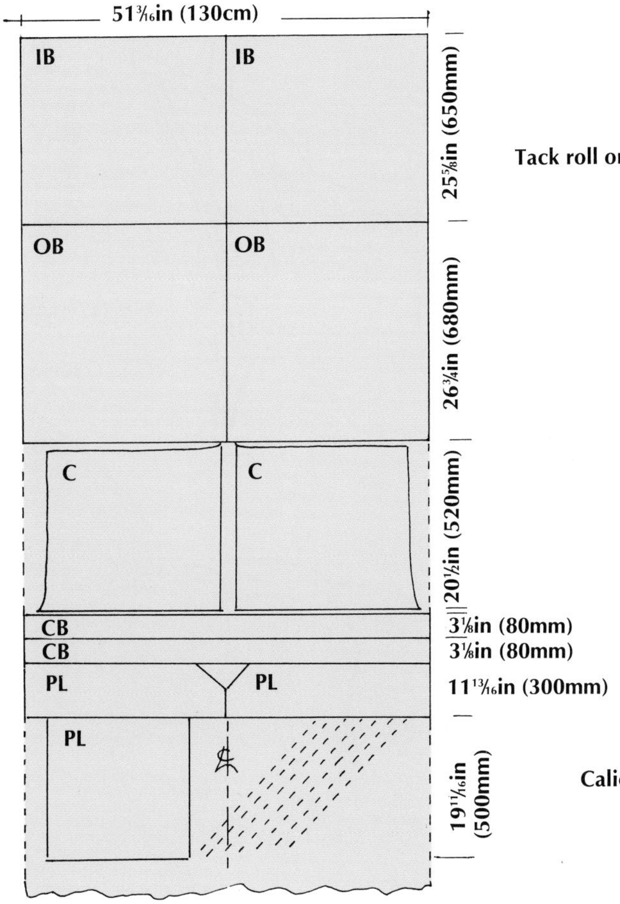

51³⁄₁₆in (130cm)

IB	IB
OB	OB
C	C
CB	
CB	
PL	PL
PL	

25⅝in (650mm)

26¾in (680mm)

20½in (520mm)

3⅛in (80mm)
3⅛in (80mm)

11¹³⁄₁₆in (300mm)

19¹¹⁄₁₆in (500mm)

Total cover length required: 9ft 2½in (2.81m)

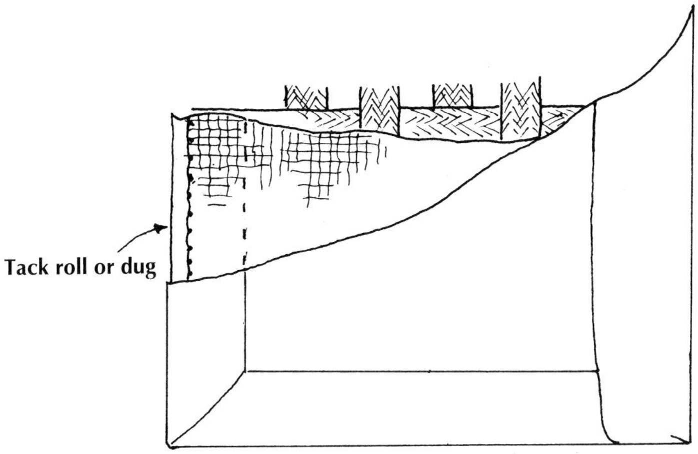

Tack roll or dug

View of platform beneath cushion

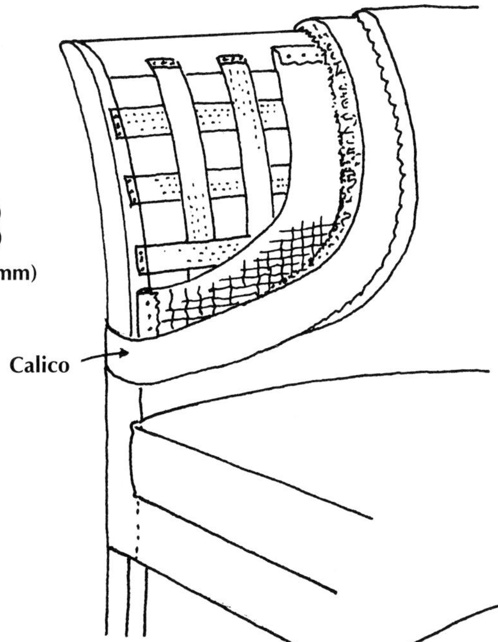

Calico

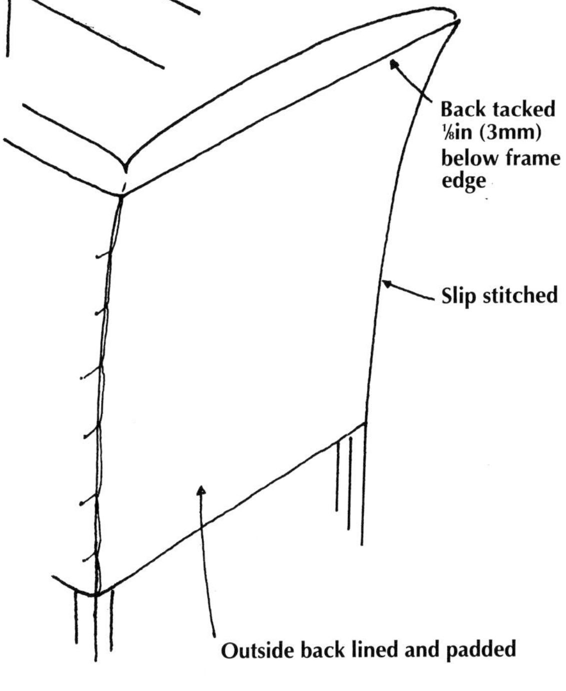

Back tacked ⅛in (3mm) below frame edge

Slip stitched

Outside back lined and padded

Notes

Inside back facings are shown but may not be needed; the width of the cover will determine this. Or they may be used simply to enhance the end shape.

Cushion panels are carefully shaped to fit the curves of the inside backs. Cushions are reversible from one seat to the other and may be fitted with zip borders if preferred.

About 19ft 8in (6m) of upholstery weight fabric would be ample to cover the pair of seats. Savings could be made by using a platform cloth and by using straight cut piping strips.

13. A late Victorian armchair

This large and comfortable chair is an interesting demonstration of the traditional upholsterer's art, with buttons and pleated surfaces arranged around a deep, fully sprung seat. The chair's framework is elaborate, and required plenty of shaped cuts from 2in (50mm) thick timber. Large tub chairs of the period were often made with iron back frames to save on frame-making materials and labour.

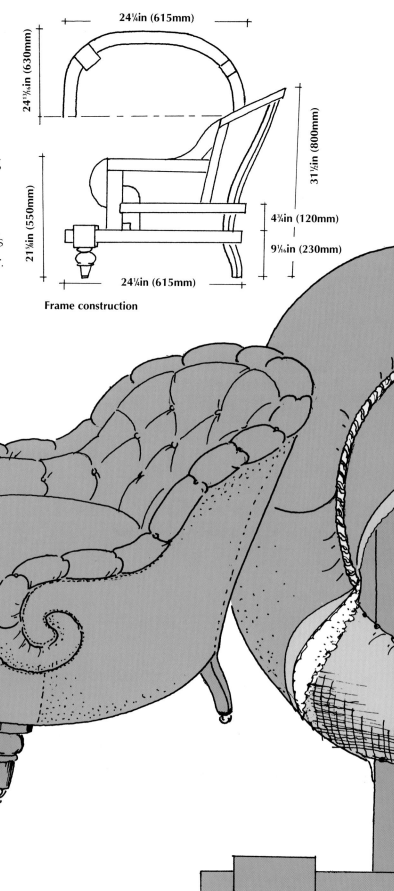

Frame construction

24¼in (615mm)
24¹¹⁄₁₆in (630mm)
31½in (800mm)
4¾in (120mm)
9¹⁄₁₆in (230mm)
21⅝in (550mm)
24¼in (615mm)

Edge roll

Plenty of second stuffing to give the seat a high crown

Seat stitch up and under edge border

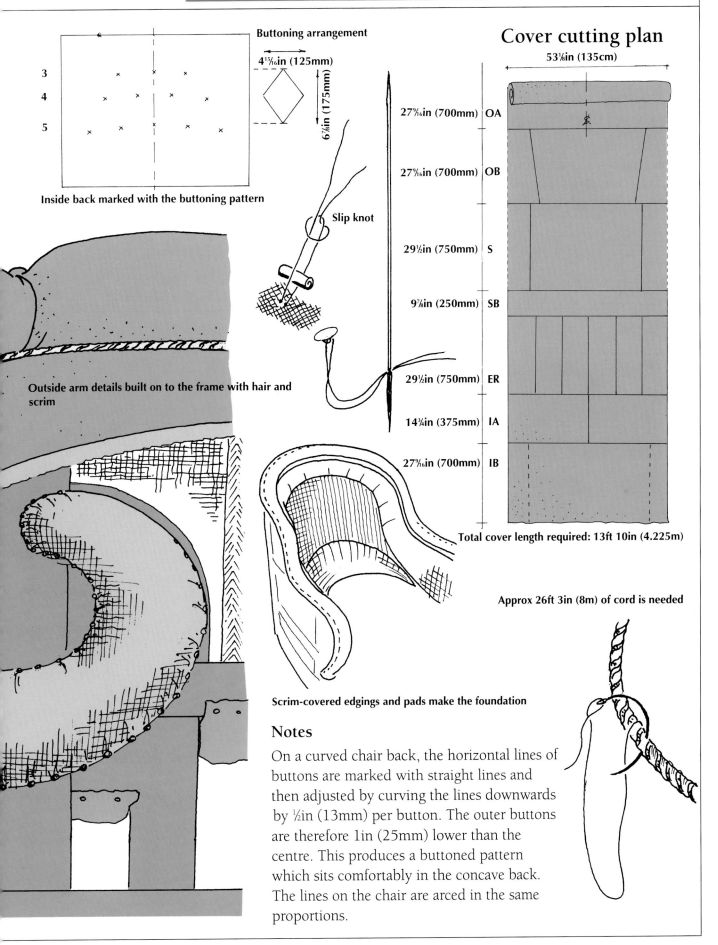

Buttoning arrangement

3
4
5

Inside back marked with the buttoning pattern

4¹⁵⁄₁₆in (125mm)

6⅞in (175mm)

Slip knot

Outside arm details built on to the frame with hair and scrim

Scrim-covered edgings and pads make the foundation

Cover cutting plan

53⅛in (135cm)

27%₁₆in (700mm)	OA
27%₁₆in (700mm)	OB
29½in (750mm)	S
9⅞in (250mm)	SB
29½in (750mm)	ER
14¾in (375mm)	IA
27%₁₆in (700mm)	IB

Total cover length required: 13ft 10in (4.225m)

Approx 26ft 3in (8m) of cord is needed

Notes

On a curved chair back, the horizontal lines of buttons are marked with straight lines and then adjusted by curving the lines downwards by ½in (13mm) per button. The outer buttons are therefore 1in (25mm) lower than the centre. This produces a buttoned pattern which sits comfortably in the concave back. The lines on the chair are arced in the same proportions.

14. A late nineteenth-century box ottoman

This upholstered and lined box provided an occasional seat, but was primarily used for storage. Velvet, printed cottons and needlework were usual coverings. Larger versions of the ottoman often had an upholstered end or support and were commonly found in the bedroom. The term ottoman was also used to describe a box seat, a large stool or Victorian pouffe.

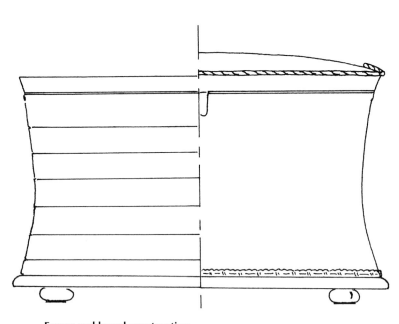

Frame and board construction

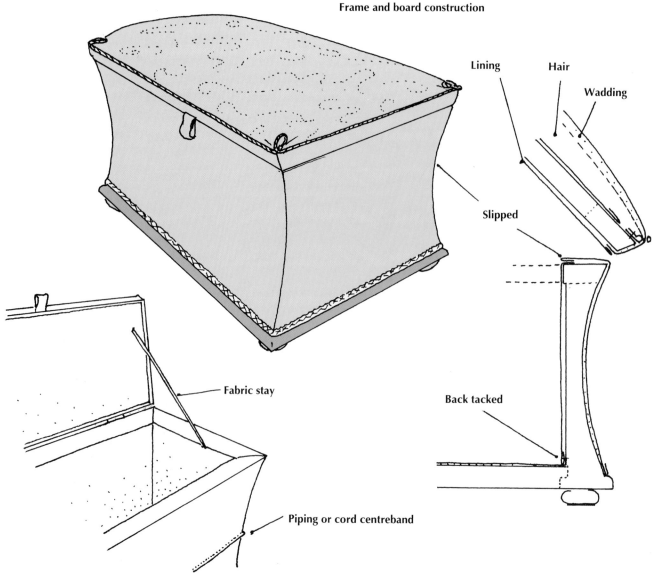

Lining

Hair

Wadding

Slipped

Fabric stay

Back tacked

Piping or cord centreband

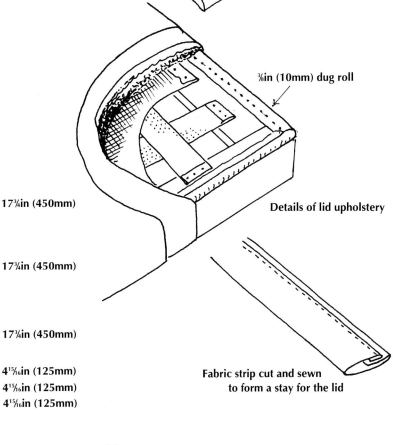

Lifting tab cut from waste

Plain sewn

Turned and folded

⅜in (10mm) dug roll

Details of lid upholstery

Fabric strip cut and sewn
to form a stay for the lid

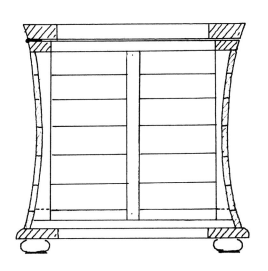

Cover cutting plan for box and lid

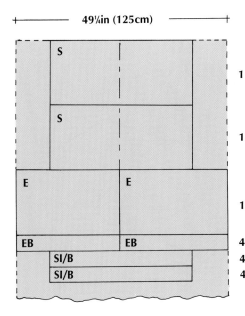

49¼in (125cm)

S	17¾in (450mm)
S	17¾in (450mm)
E E	17¾in (450mm)
EB EB	4¹⁵⁄₁₆in (125mm)
SI/B	4¹⁵⁄₁₆in (125mm)
SI/B	4¹⁵⁄₁₆in (125mm)

Top

23⅝in (600mm)

Notes

Using 49⁹⁄₁₆in (125cm) wide cover, a suggested cutting plan is shown with a separate box and lid layout where two fabrics are being used.

About 5ft 11in (1.8m) is needed to cover the box, and 8 ft 2½in (2.5m) of lining.

The ottoman top requires approximately 23⅝in (600mm) of tapestry or patterned fabric.

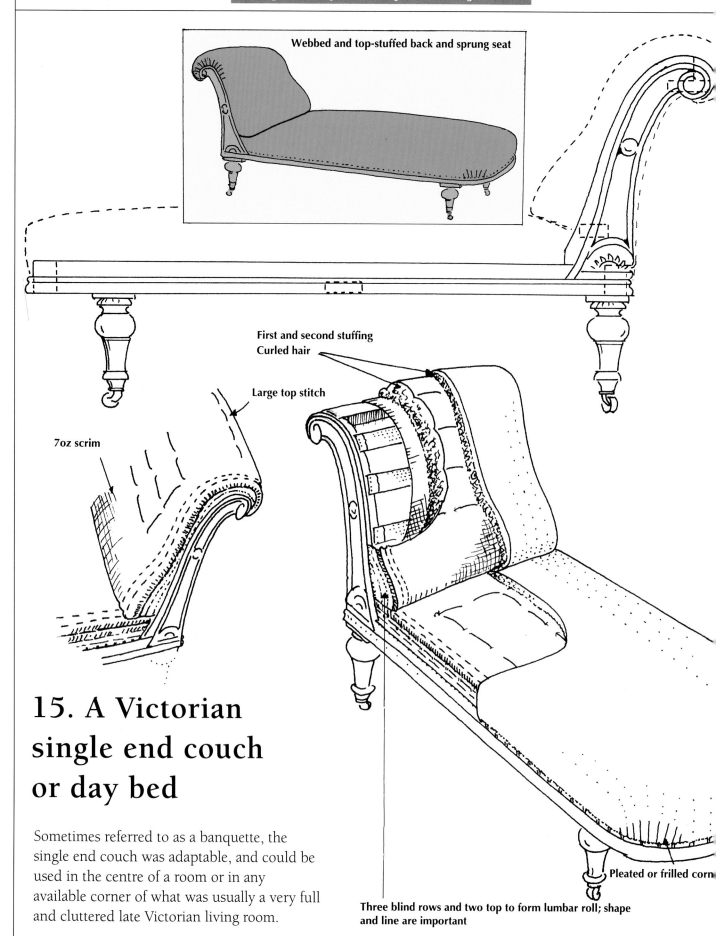

Webbed and top-stuffed back and sprung seat

First and second stuffing
Curled hair

Large top stitch

7oz scrim

15. A Victorian single end couch or day bed

Sometimes referred to as a banquette, the single end couch was adaptable, and could be used in the centre of a room or in any available corner of what was usually a very full and cluttered late Victorian living room.

Three blind rows and two top to form lumbar roll; shape and line are important

Pleated or frilled corn

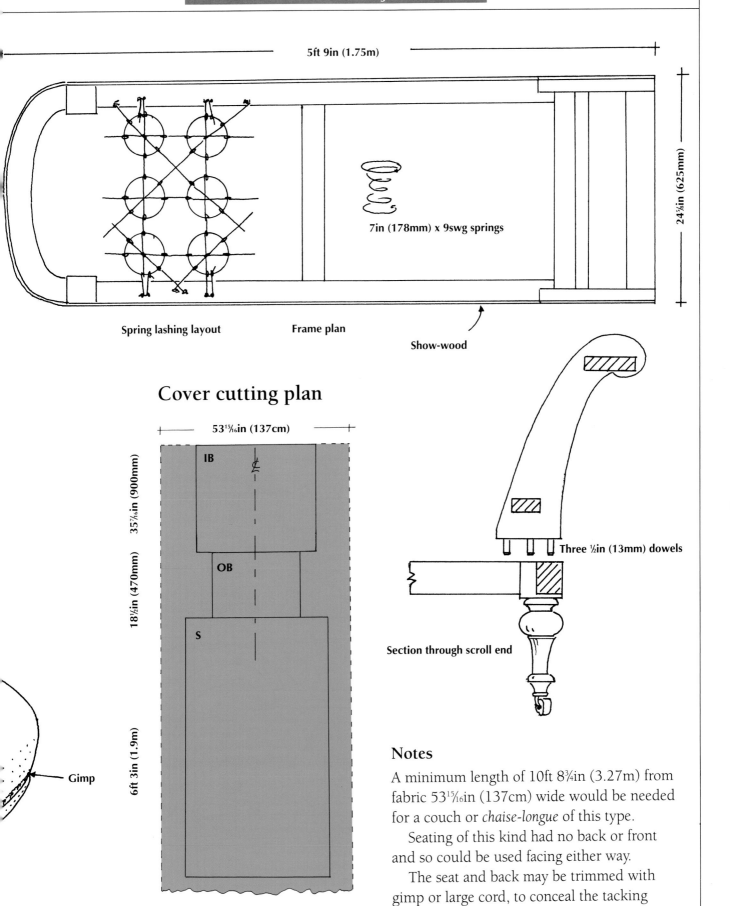

5ft 9in (1.75m)

24⅝in (625mm)

7in (178mm) x 9swg springs

Spring lashing layout   **Frame plan**

Show-wood

Cover cutting plan

53¹⁵⁄₁₆in (137cm)

35⁷⁄₁₆in (900mm)

IB

₵

OB

18½in (470mm)

S

6ft 3in (1.9m)

Gimp

Three ½in (13mm) dowels

Section through scroll end

Notes

A minimum length of 10ft 8¾in (3.27m) from fabric 53¹⁵⁄₁₆in (137cm) wide would be needed for a couch or *chaise-longue* of this type.

Seating of this kind had no back or front and so could be used facing either way.

The seat and back may be trimmed with gimp or large cord, to conceal the tacking along the show-wood edges.

16. Two nineteenth-century footstools and a low fender stool

The footstool was a typical feature of the Victorian interior where small functional objects were provided for every comfort. Oval and round stools were often good subjects for embroidered and stitched work panels.

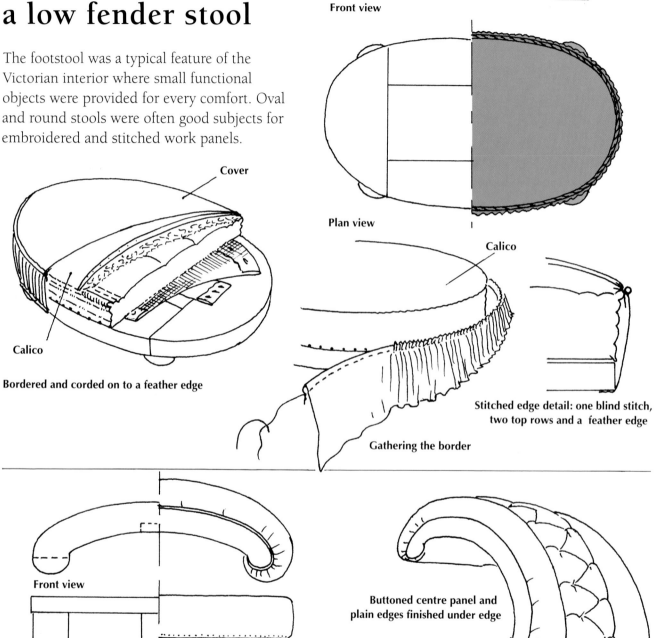

Front view

Plan view

Cover

Calico

Calico

Bordered and corded on to a feather edge

Gathering the border

Stitched edge detail: one blind stitch, two top rows and a feather edge

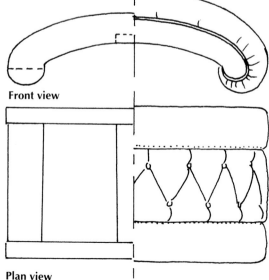

Front view

Plan view

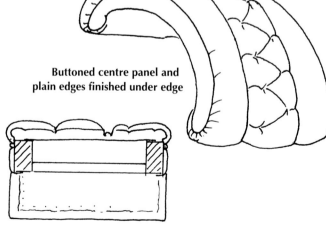

Buttoned centre panel and plain edges finished under edge

End section

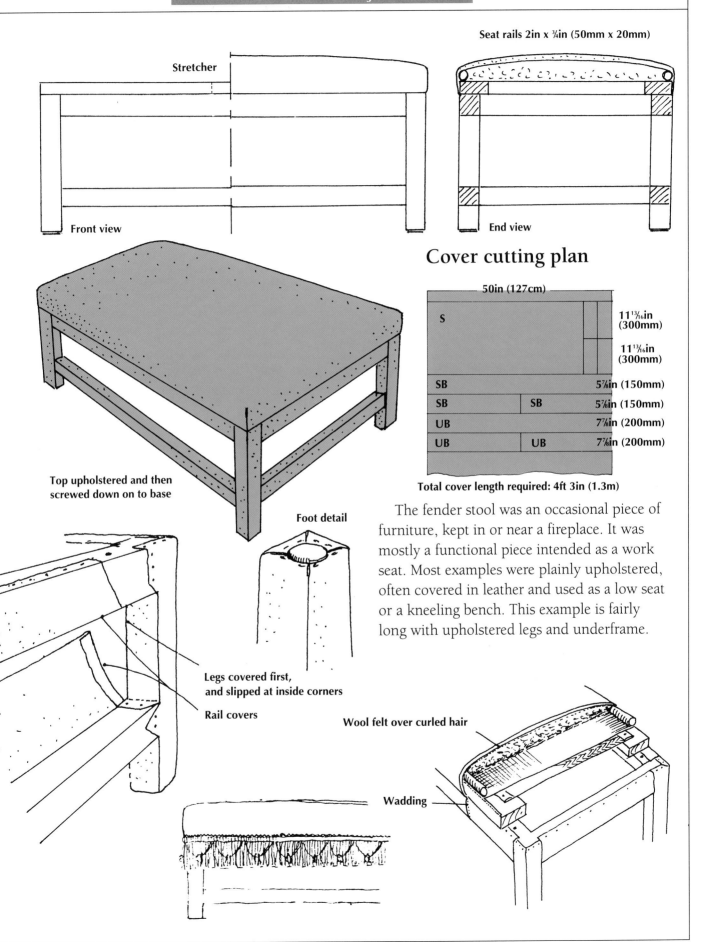

Seat rails 2in x ¾in (50mm x 20mm)

Stretcher

Front view

End view

Cover cutting plan

50in (127cm)

S			11¹³⁄₁₆in (300mm)
			11¹³⁄₁₆in (300mm)
SB			5⅞in (150mm)
SB	SB		5⅞in (150mm)
UB			7⅞in (200mm)
UB	UB		7⅞in (200mm)

Total cover length required: 4ft 3in (1.3m)

The fender stool was an occasional piece of furniture, kept in or near a fireplace. It was mostly a functional piece intended as a work seat. Most examples were plainly upholstered, often covered in leather and used as a low seat or a kneeling bench. This example is fairly long with upholstered legs and underframe.

Top upholstered and then screwed down on to base

Foot detail

Legs covered first, and slipped at inside corners

Rail covers

Wool felt over curled hair

Wadding

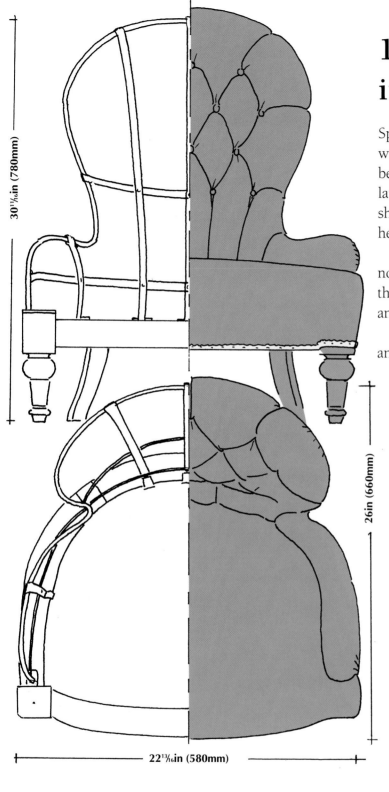

30¹⁵⁄₁₆in (780mm)

22¹³⁄₁₆in (580mm)

26in (660mm)

17. A Victorian iron back chair

Spoon back chairs of the mid-Victorian era were produced in large numbers for use in bedrooms and living rooms. The use of metal lath and rod allowed compound curves and shapes to be produced which would have been heavy and cumbersome if made from timber.

The ironwork technique originated from northern Europe, some using iron rod throughout, and others produced from heated and forged metal strips.

Many have survived a hundred years of use and are being restored or reupholstered today.

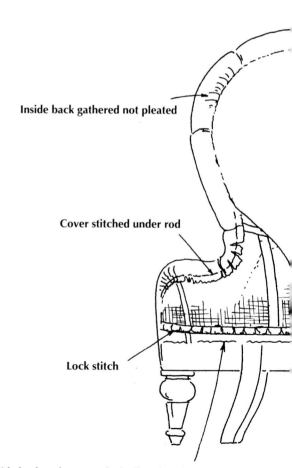

Inside back gathered not pleated

Cover stitched under rod

Lock stitch

Inside back and arms tacked off to top of rail

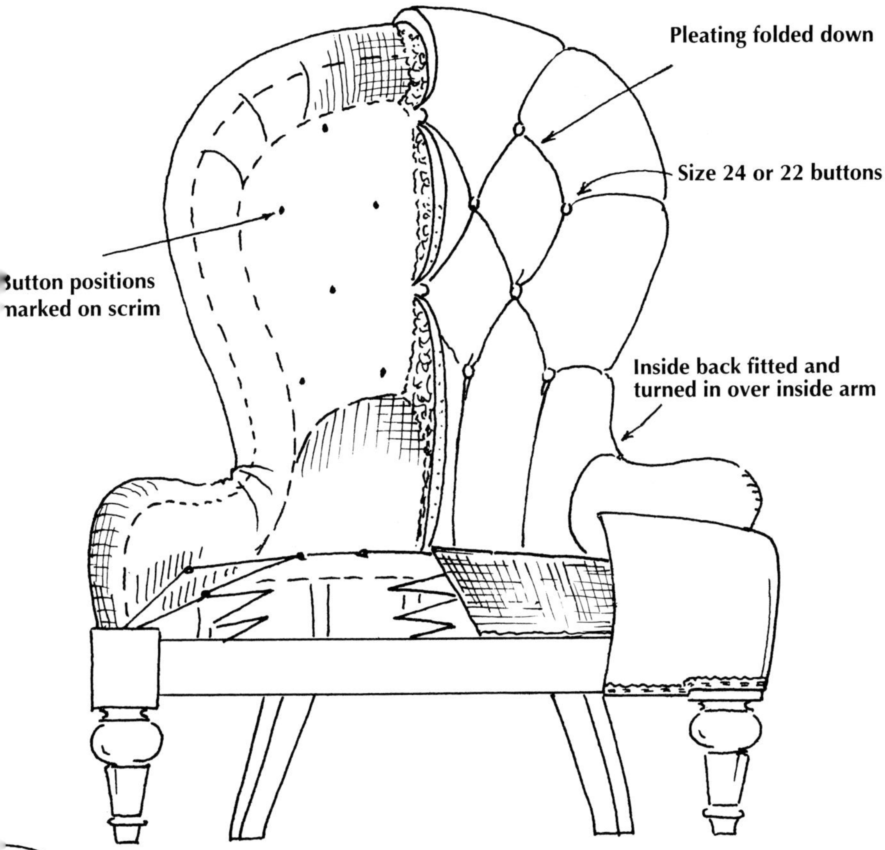
Pleating folded down
Size 24 or 22 buttons
Button positions marked on scrim
Inside back fitted and turned in over inside arm

Cover cutting plan

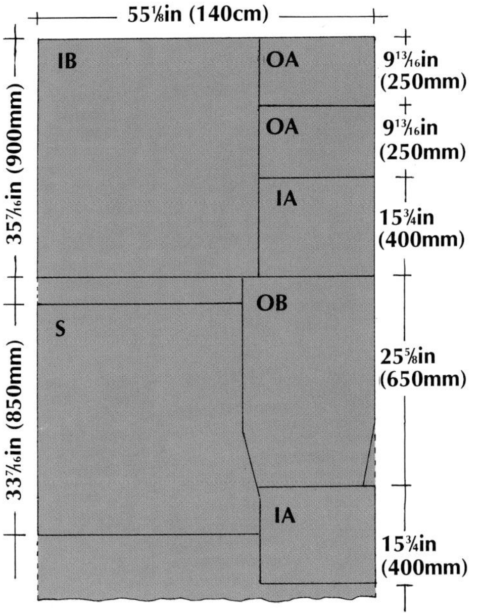
55 1/8in (140cm)
35 7/16in (900mm)
33 7/16in (850mm)
IB
OA
OA
IA
OB
S
IA
9 13/16in (250mm)
9 13/16in (250mm)
15 3/4in (400mm)
25 5/8in (650mm)
15 3/4in (400mm)

Total cover length required: 6ft 7in (2m)

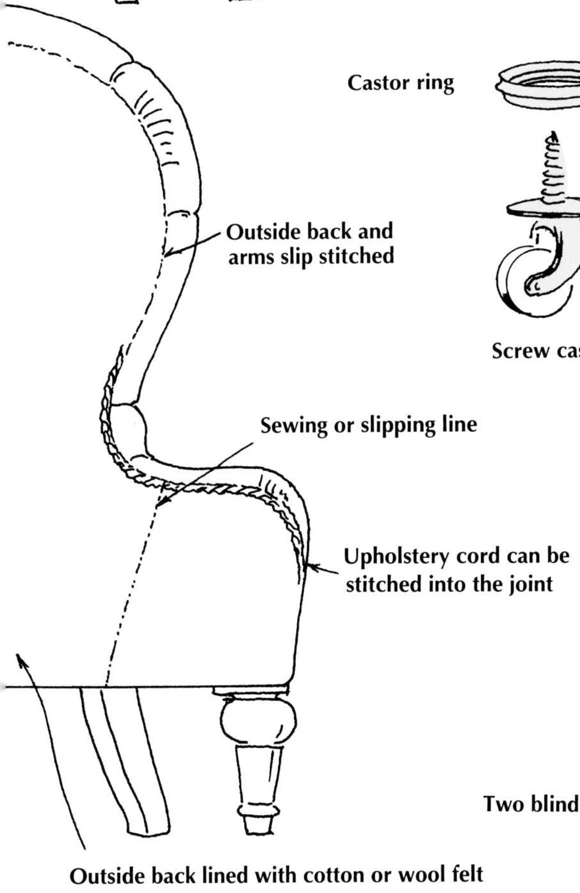
Outside back and arms slip stitched
Sewing or slipping line
Upholstery cord can be stitched into the joint
Outside back lined with cotton or wool felt

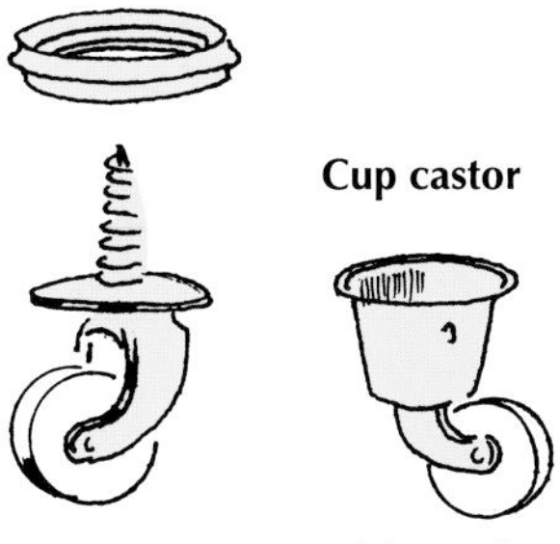
Castor ring
Cup castor
Screw castor
China or brass wheel

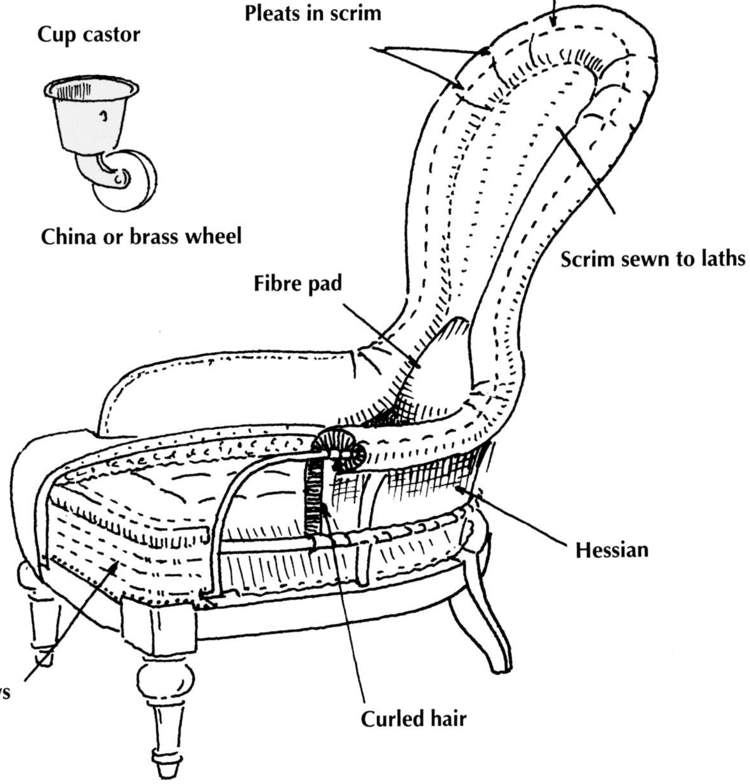
Top stitched roll
Pleats in scrim
Scrim sewn to laths
Fibre pad
Hessian
Two blind rows
Curled hair

18. A Victorian sewing chair with bible edge front

Hair-seated chairs are typically Victorian and were designed and made as sewing or nursing chairs. The upholstery was usually very firm and edges and facings trimmed and corded. With its curved seat and fairly upright back, the sitter was well supported. Very similar proportions were used for the slipper chair and the prayer chair.

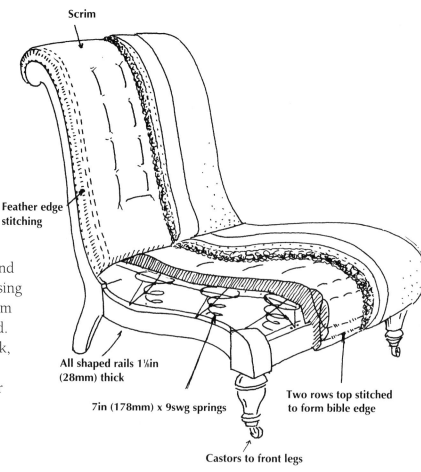

Scrim

Feather edge stitching

All shaped rails 1⅛in (28mm) thick

7in (178mm) x 9swg springs

Two rows top stitched to form bible edge

Castors to front legs

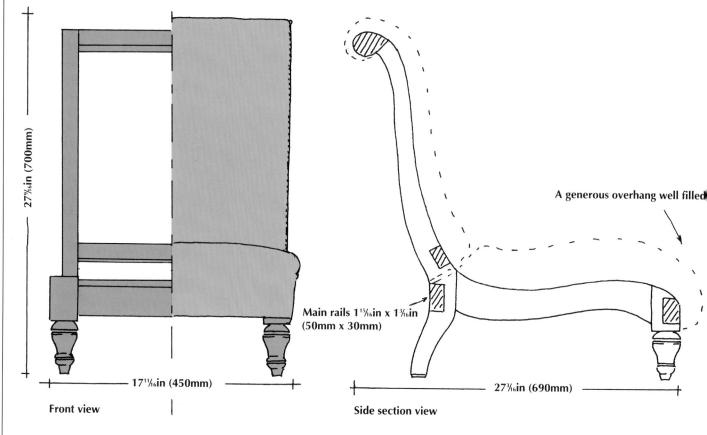

27¹¹⁄₁₆in (700mm)

17¹¹⁄₁₆in (450mm)

Front view

Main rails 1¹⁵⁄₁₆in x 1³⁄₁₆in (50mm x 30mm)

A generous overhang well filled

27³⁄₁₆in (690mm)

Side section view

Cover cutting plan

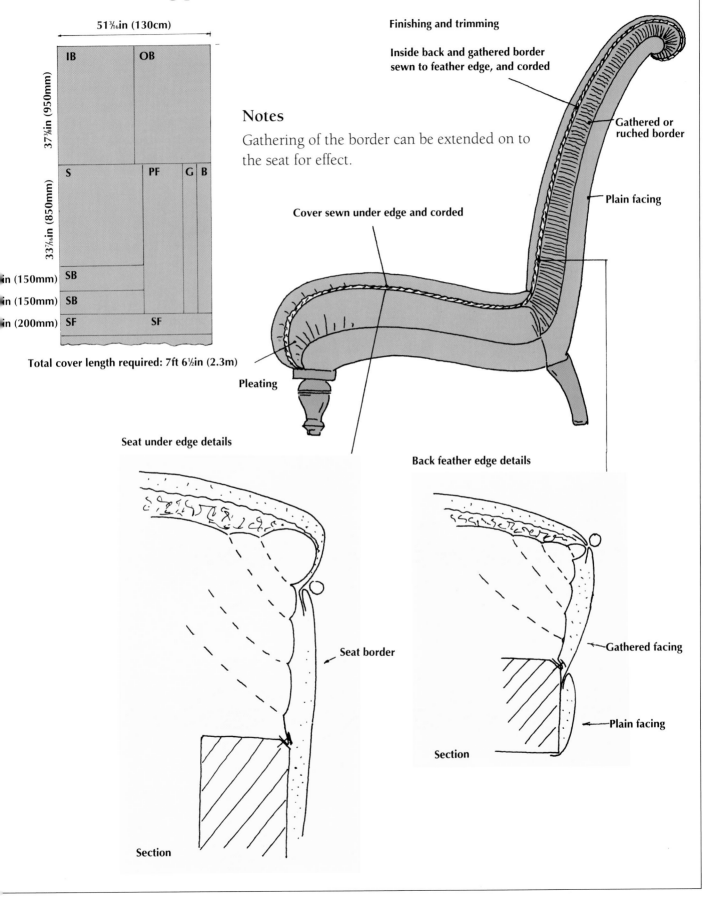

51³⁄₁₆in (130cm)

37⁷⁄₁₆in (950mm)

33⁷⁄₁₆in (850mm)

| IB | OB | | |
| S | PF | G | B |

in (150mm) SB

in (150mm) SB

in (200mm) SF SF

Total cover length required: 7ft 6½in (2.3m)

Finishing and trimming

Inside back and gathered border sewn to feather edge, and corded

Gathered or ruched border

Plain facing

Notes

Gathering of the border can be extended on to the seat for effect.

Cover sewn under edge and corded

Pleating

Seat under edge details

Seat border

Section

Back feather edge details

Gathered facing

Plain facing

Section

193

19. A drawing room chair with mock cushion seat

A well-proportioned, low-back drawing room chair with a sprung seat and back. The mock cushion gives a pillow effect to the seat and provides a soft and flexible front edge, which is much more comfortable than its conventional stitched firm edge.

Fixed feather pillows were often used as second stuffings in the backs of armchairs of this type.

Cover cutting plan

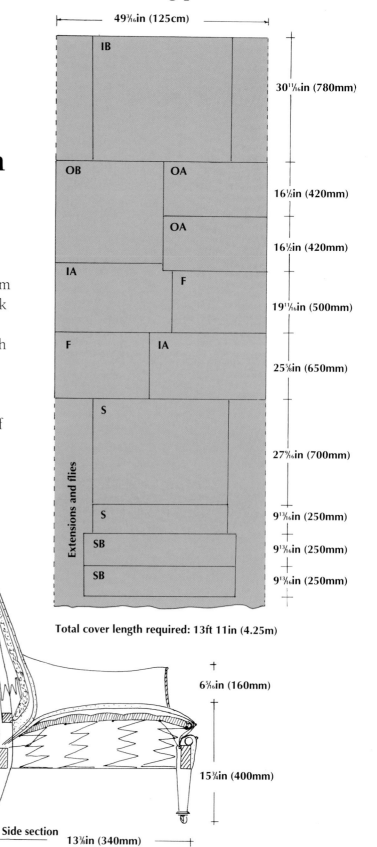

49³⁄₁₆in (125cm)

IB — 30¹¹⁄₁₆in (780mm)

OB / OA — 16½in (420mm)

OA — 16½in (420mm)

IA / F — 19¹¹⁄₁₆in (500mm)

F / IA — 25⅝in (650mm)

S — 27⁹⁄₁₆in (700mm)

Extensions and flies

S — 9¹³⁄₁₆in (250mm)

SB — 9¹³⁄₁₆in (250mm)

SB — 9¹³⁄₁₆in (250mm)

Total cover length required: 13ft 11in (4.25m)

29⅛in (740mm)

6⁵⁄₁₆in (160mm)

15¾in (400mm)

Front view — 13in (330mm)

Side section — 13⅜in (340mm)

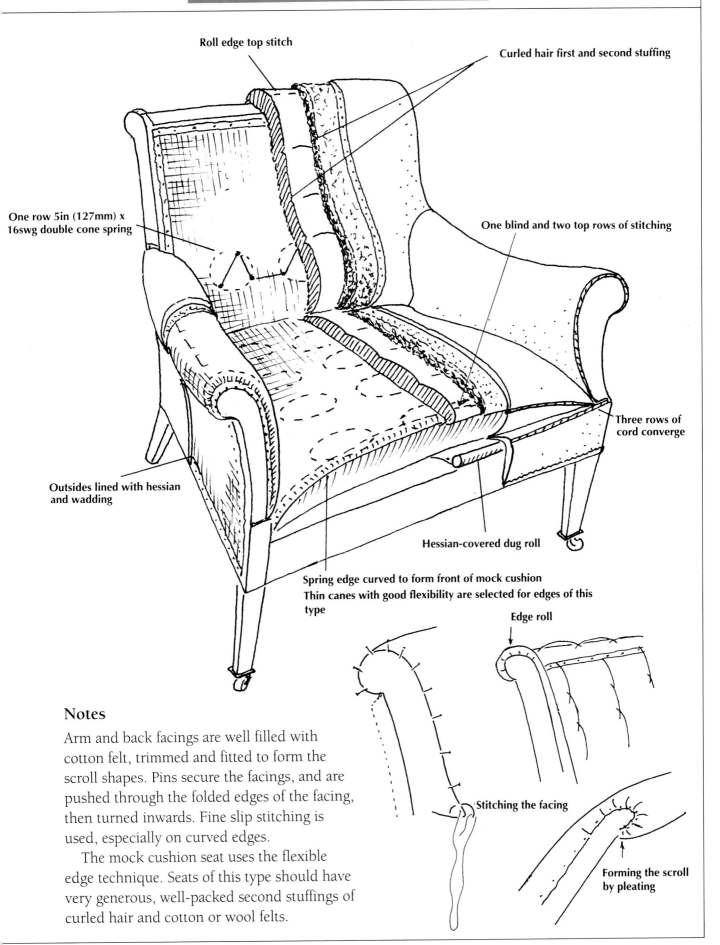

Roll edge top stitch

Curled hair first and second stuffing

One row 5in (127mm) x 16swg double cone spring

One blind and two top rows of stitching

Outsides lined with hessian and wadding

Three rows of cord converge

Hessian-covered dug roll

Spring edge curved to form front of mock cushion
Thin canes with good flexibility are selected for edges of this type

Edge roll

Stitching the facing

Forming the scroll by pleating

Notes

Arm and back facings are well filled with cotton felt, trimmed and fitted to form the scroll shapes. Pins secure the facings, and are pushed through the folded edges of the facing, then turned inwards. Fine slip stitching is used, especially on curved edges.

The mock cushion seat uses the flexible edge technique. Seats of this type should have very generous, well-packed second stuffings of curled hair and cotton or wool felts.

20. A tall back settle-style settee

A Victorian upholstered version of the settle, often used as hall or reception seating for hotels and clubs. It is a very upright piece of furniture with a comfortable seat and large enclosed ends which give protection from draughts.

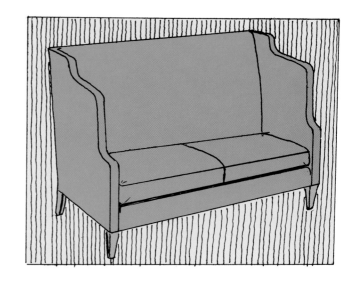

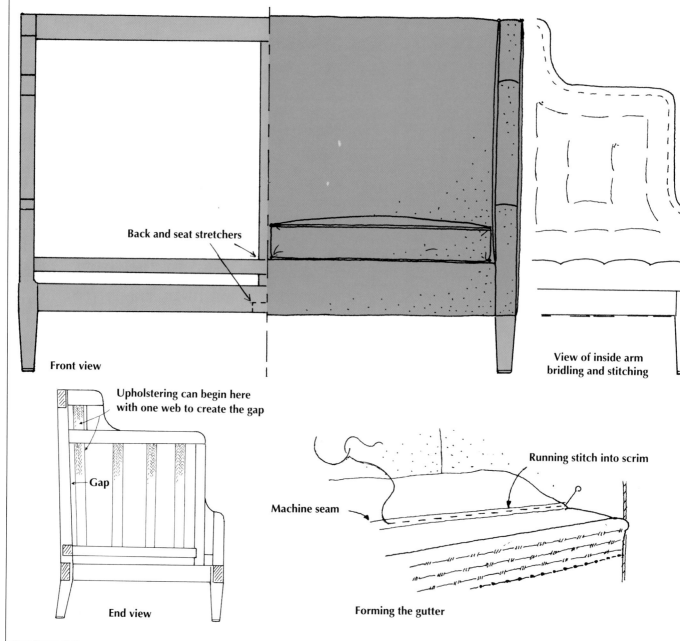

Back and seat stretchers

Front view

View of inside arm bridling and stitching

Upholstering can begin here with one web to create the gap

Gap

End view

Machine seam

Running stitch into scrim

Forming the gutter

Cover cutting plan

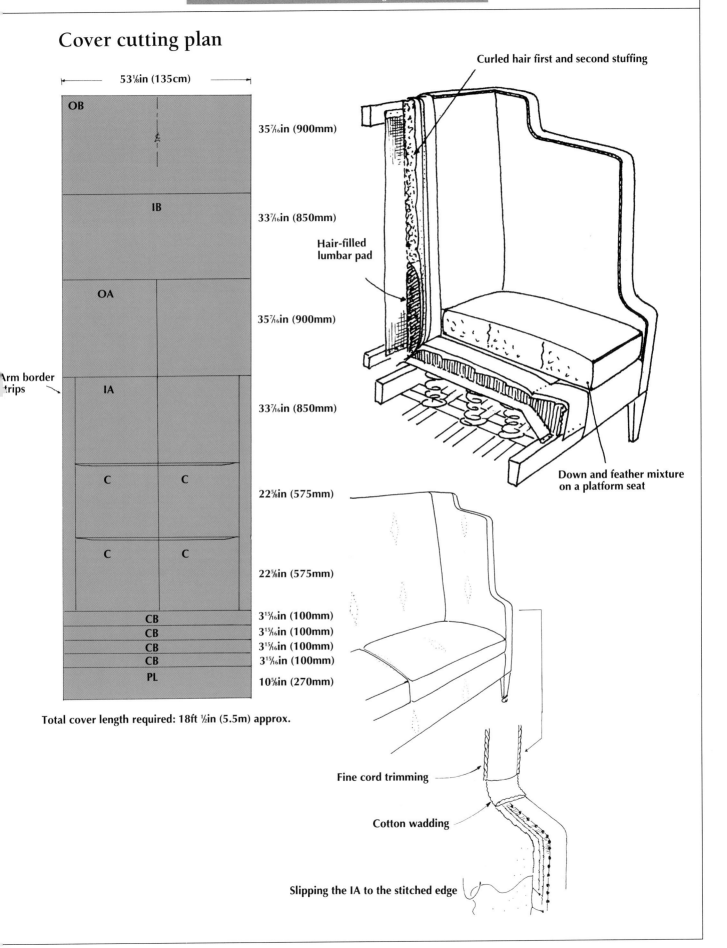

53⅛in (135cm)

OB

35⁷⁄₁₆in (900mm)

IB

33⁷⁄₁₆in (850mm)

OA

35⁷⁄₁₆in (900mm)

Arm border strips

IA

33⁷⁄₁₆in (850mm)

C   C

22⅝in (575mm)

C   C

22⅝in (575mm)

CB   3¹⁵⁄₁₆in (100mm)
CB   3¹⁵⁄₁₆in (100mm)
CB   3¹⁵⁄₁₆in (100mm)
CB   3¹⁵⁄₁₆in (100mm)
PL   10⅝in (270mm)

Total cover length required: 18ft ½in (5.5m) approx.

Curled hair first and second stuffing

Hair-filled lumbar pad

Down and feather mixture on a platform seat

Fine cord trimming

Cotton wadding

Slipping the IA to the stitched edge

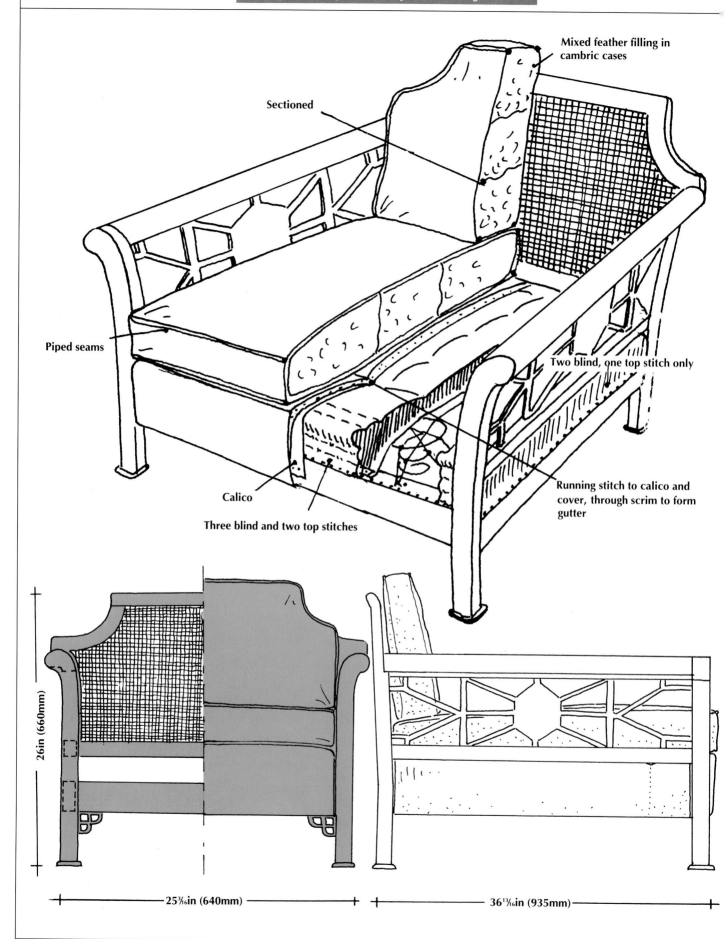

Mixed feather filling in cambric cases

Sectioned

Piped seams

Two blind, one top stitch only

Calico

Running stitch to calico and cover, through scrim to form gutter

Three blind and two top stitches

26in (660mm)

25³⁄₁₆in (640mm)

36¹³⁄₁₆in (935mm)

21. A *bergère* chair c. 1930 with cane back and sprung seat

A development of the Edwardian *bergère* with fretwork below the arms in place of the usual canework. Earlier Victorian *bergère* chairs and settees were black lacquered and painted with Chinese art in rich colours. Figured velvets and printed cottons were popular coverings for the *bergère* suite of the 1930s.

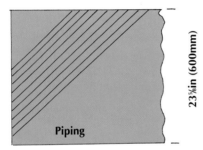

Piping

23⅝in (600mm)

Total cover length required: 11½ft (3.5m)

Notes

Because of its large size and depth, the seat of the *bergère* chair should be strong and well-sprung. Well-filled feather cushions produce the necessary comfort and support. Extra scatter cushions are usually provided so that the chairs are adaptable for different people.

The *bergère*-style chair or suite often has spring edge or cane edge seat fronts to add height and comfort.

The cover width and cutting plan shown allows for seat and back width cushions of 22⅝in (575mm). Extra fabric length will be required for fabrics with large design repeats.

Cover cutting plan

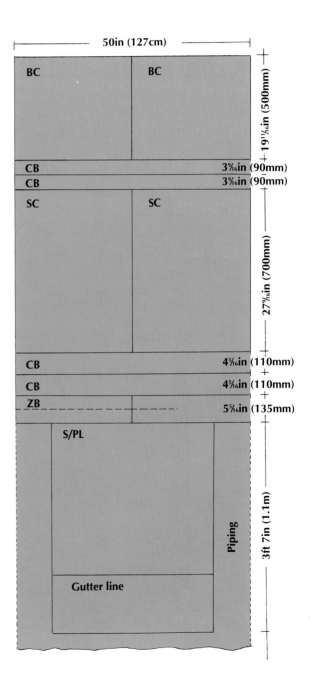

50in (127cm)

BC	BC

19¹¹⁄₁₆in (500mm)

CB — 3⁹⁄₁₆in (90mm)
CB — 3⁹⁄₁₆in (90mm)

SC	SC

27⁹⁄₁₆in (700mm)

CB — 4�5⁄₁₆in (110mm)
CB — 4�5⁄₁₆in (110mm)
ZB — 5�5⁄₁₆in (135mm)

S/PL

Piping

Gutter line

3ft 7in (1.1m)

22. An art nouveau drawing room chair

A tall chair with lots of interesting detail in the decorative Parisienne style. Rebated show-wood frames supported the slim arm and back upholstery above a well-sprung seat. Fine-patterned tapestries and damasks were used to cover ornate and simpler versions of these chairs.

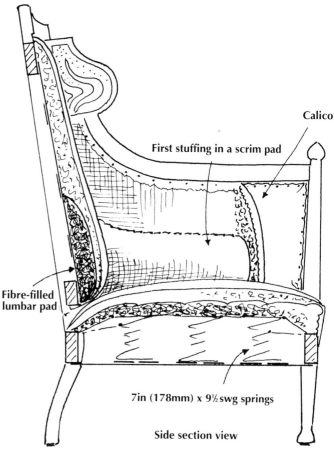

Calico

First stuffing in a scrim pad

Fibre-filled lumbar pad

7in (178mm) x 9½ swg springs

Side section view

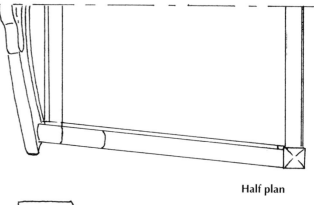

Half plan

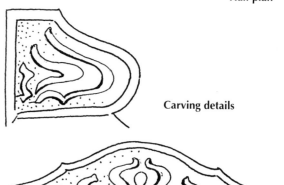

Carving details

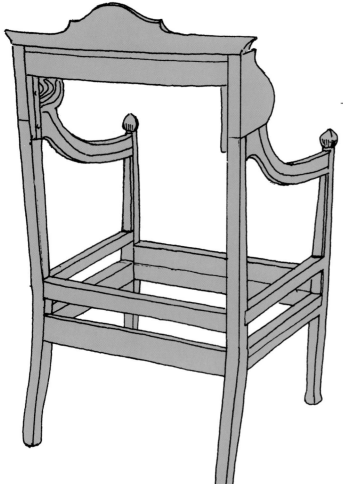

The frame showing position of stuffing rails and tacking strips

Cover cutting plan

Cover width: 53⅛in (135cm)

IA	IA
IB	OB
S	
OA	OA

21⅝in (550mm)

33⁷⁄₁₆in (850mm)

31½in (800mm)

22¼in (565mm)

Total cover length required: 9ft 1in (2.765m)

Cover cutting plan

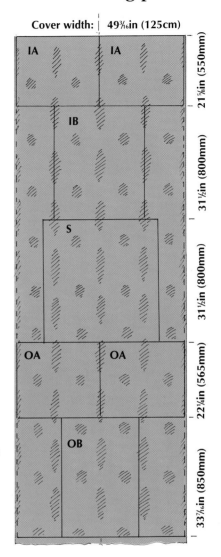

Cover width: 49⅜in (125cm)

IA	IA
IB	
S	
OA	OA
OB	

21⅝in (550mm)

31½in (800mm)

31½in (800mm)

22¼in (565mm)

33⁷⁄₁₆in (850mm)

Minimum cover length required: 11ft 8in (3.565m)

Notes

Variations in cover width can influence the cutting plan and the length of fabric required. A longer length will be needed for narrow width covers used on large chairs etc.

Patterns generally will also take up more length when matching requires the design to be centred and aligned across the job. One to one and a half metres extra is about the average requirement depending on the size of the repeat.

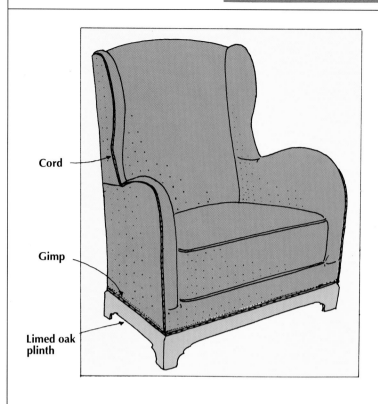

Cord

Gimp

Limed oak
plinth

23. A small wing chair with spring cushion seat on wood slats c. 1925

A chair with an interesting frame construction and a lath seat. Comfort depends on a good spring cushion (which is not reversible).

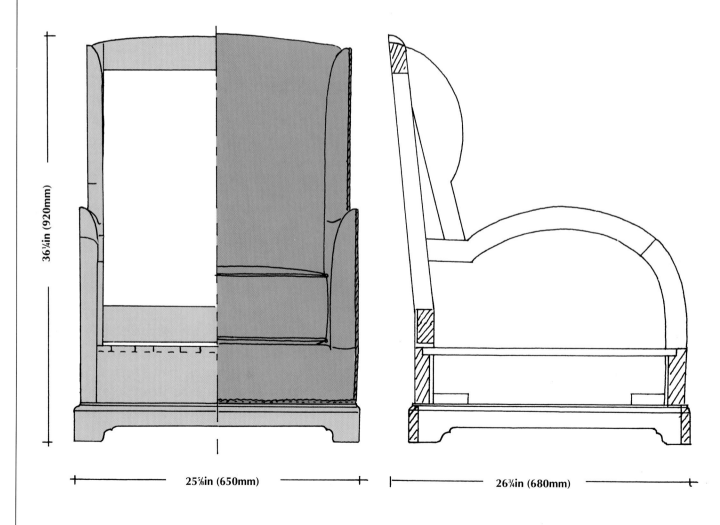

36¼in (920mm)

25⅝in (650mm)

26¾in (680mm)

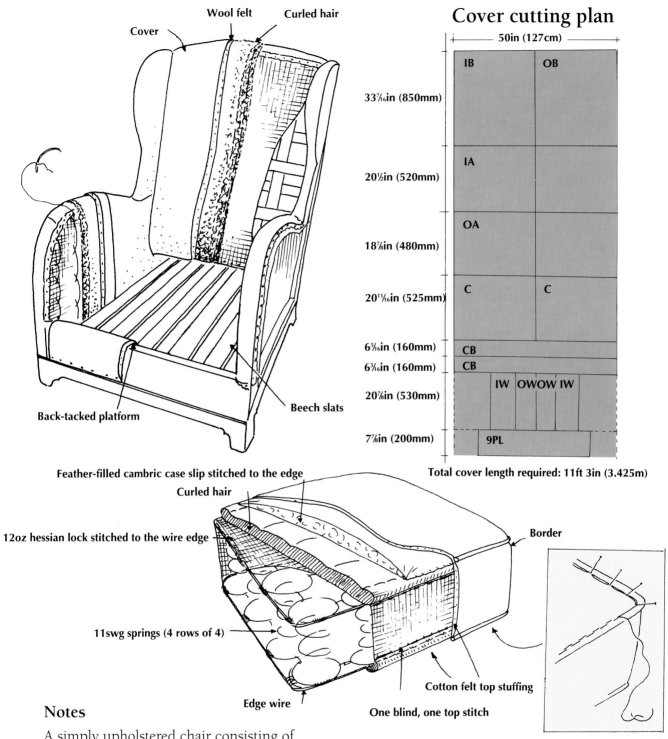

Cover

Wool felt

Curled hair

Cover cutting plan

50in (127cm)

| IB | OB |

33⁷⁄₁₆in (850mm)

| IA |

20½in (520mm)

| OA |

18⅞in (480mm)

| C | C |

20¹¹⁄₁₆in (525mm)

| CB |

6⁵⁄₁₆in (160mm)

| CB |

6⁵⁄₁₆in (160mm)

| IW | OW | OW | IW |

20⅞in (530mm)

| 9PL |

7⅞in (200mm)

Total cover length required: 11ft 3in (3.425m)

Back-tacked platform

Beech slats

Feather-filled cambric case slip stitched to the edge

Curled hair

12oz hessian lock stitched to the wire edge

Border

11swg springs (4 rows of 4)

Cotton felt top stuffing

Edge wire

One blind, one top stitch

Notes

A simply upholstered chair consisting of padded back and arms on well-tensioned webs and hessian. The large sprung seat cushion rests on 2in x ½in (51mm x 13mm) beech slats, which is typical of the period. Hand-slipped, piped or corded edges accentuate the slim outlines.

The size of the chair lends itself well to a cover cutting plan in which the half width conveniently covers most of the main parts. Very little waste occurs with a layout of this kind.

If there is a patterned fabric to be matched and bias cut pipings, an additional 4ft 11in (1.5m) would be needed, giving a total of 16ft 5in (5m).

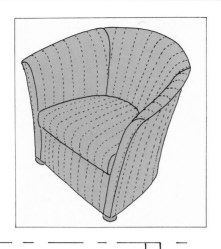

24. A small beech frame tub chair with cushion seat or fixed seat

The tub chair never seems to go out of fashion. Its inviting style and low back make it ideal for both domestic and contract use.

Striped fabrics show off its distinct and elegant line.

Shaping block

Corner block

Frame details

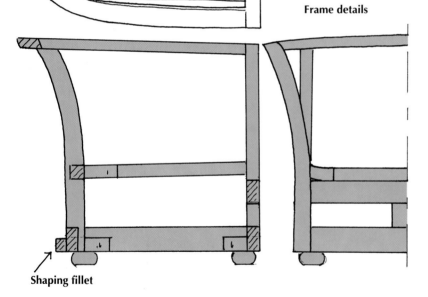

Shaping fillet

Curled hair

Coir fibre

8in (203mm) x 9swg springs

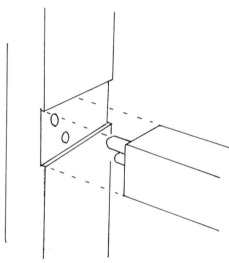

Housed and dowelled stuffing rails

6in (152mm) x 9swg springs

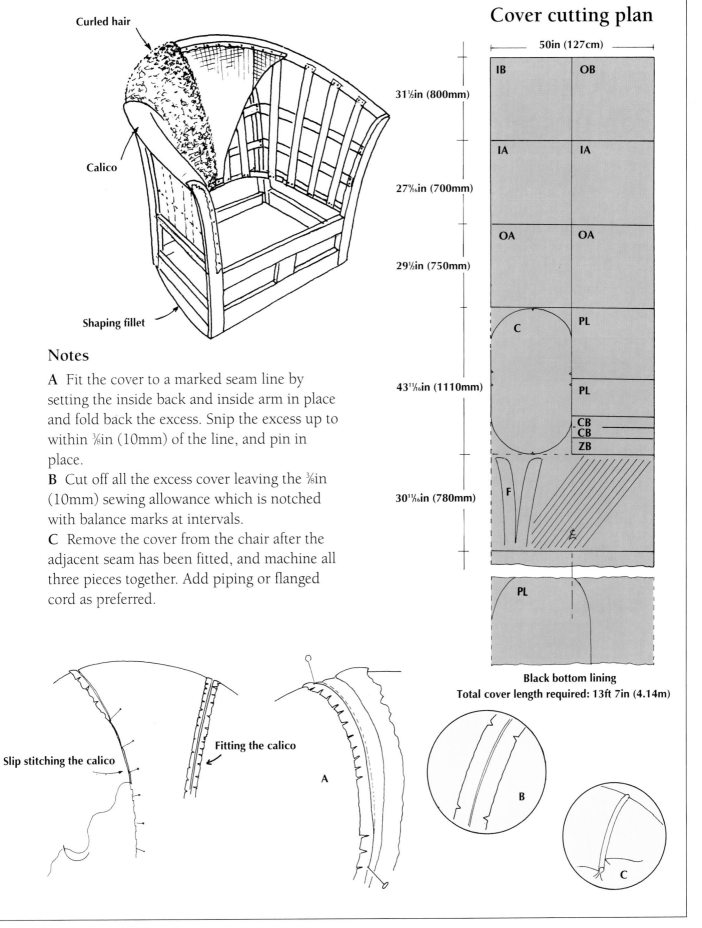

Curled hair

Calico

Shaping fillet

Cover cutting plan

50in (127cm)

IB	OB
IA	IA
OA	OA

31½in (800mm)

27%₆in (700mm)

29½in (750mm)

43¹¹⁄₁₆in (1110mm)

30¹⁄₁₆in (780mm)

C PL

PL

CB
CB
ZB

F

PL

Black bottom lining
Total cover length required: 13ft 7in (4.14m)

Notes

A Fit the cover to a marked seam line by setting the inside back and inside arm in place and fold back the excess. Snip the excess up to within ⅜in (10mm) of the line, and pin in place.

B Cut off all the excess cover leaving the ⅜in (10mm) sewing allowance which is notched with balance marks at intervals.

C Remove the cover from the chair after the adjacent seam has been fitted, and machine all three pieces together. Add piping or flanged cord as preferred.

Slip stitching the calico

Fitting the calico

A

B

C

25. A framed drop-in seat

Supported in a rebated chair frame, the drop-in or loose seat is well known by all upholsterers. There have been many variations of the same theme beginning as early as Queen Anne at the start of eighteenth century.

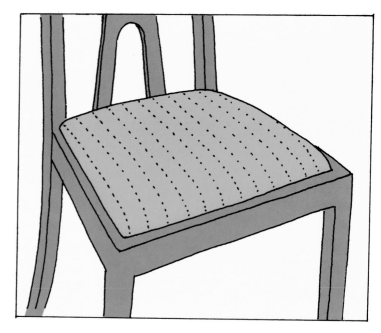

2in (52mm)

1in (24mm)

Single corner pleat

15¾in (400mm)

17¾in (450mm)

Sharp edges and corners removed

Cover cutting plan

51³⁄₁₆in (130cm)

21⅝in (550mm)

21⅝in (550mm)

21⅝in (550mm)

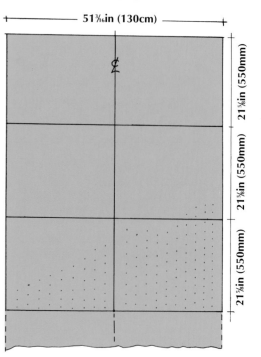

Cover cutting layout for a set of six loose seats.
Minimum cover length required: 5ft 5in (1.65m)

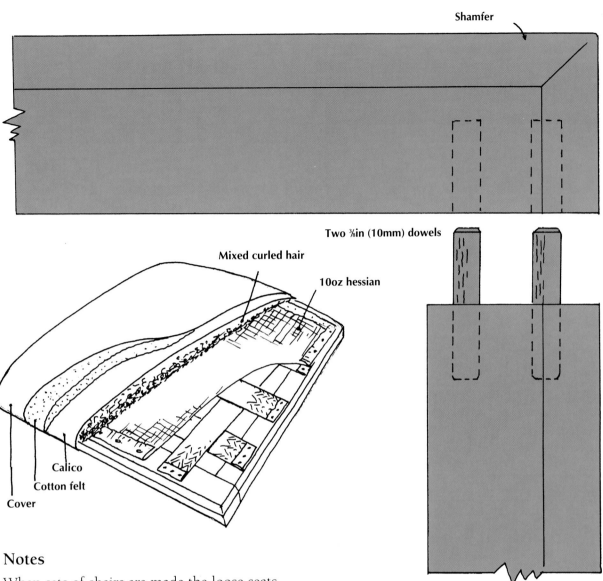

Shamfer

Two ⅜in (10mm) dowels

Mixed curled hair

10oz hessian

Calico

Cotton felt

Cover

Notes

When sets of chairs are made the loose seats are fitted and numbered to correspond with the chairs.

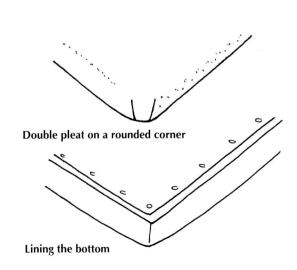

Double pleat on a rounded corner

Lining the bottom

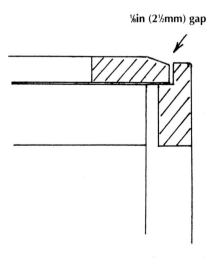

⅛in (2½mm) gap

Corner section of chair leg and loose seat frame: a ⅛in (2½mm) gap all round allows for cover

26. A waisted pouffe or footstool

In its simplest form the Edwardian pouffe was stuffed with woollen rags or straw, and waisted with a pull cord.

An alternative modern version uses high density urethane chipfoam cut and shaped to reproduce the rounded outlines of the original.

Corner rosettes   **End view**

Plan

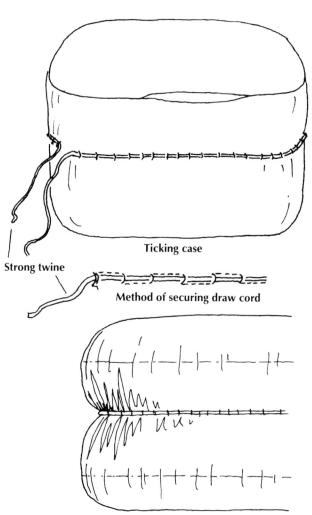

Ticking case

Strong twine

Method of securing draw cord

Inner case stuffed and drawn in to form waist

Heavy trimming cord knotted at rosettes

Notes

The main construction can be made by stuffing a calico or ticking case, and producing a shape with a draw string, or building the interior from high density 6lb chipfoam. The foam interior has a centre board of MDF (medium density fibre board) which can be stapled or tacked into.

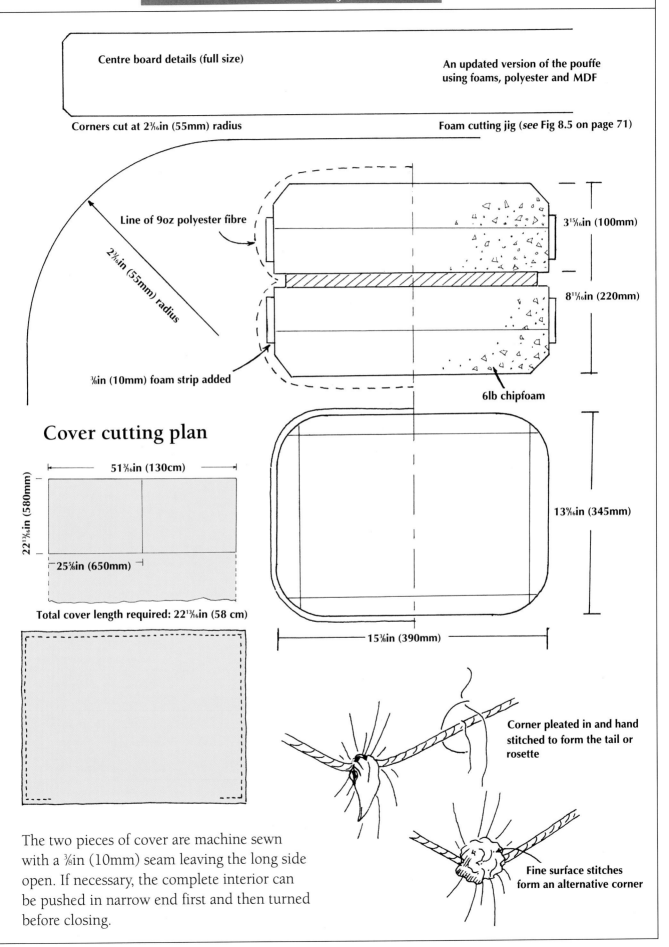

Centre board details (full size)

An updated version of the pouffe using foams, polyester and MDF

Corners cut at 2⅜in (55mm) radius

Foam cutting jig (see Fig 8.5 on page 71)

Line of 9oz polyester fibre

2⅜in (55mm) radius

⅜in (10mm) foam strip added

3¹⁵⁄₁₆in (100mm)

8¹¹⁄₁₆in (220mm)

6lb chipfoam

Cover cutting plan

51³⁄₁₆in (130cm)

22¹³⁄₁₆in (580mm)

25⅝in (650mm)

Total cover length required: 22¹³⁄₁₆in (58 cm)

13⁹⁄₁₆in (345mm)

15⅜in (390mm)

Corner pleated in and hand stitched to form the tail or rosette

Fine surface stitches form an alternative corner

The two pieces of cover are machine sewn with a ⅜in (10mm) seam leaving the long side open. If necessary, the complete interior can be pushed in narrow end first and then turned before closing.

27. A fully upholstered bedroom chair

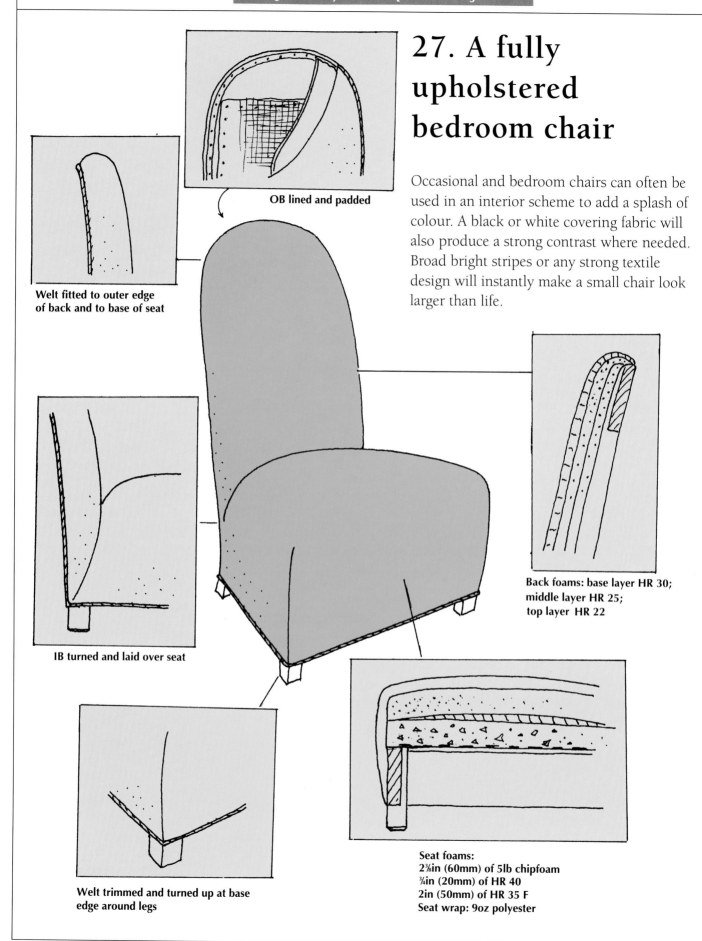

OB lined and padded

Welt fitted to outer edge of back and to base of seat

Occasional and bedroom chairs can often be used in an interior scheme to add a splash of colour. A black or white covering fabric will also produce a strong contrast where needed. Broad bright stripes or any strong textile design will instantly make a small chair look larger than life.

IB turned and laid over seat

Back foams: base layer HR 30; middle layer HR 25; top layer HR 22

Welt trimmed and turned up at base edge around legs

Seat foams:
2⅜in (60mm) of 5lb chipfoam
¾in (20mm) of HR 40
2in (50mm) of HR 35 F
Seat wrap: 9oz polyester

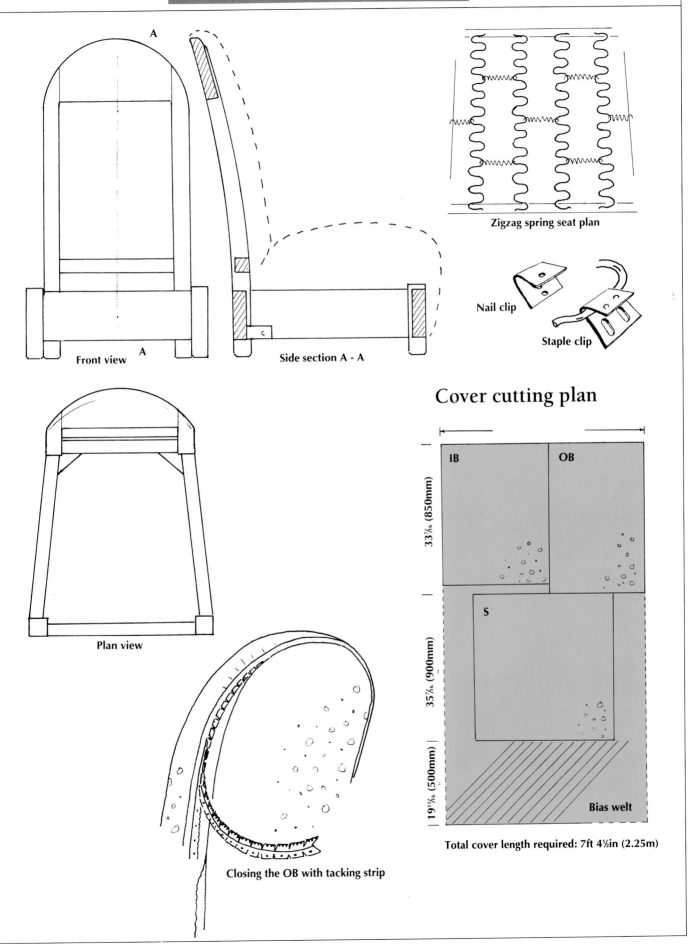

A

Front view   A

Side section A - A

Zigzag spring seat plan

Nail clip

Staple clip

Plan view

Cover cutting plan

IB

OB

S

33⁷/₁₆ (850mm)

35⁷/₁₆ (900mm)

19¹¹/₁₆ (500mm)

Bias welt

Closing the OB with tacking strip

Total cover length required: 7ft 4½in (2.25m)

28. A wing fireside chair

The unsung hero of the fireside, typical of the mid-twentieth century, these types of chair have surely topped the million mark. They have been reupholstered, re-covered and loose covered to maintain their appeal and keep them abreast of fashion. Well-made examples seem to go on for ever but no doubt the design has seen its best days.

Front view

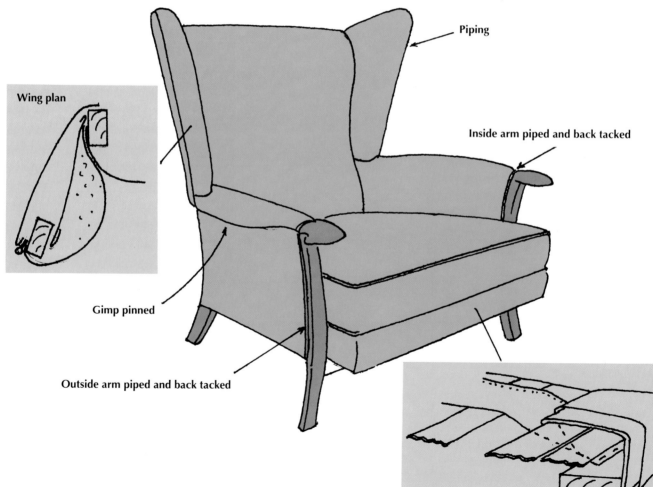

Wing plan

Piping

Inside arm piped and back tacked

Gimp pinned

Outside arm piped and back tacked

Platform

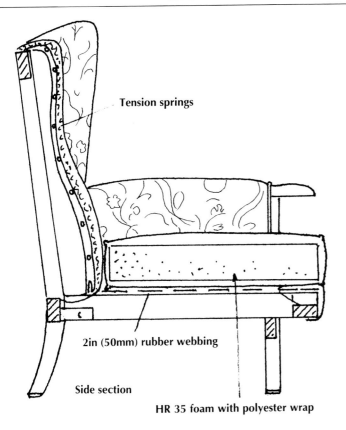

Tension springs

Side section

2in (50mm) rubber webbing

HR 35 foam with polyester wrap

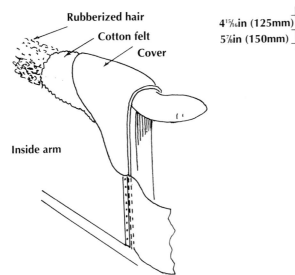

Rubberized hair

Cotton felt

Cover

Inside arm

4¹⁵⁄₁₆in (125mm)

5⅞in (150mm)

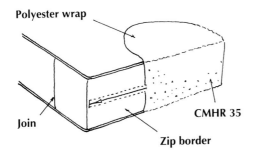

Polyester wrap

Join

CMHR 35

Zip border

Suggested cutting plan

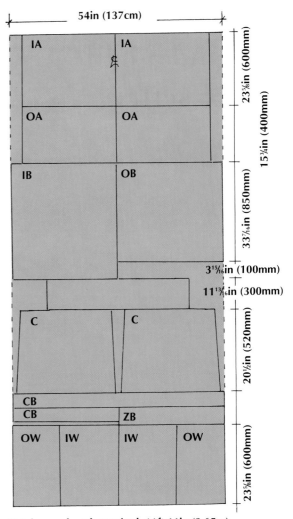

54in (137cm)

IA	IA
OA	OA
IB	OB

23⅝in (600mm)

15¾in (400mm)

33⅐⁄₁₆in (850mm)

3¹⁵⁄₁₆in (100mm)

11¹³⁄₁₆in (300mm)

C	C
CB	
CB	ZB
OW	IW	IW	OW

20½in (520mm)

23⅝in (600mm)

Total cover length required: 11ft 11in (3.65m)

Notes

The suggested cutting plan is based on a 50in to 54in (127cm to 137cm) width cover. The arrangement will suit most plain or pattern fabrics, except for some pattern types with large pattern repeats.

Piping may be straight cut from small amounts of waste, depending on the cover width chosen. Bias cut piping will require an extra 2ft 3½in (0.7m).

Approximately 19¹¹⁄₁₆in (0.5m) of strong platform cloth will be needed for covering the seat webbings. Fly pieces may be used on the IB and PL to make small savings on cover length.

29. A modern two-and-a-half seater settee

A design with a European influence which would look acceptable in a reception area or a domestic room. Manufactured to a stringent costing schedule, using modern techniques and materials, the KD (knock down) system has been successful over the last twenty-five years. The tee nut is at the heart of this production method.

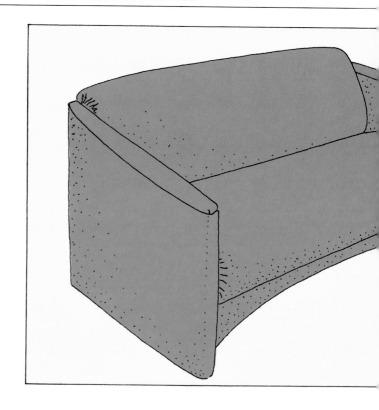

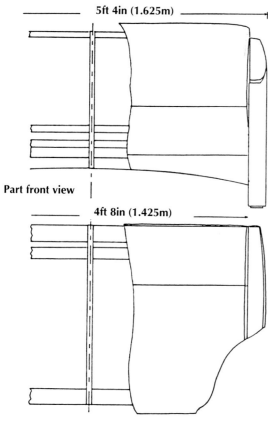

Part front view

Part plan view

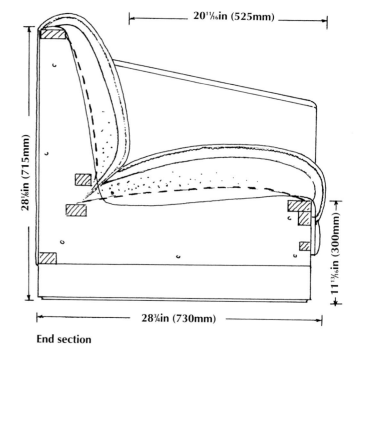

End section

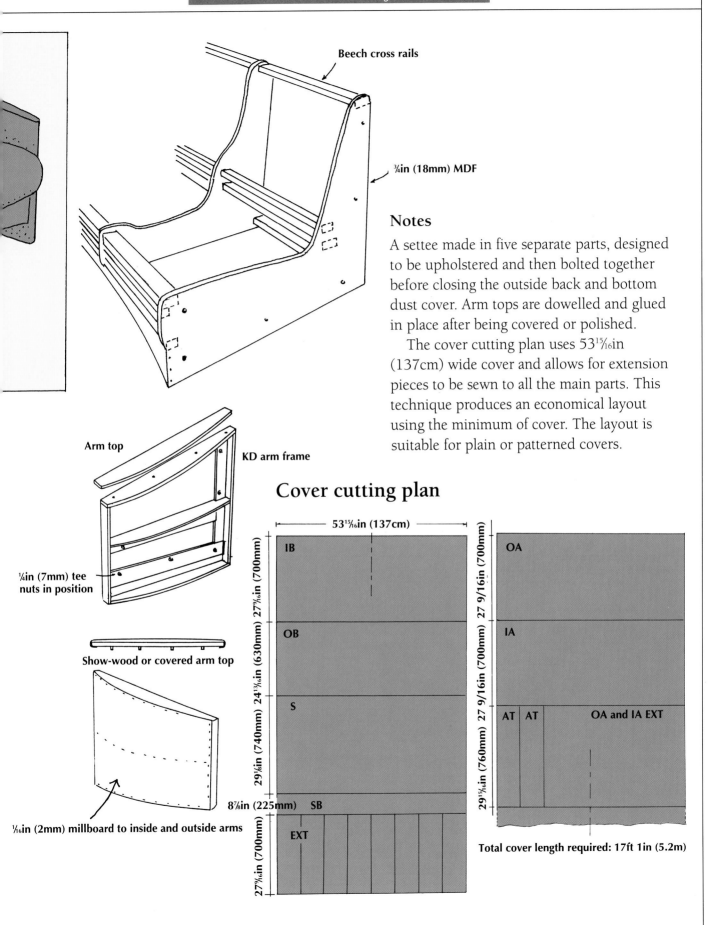

Beech cross rails

¾in (18mm) MDF

Arm top

KD arm frame

¼in (7mm) tee nuts in position

Show-wood or covered arm top

1/16in (2mm) millboard to inside and outside arms

Notes

A settee made in five separate parts, designed to be upholstered and then bolted together before closing the outside back and bottom dust cover. Arm tops are dowelled and glued in place after being covered or polished.

The cover cutting plan uses 53¹⁵/₁₆in (137cm) wide cover and allows for extension pieces to be sewn to all the main parts. This technique produces an economical layout using the minimum of cover. The layout is suitable for plain or patterned covers.

Cover cutting plan

53¹⁵/₁₆in (137cm)

IB

OB

S

8⅞in (225mm) SB

EXT

27⁹/₁₆in (700mm)

24¹³/₁₆in (630mm)

29⅛in (740mm)

27⁹/₁₆in (700mm)

OA

IA

AT | AT | OA and IA EXT

27 9/16in (700mm)

27 9/16in (700mm)

29¹⁵/₁₆in (760mm)

Total cover length required: 17ft 1in (5.2m)

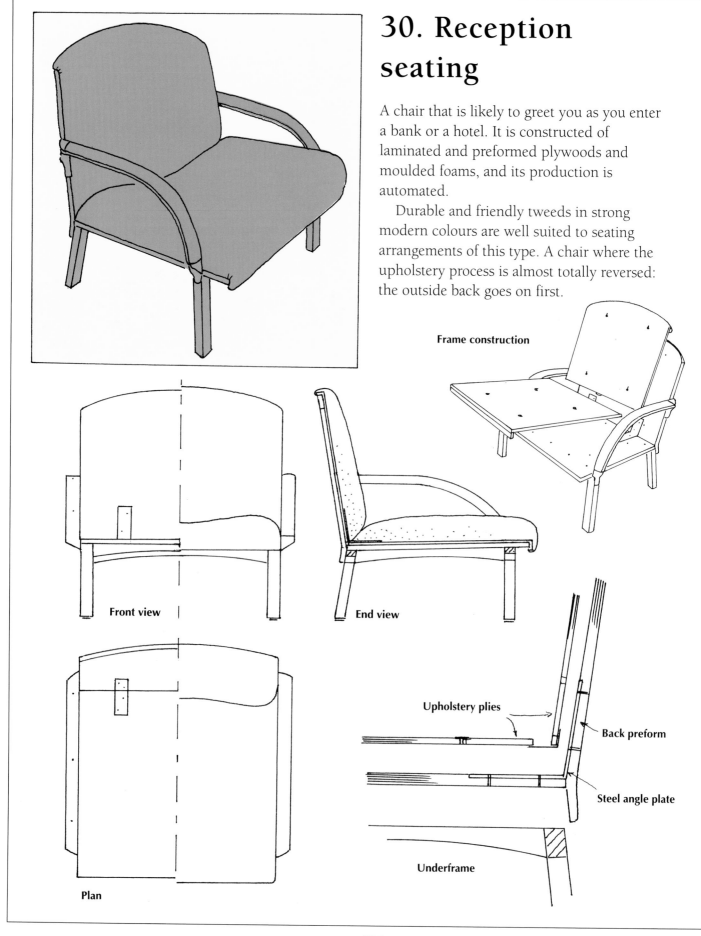

30. Reception seating

A chair that is likely to greet you as you enter a bank or a hotel. It is constructed of laminated and preformed plywoods and moulded foams, and its production is automated.

Durable and friendly tweeds in strong modern colours are well suited to seating arrangements of this type. A chair where the upholstery process is almost totally reversed: the outside back goes on first.

Frame construction

Front view

End view

Upholstery plies

Back preform

Steel angle plate

Underframe

Plan

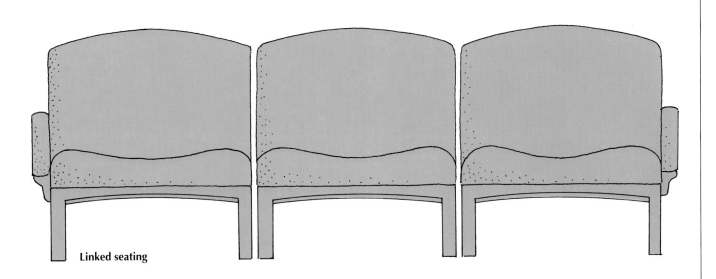

Linked seating

Cover cutting plans
for two seats

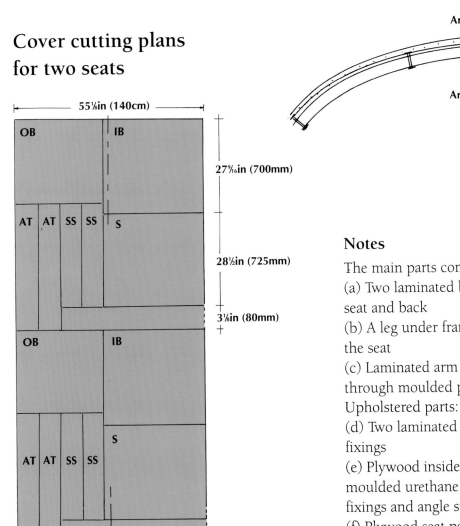

55⅛in (140cm)

| OB | IB |
| AT | AT | SS | SS | S |

27⁹⁄₁₆in (700mm)

28½in (725mm)

3⅛in (80mm)

OB	IB
	S
AT	AT	SS	SS	

Cover length required for one seat: 4ft 11in (1.505m)

Arm cap

Arm details

Notes

The main parts comprise:

(a) Two laminated beech panels, forming the seat and back

(b) A leg under frame with bolt connections to the seat

(c) Laminated arm supports with bolt fittings through moulded plastic ends

Upholstered parts:

(d) Two laminated curved arm caps with tee nut fixings

(e) Plywood inside back panel supporting moulded urethane foam with keyhole slot fixings and angle stay plate at base

(f) Plywood seat panel upholstered with moulded urethane foam unit, and tee nut inserts.

Part Three

Chapter 16
Upholsterers
at Work

David Haines

David Haines became self-employed in reupholstery in 1968, and since then he has built up a successful business in Heytesbury, Wiltshire. Seven years ago, the firm changed over to manufacturing upholstery and David was joined in the business by his son Nick.

The changeover to manufacturing occurred when David happened to make a small chair for his two-year-old goddaughter. A friend suggested they try making a few more to sell. To their surprise, the design took off, and they now produce for both the home and export markets. Their overseas commitments are mainly in the USA.

D. A. Haines and Son specialize in new work, including furniture making, polishing and upholstery.

Photo courtesy of Vicky Lane

Dorothy Gates

Dorothy Gates was taught upholstery by her father. Both of her sons and one sister are also upholsterers. She started in business in 1955, and in 1993 she became the first woman to hold office as the President of the Association of Master Upholsterers. She is a Fellow of the Association of Master Upholsterers and a Freeman of the Worshipful Company of Upholders.

Dorothy says her work never lacks interest or variety, and takes her to many different parts of the country.

Teaching is one of her first loves. She believes it is extremely important to pass on the skills of the craft to the next generation.

Photo courtesy of John Gates

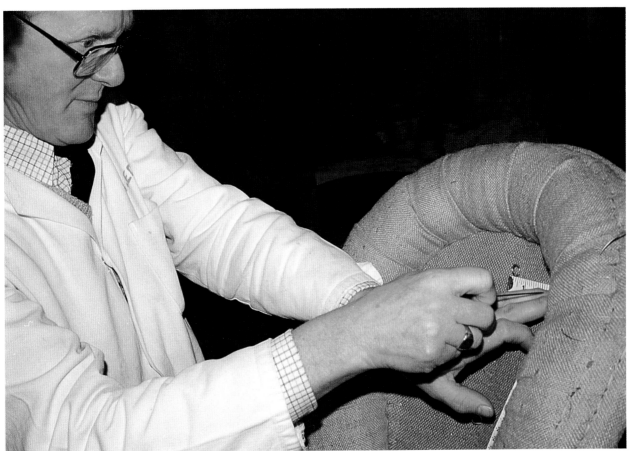

Photo courtesy of Len Rentmore

David Edgar

In 1953, David Edgar served his apprenticeship with Ewbank Turner in Hull, working alongside men who themselves had been apprentices in the 1920s and 1930s. After six years of training he gained his City and Guilds certificate and became self-employed as an upholsterer, running his own business for fifteen years.

Today, he enjoys his work with the Rural Development Commission in Salisbury as their upholstery consultant and instructor. This, he says, gives him the opportunity to pass on his skill and knowledge to young men and women who work in rural communities.

He also enjoys the world of upholstery conservation which has become an important part of the trade, involving research and a study of historical craft techniques and materials. This has increased his respect for the traditions of the craft, as well as for those who practise it. 'The upholsterer,' says David Edgar, 'uses the tactile qualities of the sculptor, the technique of the engineer and the vision of the artist.'

Heather Gilbey

Heather Gilbey (right) is particularly proud
of the fact that she is a college-trained
woman. She first became interested in
upholstery while studying furniture
restoration under the late Robert McDonald
at the London College of Furniture.

She opened her own workshop, and began
to work closely with the Victoria and Albert
Museum. For a time she specialized in 18th
century upholstery stuffing and stitching
techniques, and this work led to research both
at the V & A and Holyrood House.

She is now in her fifth year as senior
lecturer in upholstery at the London Guildhall
University, teaching all aspects of upholstery
craft and design.

Photo courtesy of Jan Jarosz

Bevan Guy

Bevan Guy started his career in 1975, working
for a local manufacturer called Vale
Upholstery. He was employed on a six-year
apprenticeship scheme and went to
Manchester College on a day release to take a
City and Guilds course in advanced furniture
making. During his employment with Vale
Upholstery he was placed in many different
areas, from design and development, through
to cutting and sewing upholstery, in order to
obtain as broad an experience of the trade as
possible.

Some years later he went to work for a

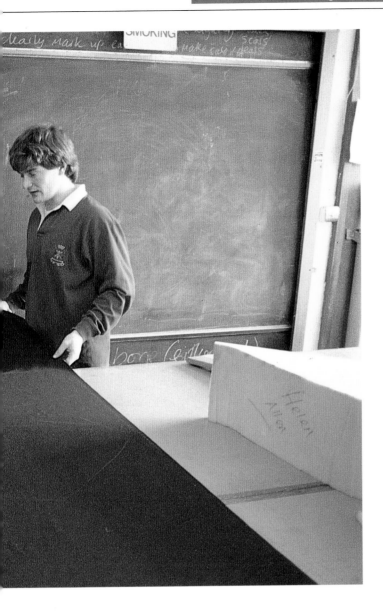

Photo courtesy of Harriet Lane

Vicky Lane

A student on the three-year Fine Craftsmanship course at Buckinghamshire College, Vicky Lane came across upholstery almost by accident, where the subject was a lesser part of the curriculum.

She graduated in 1988 and now runs a flourishing reupholstery business from her workshop in Wiltshire. Her two-storey workshop is a converted barn situated in idyllic surroundings with a catchment area of Hampshire, Wiltshire and Dorset.

She specializes in traditional, handmade upholstery and the restoration of period pieces, conserving and reusing good materials whenever possible. Vicky enjoys the challenge and variety of running her own business. 'The work often involves long hours,' she says. 'It is busy but rewarding.'

family-run company called Craft Upholstery based in Elland, West Yorkshire. The company used mostly traditional hand methods and this gave Bevan the opportunity to develop a wide variety of skills, covering all aspects of upholstery. Bevan believes there is no greater pleasure than to learn about the traditional methods by studying a well-crafted piece of furniture. 'This to me,' he says, 'is the most satisfying part of the upholstery trade.'

Now he is teaching at Burnley College, relishing the challenges presented by his students. 'My time in the upholstery trade has been most enjoyable,' says Bevan, 'because every day has something different to offer.'

Peter Humble

'If I were asked my preference,' says Peter Humble, 'I would have to say traditional upholstery as opposed to modern. I am in no way a Luddite, having a great regard for modern materials and methods, but it must also be appreciated that to make best use of these materials and methods, we have to possess an understanding of the original concept and the techniques which were employed to produce it.'

Peter's early instruction as an apprentice in the 1930s, gave him a respect and delight for the manner in which craftsmen or craftswomen used their skills to interpret the requirements of the designer and the artifact. The techniques used in upholstery then were still very traditional, even under the stress of great production demands. Life as an apprentice, pre-war, was hard, with long hours, a strict workshop discipline and a very low wage.

'At the time,' Peter recalls, 'it was accepted as the norm, so you got on with your job of learning your craft, never thinking further ahead than next week. A senior member of the workshop was given responsiblity for apprentice tuition and we had ample opportunity to observe the varying techniques of the upholsterers.'

Two years in the pinstuffing shop followed by two years deepstuffing constituted the period of apprenticeship, followed by one year as an improver. Peter's time was served at William Birch Ltd in High Wycombe. Now defunct, it was then one of the premier firms in the country.

Says Peter, 'I feel that I have been fortunate to spend my working life at a craft that has given me so much pleasure. The restoration of older furniture in the manner and style of the original gives me a feeling that is hard to describe. Perhaps well-being, happiness and satisfaction gives a fair indication of my attitude.'

Angela Burgin

Angela runs a successful business in Luton, Bedfordshire, specializing in high class, handmade drapery, curtaining, walling and upholstery.

She says: 'Walling is one particular aspect of our work that I find fascinating and rewarding. Such work was part of the upholsterer's job in the 18th century and remains so today. Schemes of this kind depend on good planning, accurate measuring and perfectly joined widths of fabric that must match exactly. Large rooms may often need as many as seven widths of fabric with drops of up to fifteen feet.'

Angela employs a number of skilled staff in her workshops where drapes, curtains and covers are prepared and made up for a variety of house furnishings. Among the other products she offers are swags and tails for window treatments and drapes for four-poster beds.

Chapter 17
Useful
Information

Suppliers of upholstery materials and fabrics

There are usually two sources of supply for upholstery materials in most areas of the country. Your local upholsterer is often the most likely and in many cases will advertise the fact that small quantities can be purchased.

The other source is either a shop which specializes in furnishing and upholstery materials, or an upholstery warehouse. The upholstery warehouse deals mainly with the trade on an account basis and in bulk quantities. Upholstery material suppliers for DIY users can usually be found in British Telecom *Yellow Pages*.

Upholstery and furnishing fabrics can also be obtained by companies listed in the *Yellow Pages*. Both small and large quantities are available from retail furnishing and retail fabric shops. The minimum sale of new furnishing fabric is one metre and when a fabric with a very large pattern repeat is chosen it may be necessary to buy a little more than the minimum.

Upholstery hides and vinyls are normally available from an upholstery warehouse, certain retailers, or direct from a factory shop. Many of the well-known furnishing fabric houses hold remnant and end-of-line sales at intervals during the year.

Courses and training in upholstery

Courses of all kinds and of varying duration are held in most counties throughout the country. There are full-time and part-time vocational courses, part-time day and evening recreational courses, as well as short courses at weekend and summer schools.

County education offices will advise on local courses, and student advisory services, attached to most colleges of further and higher education, can be consulted.

The following is a list of those colleges and institutions which have departments and schools specializing in furniture subjects. The courses offered may be vocational or recreational or both. Many offer full-time or part-time training in modern upholstery, traditional upholstery and period upholstery restoration.

Anglesey Training Ltd, Llangefni, Anglesey
Basford Hall College of Further Education, Nottingham
Bridgend College of Technology, Bridgend, Mid-Glamorgan
Brunel College of Arts and Technology, Bristol
Buckinghamshire College of Higher Education (Brunel University)
Burnley College of Technology
Central Liverpool College of Further Education
Fife College of Technology, Kirkaldy, Fife
Glasgow College of Building and Printing
Hertfordshire College of Building, St Albans, Herts
Highbury College of Technology, Portsmouth
The Jacob Kramer College, Leeds
Leeds College of Arts and Design
London Guildhall University (London College of Furniture)
Manchester College of Arts and Technology, School of Building
Newcastle College of Arts and Technology
Norwich City College of Further and Higher Education
Rycotewood College, Thame, Oxfordshire

Sandwell College of Higher and Further Education,
Gloucester
Shirecliffe College, Shirecliffe, Sheffield
Shrewsbury College of Arts and Technology
Southampton City Training
South East Essex College of Arts and Technology
West Bromwich College of Commerce and Technology,
Wednesbury

Weekend Schools and Summer Schools:

West Dean College, West Dean, West Sussex
Missenden Abbey, Gt Missenden, Bucks
Rycotewood College, Thame, Oxfordshire
Parnham House, Beaminster, Dorset
Association of Master Upholsterers, Newport, Gwent

Useful addresses

Association of Master Upholsterers,
Francis Vaughan House, 102 Commercial Street,
Newport, Gwent NP9 1LU

Association of Suppliers to the Furniture Industry
(ASFI), P.O. Box 10, Epping, Essex CM16 7RR

The British Antique Dealers' Association (BADA),
20 Rutland Gate, Knightsbridge, London SW7 1BD

The Briish Antique Furniture Restorers' Association
(BAFRA), 37 Upper Addison Gardens, Holland Park,
London W14 8AJ

British Furniture Manufacturers' Association (BFM),
30 Harcourt Street, London W1H 2AA

Business and Technician Education Council (BTEC),
Central House, Upper Woburn Place,
London WC1H 0HH

British Leather Confederation,
Kings Park Road, Moulton Park,
Northampton NN3 1JD

British Manmade Fibres Federation,
24 Buckingham Gate, London SW1E 6LB

British Rubber Manufacturers' Association
(Flexible Foam Group), 90-91 Tottenham Court Road,
London W1P 0BR

British Standards Institute,
Enquiry Service, Linford Wood,
Milton Keynes, MK14 6LE

Business Design Centre,
52 Upper Street, London N1

The Chair Frame Makers' Association,
Francis Vaughan House, 102 Commercial Street,
Newport, Gwent NP9 1LU

City and Guilds of London Institute,
76 Portland Place, London W1N 4AA

The Conservation Unit,
Museums and Galleries Commission,
16 Queen Anne Gate, London SW1 9AA

The Crafts Council,
44a Pentonville Road, Islington, London, N1 9BY

Crafts Occupational Standards Board (COSB),
Enterprise House, 25-29 Cherry Orchard Lane,
Salisbury, Wilts SP2 7LD

The Department of Trade and Industry,
Ashdown House, 123 Victoria St, London SW1E 6RB

Design Council,
28 Haymarket, London SW1Y 4SU

Design Council (Midland Office),
Norwich Union House, 31 Waterloo Road,
Wolverhampton, WV11 4BI

Design Council (Northern Office),
48 The Calls, Leeds, LS2 7EY

The Design Museum,
Butlers Wharf, London SE17

The Furniture History Society.
Enquiries to: Dr Brian Austen,
1 Mercedes Cottages,
St Johns Rd, Haywards Heath, West Sussex RH16 4EH

Furniture Industry Research Association (FIRA),
Maxwell Road, Stevenage, Herts SG1 2EW

Furniture, Timber and Allied Trades Union,
Fairfields, Roe Green, Kingsbury, London NW9 0PT

The Guild of Master Craftsmen,
166 High Street, Lewes, East Sussex BN7 1XU

The Guild of Traditional Upholsterers,
Membership Secretary, 1 Salisbury Street, Marnhull,
Sturminster Newton, Dorset DT10 1HP

**The Interior Decorators' and
Designers' Association Ltd,**
Crest House, 102-104 Church Road, Teddington,
Middlesex TW11 8PY

London and Provincial Antique Dealers' Association
(LAPADA), 535 Kings Road, London SW10 0SZ

The National Bedding Federation,
251 Brompton Road, London SW3 2EZ

The National Council for Vocational Qualifications
(NCVQ), 222 Euston Road, London NW1 2BZ

The National Fillings Trades' Association,
263a Monton Road, Eccles, Manchester M30 9LF
or Central House, 32-66 High St, Stratford,
London E15 2PS

Northern Furniture Manufacturers' Association,
Salisbury House, Salisbury Grove, Leeds,
West Yorkshire LS12 2AS

Scottish Furniture Manufacturers' Association,
Merchants House Buildings, 30 George Square,
Glasgow G2 1EG

The Textile Institute,
10 Blackfriars Street, Manchester M3 5DR

Timber Research and Development Association
(TRADA), Stocking Lane, Hughenden Valley,
High Wycombe, Bucks HP14 4ND

Rural Development Commission,
11 Cowley Street, London SW1P 2TP

The Worshipful Company of Furniture Makers,
30 Harcourt Street, London W1H 2AA

Glossary

Armchair
Armed or arming chair as distinguished from a single or side chair having no arms.

Back stool
An early single chair or side chair which developed from the stool and the chest. Later examples were upholstered.

Bergère
Louis XIV and XV style armchairs with upholstered backs and sides and squab cushion seats. Later designs often have cane backs and sides.

Binding
A narrow fabric used to support and finish an edge, such as a tape or a bias cut strip.

Bolster arm
Large upholstered arm in a bolster shape - typical late nineteenth century.

Border
A long strip or wall of fabric used to form the sides or boxing on a cushion or mattress, for example.

Box ottoman
A divan or couch with a hinged upholstered lid forming the seat, and storage space under.

Braid
A flat, narrow woven fabric, used to decorate and finish upholstery, cushions and curtains.

Bridling
A stitch used to hold down and stabilize scrim coverings, usually over first stuffings. A bridle stitch is a large running stitch, which penetrates and sets the depth of stuffing.

Buckram
A material stiffened by the use of 45 per cent weight of some agent such as size or glue.

Calico
A white or unbleached cotton fabric with no printed design.

Cambric
A fine, plain-weave cotton fabric, often glazed on one side, and used as a down-proof casing.

Cane edge
A sprung edge built on to a chair or bed using hour glass springs and a flexible cane.

Canvas
A strong, heavyweight, plain-weave fabric, traditionally made from flax or cotton. Also a term often used by upholsterers to describe the first covering over webbings or springs.

Chaise-longue
French term for a couch or day bed with an upholstered back.

Chenille
A pile fabric in which the weft thread is specially prepared and twisted by machinery, or woven and cut, before being woven into the yarn to form the pile. Cotton chenille is used in upholstery.

Chintz
A fine calico 35$\frac{7}{16}$ or 47$\frac{1}{4}$in (90 or 120cm) wide, usually roller or screen-printed and glazed or semi-glazed. Quilter chintz: Indian word meaning brightly coloured.

Circ
A commonly used abbreviation for the small circular needles used for hand sewing and slip stitching of upholstery and soft furnishings.

Collar
A strip of cover sewn into an inside back to provide a pull-in around an arm.

Couch
A long upholstered seat with a back and one or two ends. Originally a double armchair.

Cretonne
Originating from the French village of Creton and traditionally a copper-roller-printed cotton fabric. A term now more generally used to describe almost any type of lighter-weight floral printed cotton.

Damask
Figured Jacquard fabric, the weft forming the design and the warp composed of a comparatively fine yarn making the background.

Denier
The weight in grammes of 9000 metres of filament yarn, e.g. silk.

Divan chair
Fully upholstered armchair with long seat, often with scroll arms; late nineteenth century.

Drop

A curtain measurement, taken from the fixing or hook level down to the hem. Headings and turnings are added to the drop.

Dug roll

Sometimes called a tack roll or thumb roll, it is formed around frame edges using small amounts of stuffing rolled up in hessian. Preformed dugging is produced from compressed paper or reconstituted chipfoam.

Easy chair

Originally the name given to winged upholstered armchairs, introduced about 1700, but now applies to upholstered armchairs generally.

Feather down

The fine downy fibres cut and stripped from the quills of large feathers and used as a filling mixture.

Feather edge

A fine top stitch applied to a stitched edge to create a sharp edge line.

Filament

A very fine, long and usually continuous textile fibre. Several filaments of silk for example are spun together to produce one strong yarn.

Flax

Strong, lustrous bast fibre taken from the stalk of the flax plant and woven into linen cloth.

Fly piece

A narrow strip of fabric sewn to the edge of inside backs, inside arms or seats to economize on cover.

Frise

An American term used to describe a moquette with cut or uncut pile woven from mohair.

Genoa velvet

A heavy velvet with a smooth ground weave and a pile figure in various colours.

Gimp

Edgings as used in bedding and upholstery to decorate seams etc. Made from cotton, silk, rayons or mixtures.

Hair cloth

An upholstery covering material woven from the tail and mane hairs of horses, with cotton and rayons added. Plain and damask weaves are typical.

Hessian (burlap)

A plain-woven cloth of flat yarns, usually jute, and made in 7 to 12oz weights.

India tape

Twill-woven 100 per cent cotton tape similar to webbing and used to bind or reinforce edges.

Knock down (KD) furniture

Pieces of furniture which may be easily folded, broken down or flat packed for distribution.

Loose cover

A slip cover used over upholstered furniture. Traditionally employed in the summer season and made from cool linen union fabrics.

Loose seat

Also called a slip seat, drop-in seat or pallet. An upholstered frame forming the seat of a dining chair supported on rebated rails.

Mohair

The long fine hair of the Angora goat. Also describes an upholstery velvet made with a cotton base and a short mohair pile.

Monofilament

A fine continuous thread, usually synthetic. Transparent types are used as sewing threads.

Moquette

Hard-wearing pile fabric, traditionally with a wool pile and cotton ground. Moquettes may be plain, figured, cut, uncut or frise.

Nap

The surface of a fabric raised by combing or with abrasive rollers.

Nursing chair

A nineteenth-century term for a single chair with a low seat 13in to 15in (325mm to 375mm) high.

Ottoman

A long low seat without a back which originates from Turkey.

Piece

An accepted unit length of fabric, ranging from 30 to 100 metres.

Pile fabric

Fabric with a plain ground and an extra warp or weft, which projects to give the surface a fibrous nap.

Pinstuffed

Shallow padded seat or back set into a rebated show-wood frame

Piping

Narrow strip of fabric folded and sewn into a seam. Used with or without a cord.

Plain weave

A simple weave in which each warp thread interlaces over and under each weft thread. Also known as Tabby weave.

Plush

A general term for pile fabrics which have a longer pile than velvet and are less closely woven.

Pouffe

A stuffed footstool which stands high enough to be used as a seat.

Pull-in upholstery (taped)
A fly or tape sewn into a covered suface and pulled in to create a waisted effect. May also be hand stitched through the cover surface.

Repp
A heavy and firmly woven wool fabric with transverse ribs; used for upholstery.

Rollover arm
A style of easy-chair arm upholstery with a strong rollover scroll shape.

Ruching
Narrow knitted decorative trimming with a heading and a cut or looped surface. Used generally in place of piping around cushions and edges.

Scrim
Plain open-weave cloth with hard twisted yarns, woven from jute, cotton or flax. Used in upholstery to cover first stuffings.

Scrollover arm
An arm which curves inwards from the seat of a chair in the form of a double scroll, breaking into a convex sweep before curving back to form an armrest.

Seating
Upholsterers' term for hard-wearing cloths, for example hair cloth.

Settee
A name derived from the seventeenth-century settle. It is usually made from wood with a high back, large enough for several people.

Slip cover
Alternative name given to a loose or detachable cover.

Sofa
This term appeared in the late seventeenth century and described a couch for reclining.

Spoon back
The shape of a chair back, Queen Anne style, curved to fit the shape of the body.

Squab
A loose cushion.

Stitch up
A stuffed and shaped edge, reinforced with rows of blind and top stitches.

Stuffover
The name given to a chair or settee frame which is almost entirely covered with upholstery.

Tapestry
The original term applies to a wool fabric woven by hand, and later to power woven imitations, figured upholstery fabrics, and to fabric where designs are partly or wholly formed by the warp.

Trimming
The applying or forming of decorative effects using fabrics.

Tub chair
A large easy chair with a concave back.

Tufting
The technique of bridling and compressing stuffed areas in chairs, cushions and mattresses to hold fillings in place and set a depth and firmness of feel.

Upholstery
Fabric furnishings, or upholstery as we know it, began as a craft in chair making and bed making at the end of the sixteenth century.

Valance
A length of fabric which may be pleated or gathered and used to conceal a rail or frame. Generally associated with bedding.

Velour
A fine cotton velvet originating in France.

Velveteen
A very fine, lightweight cotton pile fabric with a weft pile; not of upholstery weight.

Warp
A yarn which runs in the length direction of a cloth.

Weft
A yarn which forms the cross threads in a cloth, selvedge to selvedge.

Welt
To conceal or decorate a fabric or leather joint. It also increases strength.

Worsted
Made from long wool yarn fibres, combed and twisted hard.

'X' frame chair
Early seventeenth-century chair, upholstered and decorated with nails and fringe. Became popular during the reign of James I.

Metric/Imperial Conversions

Conversion tables

Length

Centimetres	Cm or inches	Inches
2.54	1	0.39
5.08	2	0.79
7.62	3	1.18
10.16	4	1.58
12.70	5	1.97
15.24	6	2.36
17.78	7	2.76
20.32	8	3.15
22.86	9	3.54
25.40	10	3.94

Weight

Kilograms	Kg or pounds	Pounds
0.45	1	2.21
0.91	2	4.41
1.36	3	6.61
1.81	4	8.82
2.27	5	11.02
2.72	6	13.23
3.18	7	15.43
3.63	8	17.64
4.08	9	19.84
4.45	10	22.05

Conversion formulae

To convert	Multiply by
Length	
Inches to centimetres	2.54
Centimetres to inches	0.3937
Feet to metres	0.3048
Metres to feet	3.2808
Yards to metres	0.9144
Metres to yards	1.0936
Area	
Sq inches to sq centimetres	6.4516
Sq centimetres to sq inches	0.155
Sq feet to sq metres	0.0929
Sq metres to sq feet	10.7639
Sq yards to sq metres	0.8361
Sq metres to sq yards	1.1959
Volume	
Cu inches to cu centimetres	16.387
Cu centimetres to cu inches	0.06102
Cu feet to cu metres	0.02831
Cu metres to cu feet	35.3147
Cu yards to cu metres	0.76455
Cu metres to cu yards	1.30795
Weight	
Ounces to grams	28.3495
Grams to ounces	0.03527
Pounds to grams	453.59
Grams to pounds	0.002204
Pounds to kilograms	0.45359
Kilograms to pounds	2.2046

Index

About the Author

David James was born in High Wycombe and has worked in upholstery since leaving school. After a number of years as an instructor in a factory, he joined the Ministry of Public Buildings and Works as a technical officer, gaining a National Furnishing Diploma. In 1966 he became a lecturer in upholstery at Buckinghamshire College of Higher Education, near his home in Marlow, and was promoted to senior lecturer in 1971.

He is an honorary member of the City and Guilds of London Institute, and has been awarded their licentiateship. He is also a member of the Guild of Traditional Upholsterers. In recent years he has turned his talents to writing and illustrating. His first book, *Upholstery: A Complete Course*, published in 1990, has established itself as the standard work on the subject.

Notes

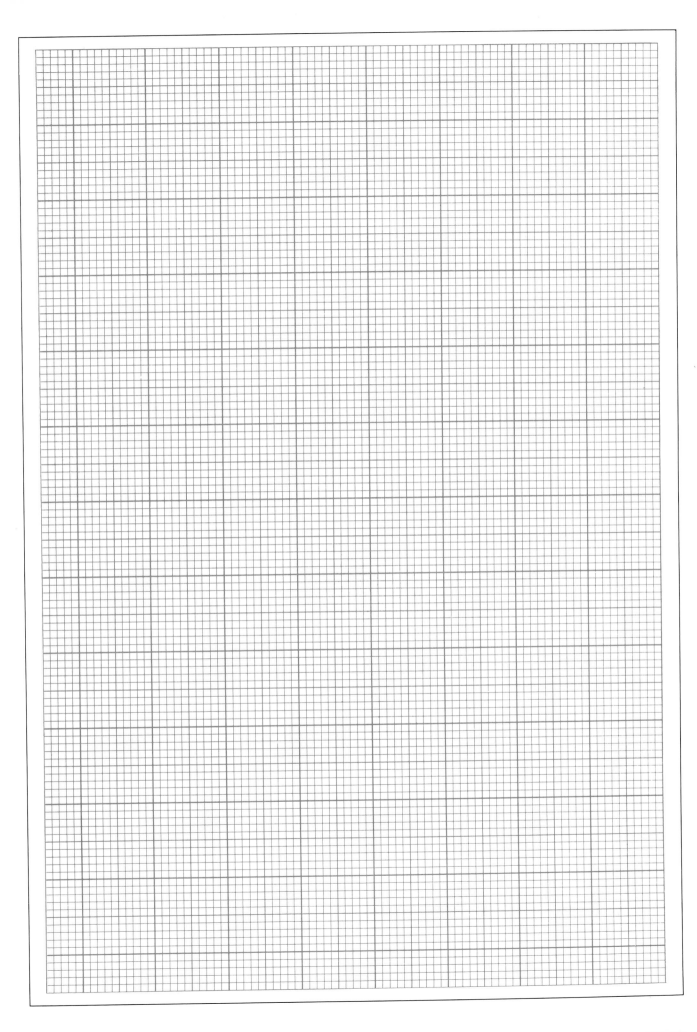

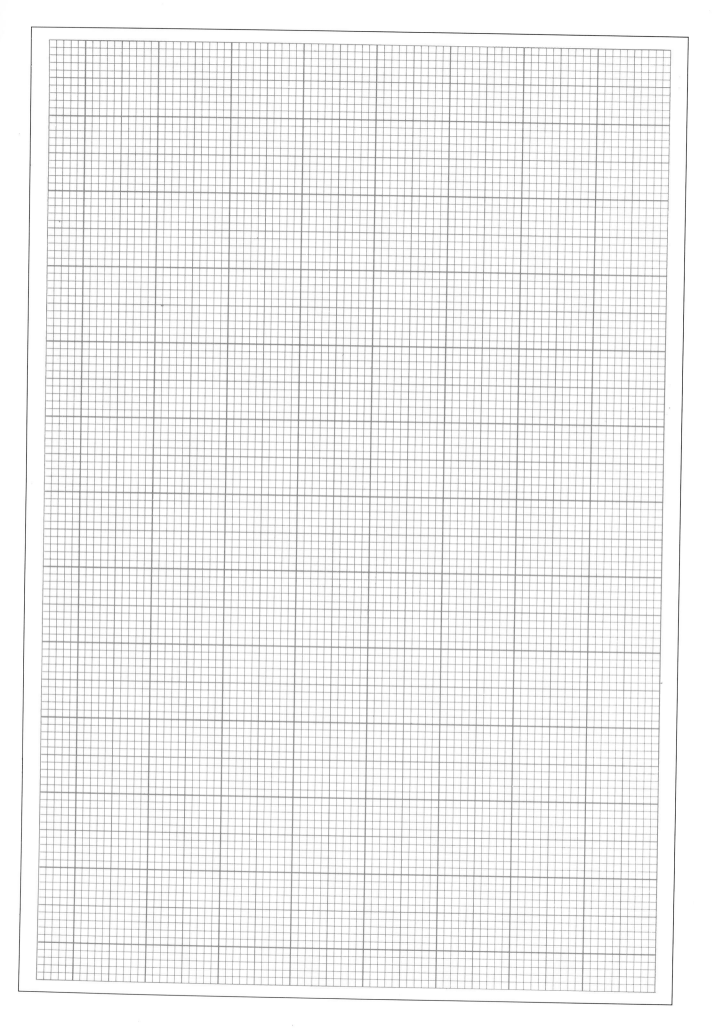

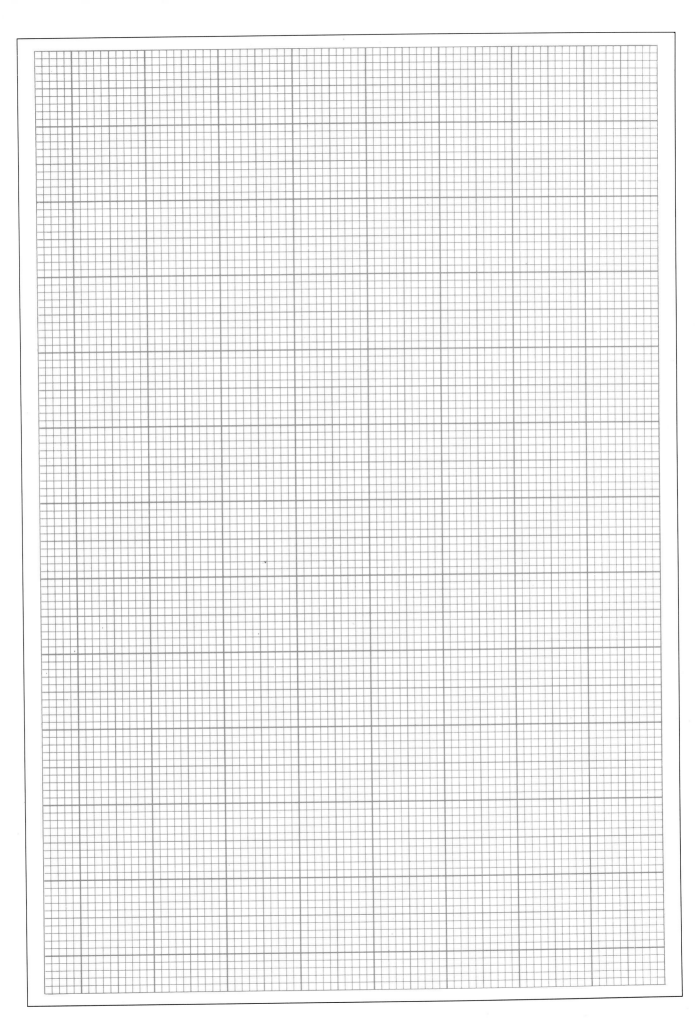

TITLES AVAILABLE FROM
GMC PUBLICATIONS
BOOKS

WOODWORKING

Advanced Scrollsaw Projects	*GMC Publications*
Bird Boxes and Feeders for the Garden	*Dave Mackenzie*
Complete Woodfinishing	*Ian Hosker*
David Charlesworth's Furniture-Making Techniques	*David Charlesworth*
The Encyclopedia of Joint Making	*Terrie Noll*
Furniture & Cabinetmaking Projects	*GMC Publications*
Furniture-Making Projects for the Wood Craftsman	*GMC Publications*
Furniture-Making Techniques for the Wood Craftsman	*GMC Publications*
Furniture Projects	*Rod Wales*
Furniture Restoration (Practical Crafts)	*Kevin Jan Bonner*
Furniture Restoration and Repair for Beginners	*Kevin Jan Bonner*
Furniture Restoration Workshop	*Kevin Jan Bonner*
Green Woodwork	*Mike Abbott*
Kevin Ley's Furniture Projects	*Kevin Ley*
Making & Modifying Woodworking Tools	*Jim Kingshott*
Making Chairs and Tables	*GMC Publications*
Making Classic English Furniture	*Paul Richardson*
Making Little Boxes from Wood	*John Bennett*
Making Screw Threads in Wood	*Fred Holder*
Making Shaker Furniture	*Barry Jackson*
Making Woodwork Aids and Devices	*Robert Wearing*
Mastering the Router	*Ron Fox*

Minidrill: Fifteen Projects	*John Everett*
Pine Furniture Projects for the Home	*Dave Mackenzie*
Practical Scrollsaw Patterns	*John Everett*
Router Magic: Jigs, Fixtures and Tricks to Unleash your Router's Full Potential	*Bill Hylton*
Routing for Beginners	*Anthony Bailey*
The Scrollsaw: Twenty Projects	*John Everett*
Sharpening: The Complete Guide	*Jim Kingshott*
Sharpening Pocket Reference Book	*Jim Kingshott*
Simple Scrollsaw Projects	*GMC Publications*
Space-Saving Furniture Projects	*Dave Mackenzie*
Stickmaking: A Complete Course	*Andrew Jones & Clive George*
Stickmaking Handbook	*Andrew Jones & Clive George*
Test Reports: The Router and Furniture & Cabinetmaking	*GMC Publications*
Veneering: A Complete Course	*Ian Hosker*
Veneering Handbook	*Ian Hosker*
Woodfinishing Handbook (Practical Crafts)	*Ian Hosker*
Woodworking with the Router: Professional Router Techniques any Woodworker can Use	*Bill Hylton & Fred Matlack*
The Workshop	*Jim Kingshott*

WOODTURNING

Adventures in Woodturning	*David Springett*
Bert Marsh: Woodturner	*Bert Marsh*
Bowl Turning Techniques Masterclass	*Tony Boase*
Colouring Techniques for Woodturners	*Jan Sanders*
Contemporary Turned Wood: New Perspectives in a Rich Tradition	*Ray Leier, Jan Peters & Kevin Wallace*
The Craftsman Woodturner	*Peter Child*
Decorative Techniques for Woodturners	*Hilary Bowen*
Fun at the Lathe	*R.C. Bell*
Illustrated Woodturning Techniques	*John Hunnex*
Intermediate Woodturning Projects	*GMC Publications*
Keith Rowley's Woodturning Projects	*Keith Rowley*
Practical Tips for Turners & Carvers	*GMC Publications*
Turning Green Wood	*Michael O'Donnell*
Turning Miniatures in Wood	*John Sainsbury*

Turning Pens and Pencils	*Kip Christensen & Rex Burningham*
Understanding Woodturning	*Ann & Bob Phillips*
Useful Techniques for Woodturners	*GMC Publications*
Useful Woodturning Projects	*GMC Publications*
Woodturning: Bowls, Platters, Hollow Forms, Vases, Vessels, Bottles, Flasks, Tankards, Plates	*GMC Publications*
Woodturning: A Foundation Course (New Edition)	*Keith Rowley*
Woodturning: A Fresh Approach	*Robert Chapman*
Woodturning: An Individual Approach	*Dave Regester*
Woodturning: A Source Book of Shapes	*John Hunnex*
Woodturning Jewellery	*Hilary Bowen*
Woodturning Masterclass	*Tony Boase*
Woodturning Techniques	*GMC Publications*
Woodturning Tools & Equipment Test Reports	*GMC Publications*
Woodturning Wizardry	*David Springett*

WOODCARVING

The Art of the Woodcarver	*GMC Publications*
Carving Architectural Detail in Wood: The Classical Tradition	*Frederick Wilbur*
Carving Birds & Beasts	*GMC Publications*
Carving the Human Figure: Studies in Wood and Stone	*Dick Onians*
Carving Nature: Wildlife Studies in Wood	*Frank Fox-Wilson*
Carving Realistic Birds	*David Tippey*
Decorative Woodcarving	*Jeremy Williams*
Elements of Woodcarving	*Chris Pye*
Essential Woodcarving Techniques	*Dick Onians*
Further Useful Tips for Woodcarvers	*GMC Publications*
Lettercarving in Wood: A Practical Course	*Chris Pye*
Making & Using Working Drawings for Realistic Model Animals	*Basil F. Fordham*

Power Tools for Woodcarving	*David Tippey*
Practical Tips for Turners & Carvers	*GMC Publications*
Relief Carving in Wood: A Practical Introduction	*Chris Pye*
Understanding Woodcarving	*GMC Publications*
Understanding Woodcarving in the Round	*GMC Publications*
Useful Techniques for Woodcarvers	*GMC Publications*
Wildfowl Carving – Volume 1	*Jim Pearce*
Wildfowl Carving – Volume 2	*Jim Pearce*
Woodcarving: A Complete Course	*Ron Butterfield*
Woodcarving: A Foundation Course	*Zoë Gertner*
Woodcarving for Beginners	*GMC Publications*
Woodcarving Tools & Equipment Test Reports	*GMC Publications*
Woodcarving Tools, Materials & Equipment	*Chris Pye*

UPHOLSTERY

The Upholsterer's Pocket Reference Book	*David James*
Upholstery: A Complete Course (Revised Edition)	*David James*
Upholstery Restoration	*David James*

Upholstery Techniques & Projects	*David James*
Upholstery Tips and Hints	*David James*

CRAFTS

American Patchwork Designs in Needlepoint — *Melanie Tacon*
A Beginners' Guide to Rubber Stamping — *Brenda Hunt*
Blackwork: A New Approach — *Brenda Day*
Celtic Cross Stitch Designs — *Carol Phillipson*
Celtic Knotwork Designs — *Sheila Sturrock*
Celtic Knotwork Handbook — *Sheila Sturrock*
Celtic Spirals and Other Designs — *Sheila Sturrock*
Collage from Seeds, Leaves and Flowers — *Joan Carver*
Complete Pyrography — *Stephen Poole*
Contemporary Smocking — *Dorothea Hall*
Creating Colour with Dylon — *Dylon International*
Creative Doughcraft — *Patricia Hughes*
Creative Embroidery Techniques Using Colour Through Gold — *Daphne J. Ashby & Jackie Woolsey*
The Creative Quilter: Techniques and Projects — *Pauline Brown*
Decorative Beaded Purses — *Enid Taylor*
Designing and Making Cards — *Glennis Gilruth*
Glass Engraving Pattern Book — *John Everett*
Glass Painting — *Emma Sedman*
Handcrafted Rugs — *Sandra Hardy*
How to Arrange Flowers: A Japanese Approach to English Design — *Taeko Marvelly*
How to Make First-Class Cards — *Debbie Brown*
An Introduction to Crewel Embroidery — *Mave Glenny*
Making and Using Working Drawings for Realistic Model Animals — *Basil F. Fordham*
Making Character Bears — *Valerie Tyler*
Making Decorative Screens — *Amanda Howes*
Making Fairies and Fantastical Creatures — *Julie Sharp*
Making Greetings Cards for Beginners — *Pat Sutherland*
Making Hand-Sewn Boxes: Techniques and Projects — *Jackie Woolsey*
Making Knitwear Fit — *Pat Ashforth & Steve Plummer*
Making Mini Cards, Gift Tags & Invitations — *Glennis Gilruth*
Making Soft-Bodied Dough Characters — *Patricia Hughes*
Natural Ideas for Christmas: Fantastic Decorations to Make — *Josie Cameron-Ashcroft & Carol Cox*
Needlepoint: A Foundation Course — *Sandra Hardy*
New Ideas for Crochet: Stylish Projects for the Home — *Darsha Capaldi*
Patchwork for Beginners — *Pauline Brown*
Pyrography Designs — *Norma Gregory*
Pyrography Handbook (Practical Crafts) — *Stephen Poole*
Ribbons and Roses — *Lee Lockheed*
Rose Windows for Quilters — *Angela Besley*
Rubber Stamping with Other Crafts — *Lynne Garner*
Sponge Painting — *Ann Rooney*
Stained Glass: Techniques and Projects — *Mary Shanahan*
Step-by-Step Pyrography Projects for the Solid Point Machine — *Norma Gregory*
Tassel Making for Beginners — *Enid Taylor*
Tatting Collage — *Lindsay Rogers*
Temari: A Traditional Japanese Embroidery Technique — *Margaret Ludlow*
Theatre Models in Paper and Card — *Robert Burgess*
Trip Around the World: 25 Patchwork, Quilting and Appliqué Projects — *Gail Lawther*
Trompe l'Oeil: Techniques and Projects — *Jan Lee Johnson*
Wool Embroidery and Design — *Lee Lockheed*

GARDENING

Auriculas for Everyone: How to Grow and Show Perfect Plants — *Mary Robinson*
Beginners' Guide to Herb Gardening — *Yvonne Cuthbertson*
Bird Boxes and Feeders for the Garden — *Dave Mackenzie*
The Birdwatcher's Garden — *Hazel & Pamela Johnson*
Broad-Leaved Evergreens — *Stephen G. Haw*
Companions to Clematis: Growing Clematis with Other Plants — *Marigold Badcock*
Creating Contrast with Dark Plants — *Freya Martin*
Creating Small Habitats for Wildlife in your Garden — *Josie Briggs*
Gardening with Wild Plants — *Julian Slatcher*
Growing Cacti and Other Succulents in the Conservatory and Indoors — *Shirley-Anne Bell*
Growing Cacti and Other Succulents in the Garden — *Shirley Anne Bell*
Hardy Perennials: A Beginner's Guide — *Eric Sawford*
The Living Tropical Greenhouse: Creating a Haven for Butterflies — *John & Maureen Tampion*
Orchids are Easy: A Beginner's Guide to their Care and Cultivation — *Tom Gilland*
Plant Alert: A Garden Guide for Parents — *Catherine Collins*
Planting Plans for Your Garden — *Jenny Shukman*
Plants that Span the Seasons — *Roger Wilson*
Sink and Container Gardening Using Dwarf Hardy Plants — *Chris & Valerie Wheeler*

VIDEOS

Drop-in and Pinstuffed Seats — *David James*
Stuffover Upholstery — *David James*
Elliptical Turning — *David Springett*
Woodturning Wizardry — *David Springett*
Turning Between Centres: The Basics — *Dennis White*
Turning Bowls — *Dennis White*
Boxes, Goblets and Screw Threads — *Dennis White*
Novelties and Projects — *Dennis White*
Classic Profiles — *Dennis White*
Twists and Advanced Turning — *Dennis White*
Sharpening the Professional Way — *Jim Kingshott*
Sharpening Turning & Carving Tools — *Jim Kingshott*
Bowl Turning — *John Jordan*
Hollow Turning — *John Jordan*
Woodturning: A Foundation Course — *Keith Rowley*
Carving a Figure: The Female Form — *Ray Gonzalez*
The Router: A Beginner's Guide — *Alan Goodsell*
The Scroll Saw: A Beginner's Guide — *John Burke*

MAGAZINES

WOODWORKING • WOODTURNING • WOODCARVING • FURNITURE & CABINETMAKING • THE ROUTER
GARDEN CALENDAR • EXOTIC & GREENHOUSE GARDENING • WATER GARDENING • BUSINESS MATTERS
THE DOLLS' HOUSE MAGAZINE • OUTDOOR PHOTOGRAPHY • BLACK & WHITE PHOTOGRAPHY

The above represents a selection of titles currently published or scheduled to be published. All are available direct from the Publishers or through bookshops, newsagents and specialist retailers. To place an order, or to obtain a complete catalogue, contact:

GMC Publications,
Castle Place, 166 High Street, Lewes, East Sussex BN7 1XU, United Kingdom
Tel: 01273 488005 Fax: 01273 478606 E-mail: pubs@thegmcgroup.com
Orders by credit card are accepted